Revisiting Children's Rights

Revisiting Children's Rights

10 Years of the UN Convention on the Rights of the Child

Edited by
Deirdre Fottrell

KLUWER LAW INTERNATIONAL
THE HAGUE – LONDON – BOSTON

Published by:
Kluwer Law International
P.O. Box 85889, 2508 CN The Hague, The Netherlands
sales@kli.wkap.nl
http://www.kluwerlaw.com

Sold and Distributed in North, Central and South America by:
Kluwer Law International
675 Massachusetts Avenue, Cambridge MA 02139, USA

Sold and Distributed in all other countries:
Kluwer Law International
Distribution Centre, P.O. Box 322, 3300 AH Dordrecht, The Netherlands

Library of Congress Cataloguing-in-Publication Data is available.

Printed on acid-free paper

ISBN 90-411-1508-0
© 2000 Kluwer Law International

Kluwer Law International incorporates the publishing programmes
of Graham & Trotman Ltd, Kluwer Law and Taxation Publishers
and Martinus Nijhoff Publishers.

Printed and bound in Great Britain by Cromwell Press Limited.

Contents

Foreword

The past decade has witnessed striking legal advances for the rights of children everywhere. Today, virtually all States are bound by international law to respect, protect and promote the human rights of children. The next step is implementation of those rights 'in small places, close to home...'

The Convention on the Rights of the Child established an innovative approach to human rights, marking a departure from earlier instruments and from traditional notions of child welfare. It was the first international human rights treaty to contain a comprehensive set of universally recognised norms, asserting the complementarity and interdependence of human rights: civil and political, economic, social and cultural. Above all, the Convention set a new vision of the child, embodying a consensus that emerged in favour of the empowerment, as well as protection, of children.

Traditionally, States have been seen to be the most important actors in the human rights arena: only States can ratify the Convention and only States can be bound by its provisions. However, the Convention on the Rights of the Child has had a clear impact on the programmes and priorities of the United Nations system. And from its earliest stages, the Convention has attracted the involvement of non-governmental organisations, whose commitment has been demonstrated by activities to implement children's rights internationally and locally. Indeed, the Convention specifically recognises the participation rights of NGOs in its implementation. Moreover, in recent years there is increasing recognition in business circles that they too have an important role to play in the implementation of child rights.

Recent developments furthering the protection of children, notably the Optional Protocols to the Convention concerning children in armed conflict, and the sale of children, child prostitution and child pornography; ILO Convention No. 182 on the prohibition and immediate action for the elimination of the worst forms of child labour; and the Statute of the International Criminal Court have kept child rights on the political agenda. And, for the first time in its history, the Security Council adopted a resolution concerning children, Resolution 1261 (1999) on children and armed conflict.

Unfortunately, despite increased international and national efforts, enormous problems remain. The rights of millions of children all over the world are violated every day, in every conceivable way. The litany is endless; girls and children with disabilities continue to experience discrimination; children are subject to all forms of ill-treatment, often at the hands of those who are expected to have their best interests at heart; they languish in prisons without adequate legal safeguards, are sold and forced into prostitution; and are victims of armed conflict.

While some States have made progress, others have made no more than symbolic gestures without creating an effective infrastructure of implementation and monitoring reaching down to the local level. Inroads are being made here with the emergence of independent national human rights institutions. In addition, human rights education – a crucial long-term contributor to prevention of human rights abuses, and an investment towards the building of a universal culture of human rights – is a priority that needs to be given increased attention through national, regional and international endeavours.

With a decade behind us since the adoption of the Convention on the Rights of the Child, the time is right to evaluate progress, re-assess strategies, and tackle the challenges that lie ahead through concrete and effective action. This collection of essays, drawn from the lecture series at the University of London, to commemorate the 10th anniversary of the Convention is an important contribution to the collective efforts towards making the Convention an everyday reality. For all those who are committed to child rights, this book will be a valuable resource.

At the start of a new century, everyone must assume their rightful ownership of the Convention. The promotion and protection of children's rights should be at the heart of all our endeavours.

Mary Robinson
United Nations High Commissioner for Human Rights
Geneva, August 2000

Acknowledgements

In the autumn of 1999 the Institute of Commonwealth Studies at the University of London hosted a series of lunchtime seminars to commemorate the 10th anniversary of the United Nations Convention on the Rights of the Child. The purpose of the seminars was to bring together leading scholars and activists working in the field of children's rights to discuss the progress of the Convention and to revisit contemporary debates in children's rights in light of the first decade of the Convention. The papers presented at the seminars are reproduced in the chapters of this book. Neither the seminars nor the book would have occurred without the enthusiastic commitment of the contributors and I am very grateful to them for their co-operation at every stage of this process.

The Institute's human rights programme was initiated in 1995 when it began to offer a postgraduate human rights degree course. In the following five years both the postgraduate programme and the subsequent expansion of human rights activities including conferences and seminars benefited from the unique multi-disciplinary approach to research and teaching of the social sciences, which was very much central to the Institute's mission. I hope that some of that multi-disciplinarity is evident in this publication. During my time at the Institute I was fortunate to work with some very supportive academic colleagues. Robert Holland, Peter Lyon, Michael Twaddle and Stephen Ashton, in particular, encouraged the various human rights projects that I undertook during my tenure as director of the human rights programme. In addition I would like to acknowledge the contribution to this and other projects of other colleagues in administration including Rowena Kochanowska, Denise Elliott and most particularly Imelda McGowan, who made an enormous contribution to the administration of the MA programme.

The preparatory work for the seminar series and this book was done while I was on a Visiting Fellowship to John Jay College, City University of New York, in the summer of 1999, which was made possible by the generosity of the College President, Dr Gerald Lynch, and I am pleased to have this opportunity to acknowledge his kindness and to thank him for facilitating a very productive stay at his college.

In addition I should like to thank the United Nations High Commissioner on Human Rights, Mary Robinson, for her early interest and continuing support of the publication. I am also grateful to Scott Jerbi from the High Commissioner's office for his assistance.

The manuscript was proofed with considerable skill, speed and good humour by Jennie Roberts. Last minute research assistance was provided by Marie Wernham. It has been great pleasure to work once again with Lindy Melman and Peter Buschman at Kluwer; the book has benefited from their professionalism and expertise.

Finally I am pleased to have the opportunity to thank my parents Patrick and Esther for their encouragement and support on this and many other endeavours; this publication is dedicated to them.

Deirdre Fottrell

London, July 2000

Deirdre Fottrell

1. ONE STEP FORWARD OR TWO STEPS SIDEWAYS? ASSESSING THE FIRST DECADE OF THE CHILDREN'S CONVENTION ON THE RIGHTS OF THE CHILD

INTRODUCTION

The United Nations Convention on the Rights of the Child (CRC) is the first binding universal treaty dedicated solely to the protection and promotion of children's rights.[1] Passed by the General Assembly in 1989, the CRC was initially delayed by a long and difficult drafting process, but the resulting document is nonetheless both ambitious and far-reaching and the potential exists within the CRC to advance considerably the rights of children all over the globe.

The CRC is a significant legal and political achievement: It elevated the child to the status of an independent rights-holder and placed children's issues at the centre of the mainstream human rights agenda. Indeed the Director of UNICEF welcomed it as 'Magna Carta for children'.[2] That the CRC also generated considerable enthusiasm among States is evidenced by the fact that on the day it opened for signature in January 1990, 61 States signed up to the CRC, and it came into force a mere seven months later. This in itself is quite exceptional, UN treaties can take years and even decades to obtain the necessary ratifications to come into force; for example the International Covenant on Civil and Political Rights (CCPR) took 10 years to obtain the 35 ratifications required to come into force.[3] The CRC, by contrast, achieved almost universal acceptance within eight years and today it is ratified by all but two States.[4] This universal ratification is unique for a human rights treaty and it gives the CRC considerable political, legal and even moral force.

This chapter provides an introduction to the CRC and more particularly an overview of its first decade. The chapter highlights certain issues around imple-

---

[1] *See* United Nations Convention on the Rights of the Child, U.N. Doc A/44/736 (1989), reprinted in 28 I.L.M. 1457 (1989).

[2] This comment was attributed to James P. Grant while he was Executive Director of UNICEF, *see* C.P. COHEN & H.A. DAVIDSON, CHILDREN'S RIGHTS IN AMERICA (1990).

[3] *See* International Covenant on Civil and Political Rights, opened for signature Dec. 16 1966, entered into force Mar. 23 1976, G.A. Res 2200 (XXI), 21 U.N. GAOR Supp. (No. 16), UN Doc.A/6316. *See generally* D. MCGOLDRICK, THE HUMAN RIGHTS COMMITTEE, (1994).

[4] The Convention has been ratified by 191 States; only the United States and Somalia have not yet ratified. The United States signed the Convention but it is considered unlikely that the Convention will pass the difficult and complex domestic procedure for ratification. *See generally* A.D. Renteln, *United States Ratification of Human Rights Treaties: Who's Afraid of the CRC?* 3 ILSA INT'L J. & COMP. L., 629 (1997). *See also* B. Hafen and J. Hafen, *Abandoning Children to their Autonomy: The UN Convention on the Rights of the Child*, 37 HARV. INT'L J. 449 (1996).

Deirdre Fottrell (ed.), Revisiting Children's Rights, 1–14
© 2000 *Kluwer Law International. Printed in Great Britain.*

mentation and some difficulties, which have arisen due to shortcomings in the protection offered by the CRC. The chapter also seeks to identify challenges which may lie ahead for the Convention in the coming decade and concludes that, while there is indeed much cause for celebration, children's rights activists need to view the CRC as a beginning rather than as an end in itself.

BACKGROUND TO THE CHILDREN'S CONVENTION[5]

The emergence of the child as an independent rights-holder is not a recent phenomenon in international law. One of the earliest international human rights instruments was the Declaration on the Rights of the Child passed by the League of Nations in 1924.[6] This early initiative was essentially paternalistic and welfare-oriented, its conceptualisation of the child stressed vulnerability and the emphasis was on protective strategies. The 1924 Declaration was non-binding and few States incorporated it into their domestic law; consequently its impact on the practice of States or international organisations was limited and its significance today is largely symbolic. It was followed in 1959, by a similar Declaration of the Rights of the Child.[7] Such early international efforts to protect children were aspirational and perhaps even tokenistic within which the child's rights were framed in broad terms.[8] Consequently, up to the 1970s the debate about the child as a rights-holder was confined very much to the domestic arena in a few Western States; on an international level children's rights were a matter of particular concern to humanitarian organisations but did not feature highly on the human rights agenda.[9]

In the US in the 1970s there emerged a coherent and robust movement for the empowerment of children in political, civil and social contexts.[10] This hinged on a move away from the welfare-oriented paternalism of earlier campaigns towards a radical liberation-oriented approach, the cornerstone of which was recognition of the child's autonomy. In addition, children's rights advocates pushed for a separate and particular canon of rights for children which reflected their needs and

---

[5] On the background to the Convention and particularly the drafting process *see generally* D. McGoldrick, *The United Nations Convention on the Rights of the Child*, 5 INT'L J. L. & FAM. 132 (1991); *see also* M. Pais, *General Introduction to the Convention on the Rights of the Child: From its Origins to Implementation*, in SELECTED ESSAYS ON CHILDREN'S RIGHTS 5 (Defence for Children International, ed. 1993).

[6] *See* Declaration on the Rights of the Child, Records of the Fifth Assembly, Supplement No. 23 League of Nations Official Journal (1924).

[7] *See* Declaration of the Rights of the Child, G.A. Res. 1386 (XIV), 14 GAOR Supplement (No. 16), UN Doc.A/4354 (1959).

[8] On the history of the rights of the child *see further*, G. VAN BUEREN, INTERNATIONAL LAW ON THE RIGHTS OF THE CHILD, (1995).

[9] On the history and background to international law and the rights of the child, *see generally* G. VAN BUEREN, INTERNATIONAL LAW ON THE RIGHTS OF THE CHILD, (1995). *See also* D. Fottrell, *Children's Rights* in HUMAN RIGHTS: AN AGENDA FOR THE 21ST CENTURY 167 (A. Hegarty & S. Leonard, eds. 1999).

[10] *See generally* J. HOLT, ESCAPE FROM CHILDHOOD, (1975); *see also* H. Rodham, *Children Under the Law* 43 HARV. ED. REV. 487 (1975).

concerns.[11] By the end of the decade a consensus emerged among States that the rights of the child were inadequately addressed in existing international human rights instruments and it was clear that international law offered little protection in particular to the many children living in extreme and difficult circumstances.

The international developments mirrored the debates taking place in the US and thus formed a loosely structured children's rights movement which sought to create awareness of the outdated tendency of many States to diminish the rights of children in matters of law and policy directly concerned with children.[12] A central objective of the movement was recognition of children's rights as human rights and that as such they merited a dedicated treaty to ensure their promotion by States.

Pressure to create a binding international instrument led to a formal proposal from the Polish delegation presented to the UN Commission on Human Rights in 1979, the International Year of the Child.[13] Over the next decade this proposal was redrafted several times as particular controversies emerged around the inclusion of certain rights. For example, consensus could not be reached on the beginning and end of childhood (particularly the issue of the point at which life begins).[14] Setting the parameters for autonomy, most notably relating to the right to freedom of religion, also proved to be highly problematic as did issues around adoption due to the non-existence of this concept in Islamic societies. Similarly, States were unable to raise the standards relating to child soldiers.[15] Moreover, the drafting process of the CRC was generally hampered by the need to strike a balance between traditional attitudes, cultural particularities and radical proposals for empowerment of children, while at the same time ensuring the rights of the child were adequately protected and the document had as wide appeal as possible. Whether the CRC struck the right balance in relation to many of its provisions is disputable; the high number of reservations suggest that for some States many of its propositions are entirely unacceptable. Moreover, the CRC is marked by the controversies and compromises during the drafting process and in some instances rights are framed in such broad terms that they are unclear in their meaning or they fail to improve on existing standards.[16] Taken as a whole, however, the CRC expands considerably

---

[11] For an authoritative overview of the development of the children's rights movement *see generally* M.D.A. Freeman, *Laws, Conventions and Rights* 7 CHILDREN & SOCIETY 37 (1993); *see also* Freeman, *Taking Children's Rights More Seriously* 6 INT'L J. L & FAM. 52 (1992). *See further* P. ADAMS, ESCAPE FROM CHILDHOOD, THE LIBERATION OF CHILDREN (1971).

[12] *See* D. Weisberg, *Evolution of the Rights of the Child in the Western World*, REV. INT'L COMM. JUR. 43 (1978).

[13] *See further* L. LEBLANC, THE CONVENTION ON THE RIGHTS OF THE CHILD 3–59 (1995).

[14] Some States argued that the definition of the child should include life from the moment of conception. *See further* P. Alston, *The Unborn Child and Abortion under the Draft Convention on the Rights of the Child*, 12 H. RTS. Q. 156–178 (1990).

[15] *See further* LEBLANC, *supra* note 13 at 3-59. *See also* M. Siraj Sait, *Islamic Perspectives on the Rights of the Child*, p. 31 in this collection.

[16] *See e.g.* Article 24(3) of the Convention which obliges State Parties to eliminate traditional cultural practices prejudicial to the health of women. The original proposal called for the elimination of female genital mutilation but was replaced as a consequence of objections from States where the practice is most common. The meaning of Article 24(3) is sufficiently unclear as to be open to a variety of local or cultural interpretations. *See* SHARON DETRICK, CONVENTION ON THE RIGHTS OF THE CHILD: A GUIDE TO THE TRAVAUX PRÉPARATOIRES (1992); *see also* VAN BUEREN, *supra* note 9 at 293.

the international law applicable to children through the sheer ambition and breath of its provisions. More significantly perhaps is the injection of a child-centred perspective into international human rights law.

THE SUBSTANCE AND CONTENT OF THE CRC

The CRC has 54 Articles, 40 of which provide substantive rights for children. Uniquely, the full range of rights is protected by the Convention including civil, political, economic, social and cultural. The inclusion of such a wide range of issues is, in itself, a departure as most previous human rights treaties drew crude distinctions between civil and political rights, which were broadly presented as being immediately applicable, and economic and social rights, which were often conceived as matters of policy and not law. As a consequence of protecting the full canon of rights the CRC apparently champions the interdependence and indivisibility of all human rights. Perhaps a downside of the range of protection offered is the problems this causes for supervision and implementation by the Committee on the Rights of the Child, particularly relating to economic and social rights where little progress has been made over the decade.

What is clear, however, is that the CRC alters considerably the character of rights which were previously considered appropriate for or relevant to children. Prior to the CRC, rights in general treaties applied in theory to both children and adults. However, in practice it was not uncommon for courts to severely limit or even deny outright the relevance of such rights to children simply by reference to their childhood status.[17] Moreover, those rights which were specific to children were limited to protective rights such as Article 24 of the CCPR or the European Convention on Human Rights provisions on education and juvenile justice.[18]

The CRC applies to all children under the age of 18. The approach of the CRC bearing in mind the range of rights protected is that as the child progresses from infant to late adolescence, different classes of rights assume greater significance.[19] Thus protective and provisory rights are overtaken in importance by the participatory rights as children move toward adulthood. The CRC is in addition underpinned by five key principles that form a backdrop against which all actions of the States are to be measured

---

[17] *See e.g.* Handyside *v* UK, Eur. Ct. H.R. Series A No. 24 (1976); for a rather extreme example of this *see also* Nielsen *v* Denmark Eur. Ct. H.R. Series A No. 144 (1987), 9 EHRR 90 (1987). It is interesting to contrast the approach of the European Court of Human Rights to children during this period with decisions of the U.S. Supreme Court *see e.g.* Tinker *v* Des Moines, 393 U.S. 503 (1969), in which the Court explicitly took the view that the First Amendment provisions on freedom of speech were equally applicable to children and adults.

[18] *See* LEBLANC *supra* note 3, at 13. *See also* European Convention on Human Rights, Article 5 (1) (d) which allows the State to detain a juvenile for education supervision and Article 2, Protocol 1 on the Right to education, *see further* U. KILKELLY, *infra* note 33.

[19] *See* Article 1 where the definition of a child is a person under 18 unless the age of majority is attained earlier under domestic law.

- First, under Article 3 the best interests of the child are a primary consideration in all matters concerning the child. This principle is widely accepted in domestic law but is introduced by this provision into international law for the first time.
- Second, Article 5 requires that account is to be had of the evolving capacities of the child, thus children can be accorded greater autonomy and responsibility as they get older.
- Third, Article 12 very radically requires that States ensure that due weight be given to the views of the child, and that children who are capable of expressing views be heard in all matters concerning them.
- Fourth, Article 2 requires that all the rights in the CRC be accorded to all children without discrimination.
- Finally, Article 6 protects the right to life, survival and development (see below).

These key themes underpin all other provisions of the CRC and they provide a strong framework for the adoption of a child-friendly focus in all of the obligations imposed on the State. The remaining Articles of the CRC cover a range of issues many of which were already protected in existing treaties, for example the prohibition on torture, the right to privacy and the right to education, freedom of expression, freedom of association, etc.[20] However, the CRC also introduced new rights and reconstructed existing rights so as to promote a child-centered perspective. For example the issue of adoption and the right to identity had not previously been protected by international law.[21] Similarly, the right to life, though protected in all international human rights documents, is expanded beyond the traditional focus on prevention of arbitrary deprivation of life to include considerations of the quality of life through imposing obligations regarding the survival and development of the child.[22]

Not surprisingly, certain provisions are considered to be extreme and radical in their application to children, particularly those contained in Articles 12–17, the participatory rights, which include the rights to freedom of expression, association, privacy and, most controversially, freedom of religion.[23] The inclusion of such rights threatened the acceptance of the CRC by certain States and provoked fears that it would promote the rights of the child at the expense of the parents and the family. Such objections overlook the fact that in most cases the rights of the child and the family will coincide and furthermore these claims distort both the spirit and the letter of the CRC. The CRC recognises the family as the fundamental unit of society in the Preamble[24] and the importance of the family to the development of

---

[20] *See* Convention on the Rights of the Child, *supra* note 1, Articles 37, 17 & 28 respectively.
[21] The right to identity is governed by Article 8, and Article 21 covers the issue of adoption. On new rights in the Convention *see*, J.S. Cerda, *The Draft Convention on the Rights of the Child: New Rights*, 12 H. RTS. Q.,115–119 (1990). *See also* G.A. Stewart *Implementing the Child's Right to Identity in the United Nations Convention on the Rights of the Child*, 26 FAM L.Q. 221 (1992).
[22] *See* Convention on the Rights of the Child, *supra* note 1, Article 6.
[23] *See generally* G. Van Bueren, *The Struggle for Empowerment: the Emerging Civil and Political Rights of Children*, in SELECTED ESSAYS ON INTERNATIONAL CHILDREN'S RIGHTS 45 (Defence for Children International, ed. 1993). *See also* R. HART, CHILDREN'S PARTICIPATION FROM TOKENISM TO CITIZENSHIP, 1992.
[24] *See* Convention on the Rights of the Child, *supra* note 1, Preamble ¶ 5 & 6.

the child is underscored in numerous provisions of the treaty itself; Article 9 provides that children shall not be separated from parents against their will; Article 16 prohibits arbitrary interferences with the child's family life; Article 18 recognises the equal role of both parents in the upbringing of the child; Article 20 requires the State establish a system of care when the child is separated from the family. In addition, various other provisions of the CRC reiterate that the rights of the child are most appropriately realised within the environment of the family and the ethos of the CRC does not attempt to disrupt the family unit save where the best interests of the child so demand. Thus, the CRC merely reaffirms that both the family unit and each member of it enjoy certain rights under international law and challenges to the CRC that argue it is anti-family are without merit.[25] Nonetheless, these kind of objections can mean that the participatory provisions are overlooked in some States and distorted in others and they are the target of a disturbingly high number of reservations.[26]

IMPLEMENTATION OF THE CONVENTION

The Convention has a relatively weak implementation system, which is common to other universal human rights treaties which is essentially a system of self-assessment based on the submission of periodic reports by States Parties. No provision was made for individual petitions or inter-State challenges, which are available for example under the CCPR.[27] The CRC is monitored by a Committee of experts[28] to which States are required to submit an initial report within two years of ratification and periodic reports every five years thereafter. The report should detail those measures the State has taken to bring its laws and administrative practices into line with the Convention. These reports form the basis of a discussion between the Committee and the State, after which the Committee issues concluding observations, in which it recognises where the State is in compliance, highlights areas of concern and makes recommendations for change, often drawing on the practices of other States. The reporting system, which sets the State up as a judge in its own cause, is limited in its efficacy. The Committee follows the established practice of other UN Committees, championing a constructive dialogue with States and avoiding confrontational supervision. This encourages States to view the Committee as a facilitator; States are invited to be honest in their reports and in return the Committee makes considerable efforts to assist States through constructive and creative

---

[25] *See e.g.,* R. Levesque, *The Internationalisation of Children's Rights: Too Radical for American Adolescents?* 9 CONN J. INT'L L. 327 (1994). *See further* Hafen & Hafen, *Abandoning Children to their Own Autonomy, supra* note 5. *See also* CHILDREN'S RIGHTS OFFICE, ALL RIGHT AT HOME? PROMOTING CHILDREN'S RIGHTS IN FAMILY LIFE (2000).

[26] *See e.g.,* W. Schabas, *Reservations to the Convention on the Rights of the Child,* 18 H. RTS Q. (1996) at 472–491, *see also* Schabas, *Reservations to the Convention on the Elimination of All Forms of Discrimination Against Women and the Convention on the Rights of the Child,* 3 WM & MARY J. WOM & L. 79–112 (1997). *See generally* Fottrell *supra,* note 9 on the issue of reservations and the CRC.

[27] *See* MCGOLDRICK, THE HUMAN RIGHTS COMMITTEE, *supra* note 3.

[28] *See* UN Convention on the Rights of the Child, *supra* note 1, Articles 43–45 on the role of the Committee and the nature of State obligations.

suggestions. However, the system undoubtedly works best with those States that generally have high levels of compliance with international human rights treaties. Moreover, relying entirely on supervision of human rights treaties through reporting mechanisms alone is probably unwise; international human rights regimes are most effective when reporting is combined with some kind of quasi-judicial processes allowing for inter-State cases and individual petitions from persons within the jurisdiction of States parties. The latter option was rejected outright in the CRC drafting process, suggesting that States continue to have conceptual and operational difficulties with the rights of the child. That the CRC does not offer such a procedure is rather unfortunate and it is also contrary to the international trends of the last two decades. Other issue and group specific conventions, such as the Convention Against Torture (CAT)[29] and the Convention on the Elimination of Racial Discrimination (CERD),[30] provide for supervision through both reporting and individual complaints. Further evidence that there is a growing trend towards promoting individual petitions is evidenced by the draft optional protocol to the Convention on the Elimination of All Forms of Discrimination Against Women passed in 1999, which allows for individual complaints to its supervisory Committee.[31] One of the main arguments forwarded by supporters of that draft protocol was that the absence of a petition procedure suggested the Women's Convention was somehow a less imposing document than other human rights treaties. The adoption of the draft protocol also countered arguments that the rights in the Women's Convention were inappropriate for resolution through such individual petition mechanisms, which reinforced the construction of a sphere of private life where international supervision was discouraged.[32] Such arguments are familiar to children's rights advocates; few States relish the prospect of their record on children's rights being the subject of a direct challenge before an international judicial forum. However, there are precedents; the European Court of Human Rights has for many years decided cases which touched on children's rights across a range of issues from freedom of expression to the right to respect for family life.[33] Interestingly also the African Charter on the Rights of the Child, which was inspired by the CRC and passed by the OAU Assembly in 1990, allows for both a State reporting system and an

---

[29] Convention against Torture and Other Cruel, Inhuman or Degrading Treatment or Punishment, G.A Res. 39/46, annex, 39 UN Supp (No. 51) at 197, UN Doc.A/39/51 (1984) entered into force June 26 1987, *see* Article 21.

[30] Convention on the Elimination of All Forms of Racial Discrimination, 660 UNTS 195, entered into force January 4 1969, *see* Article 14.

[31] Convention on the Elimination of All Forms of Discrimination against Women G.A Res. 34/180 34 UN GAOR Supp. (No.46) at 193 UN Doc.A/34/46 (1979) entered into force September 3 1981.

[32] *See* Draft Optional Protocol to the Convention on the Elimination of Discrimination Against Women, Commission on the Status of Women, UN Doc. E/CN.6/1999/10 (1999).

[33] On issues involving children before the European Convention on Human Rights *see generally* U. KILLKELLY, THE CHILD AND THE EUROPEAN CONVENTION ON HUMAN RIGHTS, 1999. *See also* by the same author *The Impact of the Children's Convention on the Case-law of the European Convention on Human Rights*, in this collection at 87.

individual complaints mechanism.[34] Thus, children within the jurisdiction of these mechanisms can litigate their rights before these regional bodies and those who are not can bring complaints under universal human rights treaties such as the CCPR which allow for individual petitions,[35] but the absence of such an option in the CRC itself is highly problematic and must ultimately be viewed as a weakness.

PROBLEMS WITH THE IMPLEMENTATION OF THE CRC

In the remaining part of the chapter the focus is on two issues which deserve closer examination; first, it has become apparent over the decade that the protection offered in certain areas needs strengthening because controversies in the drafting stage were not resolved and continue to cast a shadow over the CRC. Second, the chapter examines how the Committee has sought to overcome the inherent weaknesses in the substance and implementation of the treaty.

As mentioned at the outset, the CRC was both ambitious and far-reaching in terms of the sheer breadth of its provisions. However, conflicts over the content of rights and the wording of particular Articles have proven problematic and ultimately weakened the overall effect of the CRC leaving children in certain situations without adequate legal protection. There are two particular issues which will be discussed here; first, the CRC provisions on children in armed conflict and second, the insufficient way in which the CRC promotes the rights of girl children.

Article 38 of the CRC addresses specifically the issue of children and armed conflict and it requires States Parties to respect the rules of international humanitarian law without advancing on that law in any way. As such, Article 38 suffers from two major shortcomings. First, the focus of Article 38 is on child soldiers and yet it fails to raise existing standards, leaving the age of recruitment at 15 years, some 3 years lower than the Article 1 definition of the child. This inconsistency is troubling. Furthermore, Article 38 is in direct conflict with the CRC's own provision on child labour under Article 32 (1), which commits States to protecting children (i.e. persons under 18) from 'performing any work that is likely to be hazardous or to interfere with the child's education, or to be harmful to the child's health or physical, mental,

---

[34] *See* African Charter on the Rights and Welfare of the Child, O.A.U. Doc.CAB/LEG/24.9/49 (1990) Article 44 (1) which allows the Committee which supervises the Charter to receive communications from 'any person, group or non-governmental organisation' on any matter connected to the Charter. The Charter came into force in December 1999, *see generally* INTERIGHTS BULLETIN, March 2000.

[35] In order for an individual to bring a complaint to the Human Rights Committee under the Covenant on Civil and Political Rights, they must be within the jurisdiction of a State Party, which has accepted the competence of the Committee to hear such a complaint. *See* Optional Protocol to the International Covenant on Civil and Political Rights, G.A. Res. 2200A (XXI), 21 UN GAOR Supp. (No.16) at 59, UN Doc. A/6316 (1966), 999 UNTS 302, entered into force March 23 1976. The optional protocol has been signed by about 90 of the 135 States Parties to the Covenant; significantly the UK and the US are among those States which have not signed the protocol. *See generally*, MCGOLDRICK, *supra*, note 3.

spiritual, moral or social development'.[36] By any definition such a provision would be taken to include direct participation in armed conflict.[37]

This has rightly been viewed as a fundamental shortcoming and the Committee sought to remedy this by promoting an optional protocol to the CRC, which would prohibit the recruitment of children to the armed forces below the age of 18 years. Achieving consensus on this issue was difficult but a draft protocol was finally passed in early 2000 and is now open for signatures.[38] This is to be welcomed and is a symbolic achievement; it also indicates that shortcoming in the main body of the treaty can be amended through additional protocols.

A further problem with Article 38 is the focus on formal participation; Goodwin-Gill and Cohn observed that the participation of children in conflicts took place at a range of different levels and was in many cases voluntary.[39] More-over, in the decade since the CRC was passed the issue of the how conflict affects the lives of children and violates their rights has become increasingly desperate and multifarious with the growing exploitation of children in such conflicts as those in Sierra Leone and Uganda. In particular there has been a growing awareness of the very disruptive nature of war on the development of children and a recognition of the need for strategies which go beyond the prohibition of recruitment of child soldiers and examine the impact of conflict on child civilians. The Committee initi-ated the development of parallel procedures in 1993, when it requested the UN Secretary General commission a special report on the impact of armed conflict on the lives of children. The subsequent report by Graca Machel acted as a catalyst for a series of practical and political strategies, at both the universal and regional level, to limit the negative effects of conflict on the lives of children.[40] This inclu-ded the appointment of the Secretary General's Special Representative on Armed Conflict and mainstreaming the issue of the child in conflict and post-conflict societies in discussions at the Security Council. This train of events set in chain by the Committee is a very good example of the multi-disciplinary and multi-agency approach that the Committee favours in promoting and protecting the rights of children; as a consequence some of the substantive failings of the CRC in this area have been ameliorated.[41]

---

[36] *See* UN Convention on the Rights of the Child, *supra* note 1.

[37] On the issue of children and armed conflict *see generally* G.S GOODWIN-GILL & I. COHN, CHILD SOLDIERS (1994). *See also* J. Kuper, *Children and Armed Conflict – Some Problems of Law and Policy*, in this collection at 101. *See further* KUPER, CHILD CIVILIANS, (1997).

[38] *See* Optional Protocol to the Convention on the Rights of the Child on the Involvement of Children in Armed Conflicts, UN Doc.A/54/L.84 at 2 (2000), also available at < http:www.unhchr.ch.html/menu2/6/protocolchild.htm/ >, adopted 16 May 2000. *See further* 4 CHILDREN AT WAR, Dec. 1999.

[39] *See* GOODWIN-GILL & COHN, CHILD SOLDIERS, *supra* note 30.

[40] *See* G. MACHEL, REPORT ON THE IMPACT OF ARMED CONFLICT ON CHILDREN (1996), UN Doc.A/51/306, August 26th 1996. *See further* C. Hamilton & T. El Haj, *Armed Conflict: the Protection of Children under International Law*, 5 INT'L J. CHIL. RTS. 1 (1997). *See also* J. Kuper, *Children and Armed Conflict: Some Problems in Law and Policy*, in this collection at 101.

[41] The issue of children and armed conflict has become a matter for discussion by both the legal and political organs of the United Nations; in December 1997 the Secretary General established the post of Special Representative on Children in Armed Conflict. In addition child soldiers have been dis-cussed by the UN Security Council and in July 2000 the Secretary General issued a report to the

A second fundamental flaw in the substance of the CRC is found in the luke-warm provisions on the rights of girl children. There is an emerging consensus that the discrimination suffered by girls across continents, and particularly in developing States, requires further action from international bodies and that the provisions of the CRC in this regard are inadequate.[42] The CRC has been derided by feminists because of its focus on 'white, male, relatively privileged children' and because it largely ignored the particular disadvantages faced by girls in developing States.[43] It is silent on what measures States should take regarding the specific difficulties of girls in many non-Western societies. The main protection offered girls is found in Article 2, which guarantees equality and non-discrimination, but the reality of many girls' lives is beyond the scope of such declaratory provisions and this must be viewed as an oversight by the drafters.[44] Paper equality cannot be considered a cure-all for the effects of centuries of discrimination. Denial of the rights of girls results from a complex interplay of social, economic, political and religious factors which include traditional male domination of the public sphere, prejudicial cultural practices, misinterpretation of religious obligations and economic disempowerment. In the past decade concern about the position of girls generally, and particularly relating to their exclusion from education and the consequent personal and social costs of such denial, has elevated the issue of the education of girls onto the agenda of development and human rights organisations.[45] There are recent promising initiatives which may eventually have positive effects on the lives of girl children.

Nevertheless the absence of specific protection and provision for girl children in the CRC is baffling and suggests that such an issue was considered too 'controversial' for inclusion in a Convention which sought wide approval. In addition,

---

footnote continued

Security Council on aspects of children and armed conflict, *see further* DEPARTMENT OF PUBLIC INFORMATION, Press Release, July 21 2000, available at < http://www.unhchr.ch >.

[42] *See generally* S. GOONESEKERE, WOMEN'S RIGHTS AND CHILDREN'S RIGHTS: THE UNITED NATIONS CONVENTIONS AS COMPATIBLE AND COMPLEMENTARY INTERNATIONAL TREATIES, 1992. *See also* K. Backstrom, *The International Human Rights of the Child: Do They Protect the Female Child?* 30 G.W. J. INT'L L. & ECON. 541 (1997).

[43] *See* F. Olsen, *Children's Rights: Some Feminist Approaches to the United Nations Convention on the Rights of the Child* in THE BEST INTERESTS OF THE CHILD 193 (P. Alston, ed., 1992).

[44] *See* C. Price Cohen, *The United Nations Convention on the Rights of the Child: A Feminist Landmark*, 2 WM & MARY J. of WOM. & L. 29 (1997) in which she argues that the Convention should be recognised as an important feminist landmark. Cohen bases her argument largely on Article 2 and she credits the Convention with creating a generally heightened awareness of the difficulties faced by many young girls.

[45] UNICEF and UNDP have initiated programmes which seek to explore and promote new delivery systems for educating girls and also promoting community-based education taught by female teachers and taught on flexible timetables to allow for work schedules etc. The model for such programmes is that run by the Bangladesh Rural Advancement Committees, *see generally* UNICEF, THE STATE OF THE WORLD'S CHILDREN (1999). *See also* C. Heward *Introduction: the New Discourses of Gender* in GENDER, EDUCATION AND DEVELOPMENT; BEYOND ACCESS TO EMPOWERMENT 4 (C. Heward & S. Bunawaree, eds. 1999); See *further* C. Brazier, *The Great Education Scandal* NEW INTERNATIONALIST, Aug. 1999 at 7. *See also* G. Van Bueren & D. Fottrell, *The Potential of International Law to Combat Discrimination Against Girls in Education,* in RELIGIOUS FUNDAMENTALISM AND THE HUMAN RIGHTS OF WOMEN 129 (C.W. Howland, ed., 1999).

the specific provisions of the CRC dealing with education, Articles 28 and 29 make no express reference to the needs of girls and the CRC will not assist particularly those seeking to advance educational rights of girls in developing States. This oversight of the Convention is perhaps more striking given the fact that less than three years after the CRC was passed the Vienna Declaration urged States to prioritise the rights of women and girls, showing an awareness of their marginalised position which is curiously absent in the CRC.[46]

The Committee has responded relatively well to the Vienna Declaration and has shown a desire to tackle the substantive deficiencies of the Convention on gender issues. In 1995 the Committee devoted a day of discussion to the girl child which eventually fed into the Beijing World Conference on Women held the same year. The Committee has also raised gender discrimination issues with such States as Egypt, China, Jordan, Pakistan, Burkina Faso, El Salvador and Nepal.[47] Moreover, it has signaled a desire to receive information in all States' reports relating to the education of girls and measures undertaken within the State to close the gap between law and practice on matters of discrimination. These steps indicate that a dynamic interpretation of the CRC by the Committee may allow for certain obligations to be read into the CRC which would require remedial action to promote the rights of girl children.

IMPLEMENTING THE MANDATE EFFECTIVELY

From the outset the Committee on the Rights of the Child has been proactive and creative in fulfilling its functions under the CRC. There were fears that the demands of the reporting system would prove overwhelming for States given the range of rights protected and thus the Committee issued a set of guidelines to assist States in the preparation of their reports. The result was that the Committee clusters the CRC Articles into sections according to topic rather than numerical order; each section covers a specific Article or set of Articles as follows:

- General principles
- Civil rights and freedoms
- Family environment and alternative care
- Basic health and welfare
- Education, leisure and cultural activities
- Special protection measures[48]

Initially the Committee was quite timid and its conclusions on reports were short and relatively simple. However, its recent assessments are increasingly complex and detailed and often include very specific recommendations to States on ways in

---

[46] Vienna Declaration and Programme of Action, World Conference on Human Rights, Vienna 14–25th June 1993 UN Doc.A/CONF.157/24 (Part I) at 20 1993, ¶ 18.

[47] The Committee's general discussion on the girl child was held on January 23rd 1995 *see* UN Doc.CRC/C/38 (1995). On the comments of the Committee relating to education of girl children *see generally* R. HODGKIN & P. NEWELL, IMPLEMENTATION HANDBOOK FOR THE CONVENTION ON THE RIGHTS OF THE CHILD, 25 (1998).

[48] *See* LEBLANC, *supra* note 13 at 52.

which its laws and practices can be improved.[49] In addition, the Committee rejects reports it considers inadequate or it can, and does, request more information on a specific issue.[50] States report to the Committee every five years and are expected in each periodic report to address matters raised by the Committee in its earlier set of concluding comments. This method of implementation as discussed above is limited in its effectiveness. Where a State presents an overly optimistic picture of its own laws and administrative practices, the Committee is very often not in possession of the information to counter such claims as it lacks any investigatory capacity and it is grossly underresourced, both in human and financial terms. Indeed the work of the Committee is done on an almost voluntary basis. The situation is ameliorated, however, by a very active and constructive group of non-governmental organisations (NGOs), which played a significant role in the drafting of the CRC and continue to feed information to the Committee on States as their reports come before the Committee for examination. However, the ability of the Committee to conduct its own research is almost non-existent and thus NGOs and interest groups set the agenda.

A related issue is that the Committee may well find itself overwhelmed by the scale of its task. The Committee meets three times a year for sessions of four weeks and there is some concern about its ability to carry out its functions. As of June 1999 the Committee had received 133 initial reports and 23 periodic reports; it had considered 102 reports. Because its sessions are brief the Committee can only consider five reports per session and is already running almost four years behind and it is saved only by the fact that so many States are behind in the submission of reports.[51] At present, some 57 States are overdue in their submission of initial reports and a rather alarming 100 periodic reports are overdue.[52] A nightmare scenario lies ahead; compliance with the CRC requires at the very least that States Parties feel a certain pressure to submit reports on time and carry out the reviews of domestic laws and practices that such reports entail.

As the Committee itself falls behind in its own consideration of reports it will be increasingly difficult to exert the necessary pressure on States. The smooth running of the reporting system is crucial because, as discussed above, the CRC has no provision for inter-State or individual complaints. Thus the monitoring compliance rests entirely on a system which is already buckling under the inevitable strain of its various shortcomings.

A further problem for the Committee has been the content of State reports, particularly concerning those Articles of the CRC that deal with economic and social issues, some of which are framed in such broad language that States argue

---

[49] *See* R. Rios-Kohn, *The Convention on the Rights of the Child: Progress and Challenges*, 5 GEO. J FIGHTING POVERTY 139 (1998). *See also* J. Todres, *Emerging Limitation on the Rights of the Child: The U.N. Convention on the Rights of the Child and its Early Case-Law*, 30 COLUM. HUM. RTS. L. REV. 159 (1998).
[50] *See* Fottrell, *supra* note 9.
[51] *See* e.g. CRC/C/62 (1997), available at < http://www.unhchr.ch >
[52] *See*, Complete Reporting History of States Parties, 18/11/99, CRC/History.

obligations are unclear and the right itself is all but unenforceable. This has manifested itself through inadequate information regarding economic and social rights and a continuing attitude on the part of many States that such matters are issues of policy and not law. The Committee consistently asks for further information and criticises States for not following the reporting guidelines.[53] Although this is common to other treaties, notably the Covenant on Economic, Social and Cultural Rights, there is some urgency for this to be resolved given the growing number of children living in appalling economic deprivation and poverty. There is a danger that the CRC could be perceived as irrelevant if it fails to have any impact on such situations.

A final point to note is the threat posed to the CRC from an alarmingly high number of reservations, which are dangerously broad and allow States to limit considerably the likely impact of the CRC within their own jurisdiction. Both the number and the breadth of the reservations suggest that many States are taking an à la carte approach to the CRC, which ensures selective application of its provisions such that very little change is effected within the State. The Committee on the Rights of the Child has taken a strong line with States who have entered such reservations and has succeeded in encouraging states to withdraw their reservations; nevertheless, it remains problematic and some kind of robust solution may be required in the near future.

CONCLUSION

Despite these emerging problems in the implementation and application of the CRC, in its short life it has still managed to have a positive impact on the protection of children's rights internationally and domestically. The very fact that the CRC has been almost universally ratified is in itself remarkable and indicates a consensus surrounding at least the spirit if not the letter of the its provisions. What is perhaps most interesting about the performance of the CRC is the fact that children's rights have not become ghettoised or marginalised within the UN, as happened to women's rights in the first decade of the Women's Convention. In actual fact children's rights have been mainstreamed and are discussed and prioritised, at least on paper, at every level of UN activity.

In addition, the CRC was the inspiration for a number of regional initiatives in Europe and Africa and the proliferation of international instruments promoting the rights of the child is promising. The standards of the CRC have also trickled down into the jurisprudence of the ECHR, which has been influenced by the persuasive value of its principles in a number of recent cases involving children. In a number of jurisdictions domestic courts have also looked to the Convention for guidance and the result has invariably raised the existing standards within that State.[54]

Finally, the Committee itself has been both creative and proactive in its inter-

---

[53] HODGKIN & NEWELL *supra* note 47.
[54] *See e.g.* R *v* Secretary of State for the Home Department Ex Parte Venables, 3 W.L.R 23, 26/6/97. *See further* KILKELLY, *supra* note 33.

pretation of its own mandate and has attempted to circumvent such problems as arise from its restricted powers.[55] In addition to becoming more robust in its criticism of States, it has also initiated Days of Discussion, which are devoted to the consideration of thematic issues and have fed into other procedures including the Beijing Conference on Women and the Cairo Conference on the Environment. In 1997 the Committee established a working group to consider the particular needs of children with disabilities following one of these thematic discussions.

Thus, as the CRC passes its 10th birthday, much has been achieved. Children's rights are prioritised at all levels of UN activity and have appeared in recent years on the agenda not just of the Commission on Human Rights but also the General Assembly and the Security Council. There is also growing awareness of the inadequacy of legal mechanisms alone to deal with many issues and there has consequently been an exploration of other means of achieving effective realisation of the rights of the child. The greatest danger for the CRC is complacency; given its widespread ratification there is a tendency to view the CRC as an end in itself, when in fact it is merely a beginning. No State wishes to be viewed as a violator of children's rights and thus it was hardly surprising that States were in such a hurry to ratify the CRC. However, at present many States enjoy the moral benefits inherent in ratification, without giving full effect to its legal obligations. Making that transition will be a challenge for the CRC in the coming decades.

---

[55] *See* Fottrell *supra* note 13.

Michael Freeman

2. CHILDREN AND CULTURAL DIVERSITY

INTRODUCTION

In 1968 a man consulted a doctor in South London for medical treatment of a venereal disease. He introduced his young wife to the doctor and let it be known that he had already taken her to a clinic to be fitted with a contraceptive device. The doctor was concerned and reported the matter to the police who brought a complaint to the juvenile court that she was in need of care because she was being exposed to moral danger.[1] The couple were Nigerian Muslims:[2] he was in his mid-twenties and she was at most 13, but may have been as young as 11. They had married in a polygamous ceremony in northern Nigeria shortly before coming to England. The court made a 'fit person order'[3] under the Children and Young Persons Act 1963 and the girl was admitted to the care of a local authority. The reasons which led the court to conclude that she was in moral danger are encapsulated in the following statement:

> Here is a girl, aged 13, or possibly less, unable to speak English, living in London with a man twice her age to whom she has been married by Muslim law. He admits having had sexual intercourse with her at a time when, according to the medical evidence, the development of puberty had almost certainly not begun ... He further admits that since the marriage ... he has had sexual relations with a prostitute in Nigeria from whom he has contracted venereal disease. In our opinion a continuance of such an association, notwithstanding the marriage, would be repugnant to any decent-minded English man or woman. Our decision reflects that repugnance.[4]

This decision was reversed by the Divisional Court. The Lord Chief Justice, Lord Parker, conceded that it was possible to hold that a validly married wife could be in moral danger, but he refused to accept that the girl in this case was. He said:

> I would never dream of suggesting that a decision by this bench of justices, with this very experienced chairman, could ever be termed perverse: but having read that, I am convinced that they have misdirected themselves. When they say that 'a continuance of such an association notwithstanding the marriage would be repugnant to any decent-minded English man or woman', they are I

---

[1]   Alhaji Mohamed *v* Knott [1969] 1 Q.B.1.
[2]   They were domiciled in Nigeria.
[3]   Fit person orders were replaced by care orders in 1969.
[4]   *Supra* note 1 at 15.

Deirdre Fottrell (ed.), Revisiting Children's Rights, 15–29
© 2000 *Kluwer Law International. Printed in Great Britain.*

think, and can only be, considering the view of an English man or woman in relation to an English girl and our Western way of life. I cannot myself think that decent-minded Englishmen or women, realising the way of life in which this girl was brought up, and this man for that matter, would inevitably say that this is repugnant. It is certainly natural for a girl to marry at that age. They develop sooner, and there is nothing abhorrent in their way of life for a girl of 13 to marry a man of 25 ... Granted that this man may be said to be a bad lot, that he has done things in the past which perhaps nobody would approve of, it does not follow from that that this girl, happily married to this man, is under any moral danger by associating and living with him. For my part, as it seems to me, it could only be said that she was in moral danger if one was considering somebody brought up and living in our way of life and to hold that she is in moral danger in the circumstances of this case can only be arrived at, as it seems to me, by ignoring the way of life in which she was brought up, and her husband was brought up.[5]

The Divisional Court held that the marriage was entitled to recognition by the English courts. It followed from this that the husband was not committing the offence of unlawful sexual intercourse[6] – unlawful, it was held, meant outside marriage.[7]

The case, understandably, provoked considerable controversy. *The Daily Express* was outraged. So was Baroness Summerskill, who initiated a debate in the House of Lords.[8] The decision was branded as racist, a failure by white institutions to protect a vulnerable black child. Olive Stone thought the case 'disturbing'[9] and Ruth Deech believed its 'practical consequences would be disastrous'.[10] It led Ian Karsten to call for a minimum age to be prescribed for recognition purposes.[11] But other commentators welcomed the decision. It showed a willingness to embrace the customs and culture of another society.[12] What was 'moral danger' was being tested by the morality of the culture to which the couple belonged. The decision was seen to be consonant with an acceptance of moral pluralism.[13]

Whichever stance one adopted, the case had troubling features. An analysis of Lord Parker's judgment reveals prejudices and misconceptions galore, not least a concern that his understanding of Islamic culture in northern Nigeria may not have been very deep, assumptions and biases filling in gaps in his knowledge base. It is not clear what evidence, if any, was given to either court about the life realities of Muslim Nigeria. It would be nice to record a happy ending to this story but not long after the marriage ended in divorce. Indeed, the girl in this case and the hus-

---

[5] *Ibid* at 15–16.
[6] *See* Sexual Offences Act 1956 § 6(1) (intercourse with a girl under 16).
[7] On the interpretation of §19(1) of the 1956 Act, *see further* R *v* Chapman [1959] 1 QB 100.
[8] *See* 290 HANSARD H.L. cols. 1321–1323.
[9] *See* O. Stone, Vol. no. 7 FAMILY LAW 40 (1977).
[10] *See* R. Deech, *Family Law and Immigrant Practices* 123 N. L. J. 110–111 (1973).
[11] *See* I. Karsten, *Child Marriages* 32 MOD. L. REV 212, (1969) 215–216.
[12] *See* BRENDA HOGGETT, PARENTS AND CHILDREN, 110 (1977).
[13] *See* M.D.A. FREEMAN, THE LEGAL STRUCTURE, 48 (1974).

band's other wife together divorced him in the same court on the same day, a precedent which is unlikely ever to re-occur.

About the same time as *Mohamed v Knott* was going through the courts, the question arose in England in a different context in the case of *R v Derrivierre*.[14] A West Indian father was charged with an assault upon his 12-year-old son occasioning him actual bodily harm. The boy had been disobedient and the father punished him by punching him a number of times in the face. English law provides a defence to the crime of wilfully assaulting a child[15] if the purpose is chastisement and the punishment is moderate and reasonable.[16] The father was given a six-month term of imprisonment for what the Deputy Chairman of the Inner London Quarter Sessions described as a 'brutal attack'. On an appeal against sentence the Criminal Division of the Court of Appeal upheld the decision and set out the broad principle involved:

> Standards of parental correction are different in the West Indies from those which are acceptable in this country; and the Court fully accepts that immigrants coming to this country may find initially that our ideas are different from those upon which they have been brought up in regard to the methods and manner in which children are to be disciplined. There can be no doubt that once in this country, this country's laws must apply; and there can be no doubt that, according to the law of this country, the chastisement given to this boy was excessive and the assault complained of was proved. Nevertheless, had this been a first offence, and had there been some real reason for thinking that the appellant either did not understand what the standards in this country were or was having difficulty in adjusting himself, the Court would no doubt have taken that into account and given it such consideration as it could.[17]

In fact Derrivierre had a previous conviction for assaulting his daughter only a year before and thus had already received a fair warning of the unacceptable nature of this type of behaviour in England. But the case does show a willingness by English courts to take supposedly different standards of another culture into account in sentencing.[18] More recently, in a child care case,[19] the practices of a mother who was by origin Vietnamese were judged against the 'reasonable objective standards of the culture in which the children have hitherto been brought up',[20] though the judge was careful to add, 'so long as these do not conflict with our minimal acceptable

---

[14] R v Derrivierre (1969) 53 Cr. App. Rep. 637.
[15] *See* Children and Young Persons Act 1933 § 1(7).
[16] As to which *see generally* Cockburn C.J. in R v Hopley (1860) 2 F & F 202. *See further* P. NEWELL, CHILDREN ARE PEOPLE TOO (1989). On the religious roots *see* P. GREVEN, SPARE THE CHILD, (1992). Echoes of this can be detected in M. STRAUS, BEATING THE DEVIL OUT OF THEM: CORPORAL PUNISHMENT IN THE AMERICAN FAMILY, (1994).
[17] *Supra* note 14 at 638–639.
[18] *See further* S.M. POULTER, ENGLISH LAW AND ETHNIC MINORITY CUSTOMS, 271–274 (1986).
[19] Re H [1987] 2 FLR 12.
[20] *Ibid*, at 17.

standards of child care in England'.[21] But, of course, the judge heard no evidence of what the 'reasonable objective standards' of rural Vietnam were, though he was convinced that the mother's disciplinary measures were unacceptable in that culture too. Neither *Derrivierre* nor *Re H* (the Vietnamese case) provoked the interest or the controversy which *Mohamed v Knott* fuelled. But that is hardly surprising, given English ambivalence to questions of the physical chastisement of children.[22]

These extended case studies are but two examples of the problem posed when legislation comes up against the practices of another culture.[23] It is a problem well known to drafters of international conventions and the two examples drawn from England could be added to by reference to confrontations in other countries. But the temptation to document such examples will be resisted and this chapter will focus on aspects of two international conventions instead.

In 1919, the International Labour Organisation adopted a convention fixing the minimum age for admission of children to industrial employment.[24] Article 2 of this states

> Children under the age of 14 years shall not be employed or work in any public or private industrial undertaking, or in any branch thereof, other than an undertaking in which only members of the same family are employed.

For most Western States the age of 14 was accepted. But the Commission on Children's Employment, responsible for preparing the Labour Conference, met strong objection from countries in Asia where child labour under the age of 14 was and indeed still is widespread and where the financial resources for implementing rapid change did not exist. 'Should modifications of the Convention be allowed in the case of those countries with special climatic and industrial conditions?', asked Sir Malcolm Delevinge of the United Kingdom.[25] A trade unionist from Britain, Margaret Bondfield, was in no doubt that such exceptions were unacceptable but a compromise at her initiative was effected. Speaking of what became Article 6 of the Convention, she said:

> With regard to one of the main objections, namely the nature of the Indian industries. We have carefully drafted this amendment to exclude all those

---

[21] *Id.*

[22] This came to the fore yet again in Britain in 1994 over the question of the moral propriety and legality of a childminder smacking a child in her care. See London Borough of Sutton *v* Davis [1994] 1 FLR 737. It has now been 'resolved' by Government Guidance permitting a childminder to smack, but only where a parent gives consent, *see* THE TIMES, Dec. 3 1994.

[23] On scarification *see* R *v* Adesanya, THE TIMES, July 16 & 17 1974. *See also* S. Poulter, *Foreign Customs and The English Criminal Law* 24 INT'L & COMP. L. Q. 136 (1975). On West African fostering practices *see* Re O (1973) 3 FAM LAW 40, Re E O (1973) 3 FAM LAW 48 and Re A (1978) 8 FAM LAW 247. Also interesting is Re H [1978] Fam. 65 (returning an abused Pakistani child of four to her parents who were returning to Pakistan).

[24] *See* P. VEERMAN, THE RIGHTS OF THE CHILD AND THE CHANGING IMAGE OF CHILDHOOD, (1992) Chapter 13.

[25] LEAGUE OF NATIONS, INTERNATIONAL LABOUR CONFERENCE, First Annual Meeting, 1921 at 96.

industries that could be considered purely native industries or that are small industries. It is especially drafted to refer only to those industries, which are being modelled on Western ideas, which are to some extent under control of factory legislation and which are mainly supervised by Western people.[26]

And so Article 6 declares boldly that Article 2 'shall not apply to India' and then sets a lower age (12) below which children are not to be employed in factories 'working with power and employing more than 10 persons' or in mines, transport or the docks. India continued to raise reservations, in particular relating to the 'difficulties which local customs would place in the way of organising adequate primary education'.[27] In the event India did not ratify this Convention though it did ratify (in 1921) another ILO Convention adopted in 1919 on the prohibition of nightwork.[28] The 1919 Convention on minimum age has been replaced by one adopted in 1973.[29] This states that every State Party is to undertake progressively to raise the minimum age for admission to employment or work 'to a level consistent with the fullest physical and mental development of young persons'.[30] Developing countries are, nevertheless, still allowed to specify a minimum age for employment at 14 years.[31] There is currently debate ongoing on a new ILO Convention. The U.N. Convention on the Rights of the Child (CRC) recognises the right of the child to be protected from economic exploitation and from performing hazardous work or work likely to interfere with education[32] but no minimum age is specified.

But it is another provision of the CRC to which attention must now turn. Article 24, dealing with health and health services, confronts the issue of cultural difference in paragraph 3. This states, 'State Parties shall take all effective and appropriate measures with a view to abolishing traditional practices prejudicial to the health of children'. There are many traditional practices which may harm children but no one is in any doubt that one practice in particular is targeted by this provision, viz. female circumcision.[33] This is prevalent in wide areas of the

---

[26] *Id.*
[27] 3 INTERNATIONAL LABOUR REVIEW Nos. 1–2, July–August (1921) at 16.
[28] ILO Convention No. 6, it is reproduced in VEERMAN, *supra* note 24, at 420. India did originally ask for preferential treatment on this Convention too as did Japan and Belgium (whose request to except the glass industry was rejected by the Conference).
[29] ILO Convention No. 138 (reproduced in VEERMAN, *supra* note 24, at 484).
[30] Article 1.
[31] Article 2(4). They must state a reason or alternatively agree to renounce 'the right to avail itself of the provisions in question as from a stated date' (Article 2(5)). India by the Child Labour (Prohibition and Regulation) Act 1986 has prohibited those less than 14 years working in certain hazardous employment and regulated their working conditions in certain other employment.
[32] Article 32. States Parties must provide a minimum age for employment and provide for penalties or other sanctions to ensure effective enforcement. (Art. 32 (2) (a) and (c)). On India *see generally* M. WEINER, THE CHILD AND THE STATE IN INDIA, (1991).
[33] Delegates of Canada, the United Kingdom and the US were in favour of formulations of the Article that would have referred specifically to female circumcision. See D. Johnson *Cultural and Regional Pluralism in the Drafting of the UN Convention on the Rights of The Child*, THE IDEOLOGIES OF CHILDREN'S RIGHTS 95 (M. Freeman & P. Veerman, eds., 1992) 109–110.

world[34] and it takes a number of forms.[35] Infibulation – genital mutilation of the grossest kind – is particularly common in the Sudan, Somalia, Ethiopia and Mali. Several Western countries have legislated against it,[36] including the United Kingdom in 1986,[37] and France has prosecuted and imprisoned parents involved in it. Senegal has also now outlawed the practice but this was done to ensure American financial assistance (1999). Nevertheless, in formulating Article 24, paragraph 3, caution had to be taken. Senegal, for example, warned that a more direct condemnation would force the practice underground.[38]

Four examples have now been used: child marriages, child labour, female circumcision and corporal chastisement practices. Of female child circumcision more will be said. But at this stage attention must turn to the concept of cultural pluralism and its justification. And pluralism must be distinguished from two other political ethical theories, namely relativism and monism (or universalism).

CULTURAL PLURALISM

The fact of cultural pluralism was known as early as the time of the Greek historian, Herodotus,[39] and can be traced through Montaigne,[40] Vico,[41] Hume[42] and Montesquieu[43] (who perhaps was the first to try to explain cultural difference). But it is to twentieth-century anthropology that we must look for articulation of the concept.[44]

---

[34] *See* A. Slack, *Female Circumcision: A Critical Appraisal* 10 HUM. RTS. Q. 437 (1988). *See also* S. James, *Reconciling International Human Rights and Cultural Relativism: The Case of Female Circumcision* 8 BIOETHICS 1 (1994).

[35] *See* E. DORKENOO & S. ELWORTHY, FEMALE GENITAL MUTILATION: PROPOSALS FOR CHANGE (1992); *see also* E. DORKENOO, CUTTING THE ROSE, (1994).

[36] The United Kingdom has the Prohibition of Female Circumcision Act (1986). There have as yet been no prosecutions. *See* Baroness Jeger's letter to THE TIMES, April 1 1999. There is also legislation in the US, The Female Genital Mutilation Act of 1993, H.R. 3247. This is discussed at 9 BERKELEY WOMEN'S L. J., 206 (1994). In France there is no specific law but the violence involved in circumcision brings the activity within a more general proscription. The Gréon case in France, which led to a one-year suspended sentence, promoted an outcry, see THE GUARDIAN, Sept. 17 1994. Since then an African woman was sentenced to eight years for circumcising 48 young girls, THE TIMES, Feb. 8 1999.

[37] For the view of social workers towards it *see* L. Eaton, *A Fine Line*, COMMUNITY CARE, 21–27 July 1994, at 16. *See also* BRYAN HARTLEY, ARCHIVES OF DISEASES IN CHILDHOOD (1994).

[38] Senegal pointed to son preference as another harmful traditional practice.

[39] *See* his PERSIAN WARS, ('if one were to offer men to choose out of all the customs in the world such as seemed to them the best, they would examine the whole number, and end by preferring their own') (Book 3, Ch. 38).

[40] *See* C. Geertz, *Anti Anti-Relativism*, 86 AMERICAN ANTHROPOLOGIST 86, 263 at 264.

[41] THE NEW SCIENCE (1744).

[42] *See*, in particular, A DIALOGUE IN ENQUIRIES CONCERNING HUMAN UNDERSTANDING AND CONCERNING THE PRINCIPLES OF MORALS (L.A. Selby-Bigge ed. revised by P.H. Nidditch, 1975) 324.

[43] THE SPIRIT OF THE LAWS (1748).

[44] In particular to F. Boas, *see e.g.*, *The Mind of Primitive Man*, 14 JOURNAL OF AMERICAN FOLKLORE 1 (1901). *See also* R. BENEDICT, PATTERNS OF CULTURE, (1934); M. HERSKOVITS, CULTURAL RELATIVISM: PERSPECTIVES IN CULTURAL PLURALISM (1972).

Pluralism is a theory about the sources of value (as are relativism and monism).[45] Pluralists believe that there are many reasonable conceptions of a good life and many reasonable values upon which the realisation of good lives depend. There are conflicts among reasonable conceptions of a good life as well as among reasonable values. Political ethics needs to cope with these conflicts, to attempt to surmount difficulties caused by the incompatibility and incommensurability of values whose realisation is thought to be essential. Where values are incompatible – for example a belief in equality of the sexes and a belief that men are superior – the realisation of one value must exclude the other. Values are incommensurable where there is no measuring rod by which they can be compared.

Incommensurable values need not necessarily be incompatible, and where they are not they can co-exist. If values were only incommensurable the problem would not be too great – a vision which allowed for and requited discrete but compatible conceptions of the good life is not beyond the scope of imagination. It is the incompatibility of values that constitutes the stumbling-block. Pluralists accept that conflicts among values can be resolved by appealing to some reasonable ranking of the values in question. They acknowledge that a plurality of reasonable rankings also exists.

MONISM

Monism, or universalism,[46] by contrast, is committed to there being an overriding value or set of values and, if the latter, a ranking scheme on the basis of which values can be compared in a way that all reasonable people would find acceptable. Pluralists object to monism because they cannot accept the idea that there is an overriding value, that there is some consideration which always takes precedence over all other considerations. Monism also overlooks those cases of moral conflict where no standard can legitimately claim a monopoly of the truth (the issue of abortion[47] is the best example of this). Where pluralists and monists agree is in accepting the need for a reasonable method of resolving conflict.

RELATIVISM

Pluralists also reject relativism. Pluralism may have emerged out of relativism and the two are often confused.[48] Pluralists and relativists agree that there are no overriding values, that all values are conditional, that there is a plurality of incompatible and incommensurable values. They agree on the need for conflict resolution.

---

[45] *See* C. Larmore, *Pluralism and Reasonable Disagreement*, 11 SOCIAL PHILOSOPHY AND POLICY 11, 61, 64 (1994).

[46] There are different models of monism, ranging from the Platonic 'Idea of The Good' (see his REPUBLIC, and to different versions of utilitarianism, using in its simplest model a felific calculus, *see* J BENTHAM, INTRODUCTION TO THE PRINCIPLES OF MORALS AND LEGISLATION.

[47] *See* R. DWORKIN, LIFE'S DOMINION, (1993).

[48] Joseph Raz claims not to know what cultural pluralism is, *see Moral Change and Social Relativism*, 11 (1) SOCIAL PHILOSOPHY AND POLICY 139 (1994).

But relativists go beyond pluralism and think that all values are conventional. Relativism emerged in reaction to cultural evolutionism, which was European and often racist.[49] As Hatch puts it, 'It goes without saying that people who were thought to be the least cultured were also thought to be the least intelligent and the darkest in pigmentation.'[50] When cultural relativism emerged in the first third of this century it was seen as a challenge to racist, Eurocentric notions of progress.[51] Cultural relativism like pluralism is a theory about the way evaluations or judgements are made. But to the relativist, 'evaluations are relative to the cultural background out of which they arise'.[52] So to Ruth Benedict, one of the founders of relativism, tolerance is a key element of cultural relativism;[53] and to Herskovits it is necessary to recognise the 'dignity inherent in every body of custom.'[54] The philosopher Charles Taylor talks of the presumption of the equal worth of cultures.[55]

The attractions of relativism are difficult to ignore. It is rooted in egalitarianism, in liberalism and in modernism. It belongs perhaps to a disenchanted vision of the world.[56] It is anti-assimilationist, it is anti-imperialist, and it is hostile to ethnocentrism.[57] It is sympathetic to, and would wish to protect, the traditions and rights of indigenous peoples.[58] It has the value also, in a sort of Millian way,[59] of enhancing the prospects of achieving moral knowledge, though this presupposes the possibility of real communication across cultures and this is not always possible.[60]

Relativists regard all values as the products of the customs, practices and beliefs which have as a matter of fact developed within a particular tradition. They deny that any value has any authority, epistemological or moral, outside of this cultural context. They deny that conflict between values belonging to different traditions can be settled in any reasonable way, because, so they argue, what is reasonable is itself a product of particular cultures. And so they demand of us that we ask not whether social practices like child marriage or female circumcision, or for that matter purdah, suttee or polygamy, are justified by the moral considerations that we find cogent, but rather whether they are sanctioned by the relevant social understandings of the cultures within which they are practised.

---

[49] G.W. STOCKING JR., RACE, CULTURE AND EVOLUTION (1968).
[50] E. HATCH, CULTURE AND MORALITY: THE RELATIVITY OF VALUES IN ANTHROPOLOGY, 26 (1983).
[51] A.D. RENTELN, INTERNATIONAL HUMAN RIGHTS: UNIVERSALISM VERSUS RELATIVISM (1990).
[52] *Seer* M. HERSKOVITS, *supra* note 44 at 14.
[53] *Supra* note 44 at 37. *See also* HATCH, *supra* note 50 at 99–100.
[54] *See* M. HERSKOVITS, MAN AND HIS WORKS, 76 (1947).
[55] *See* C. TAYLOR, MULTICULTURALISM AND 'THE POLITICS OF RECOGNITION', 72 (1992).
[56] Charles Larmore so characterises it *supra* note 45 at 71.
[57] *See*, A. An-Na'im, *Religious Minorities under Islamic Law and The Limits of Cultural Relativism*, 9 HUM. RTS. Q. 1 (1987).
[58] *See* W. KYMLICKA, LIBERALISM, COMMUNITY AND CULTURE, (1989). *See also* A. Gewirth, *Is Cultural Pluralism Relevant To Moral Knowledge?* 11 (1) SOCIAL PHILOSOPHY AND POLICY 11(1) 22, 35 (1994).
[59] *See* J.S. MILL, ON LIBERTY (1859).
[60] *See* C. Kukarhas, Explaining Moral Variety, 11 (1) SOCIAL PHILOSOPHY AND POLICY, 1, 18 (1994).

But, if that means that a culture can only be judged by endogenous value judgements, and that moral principles which derive from outside that culture have no validity, morality has become a slave to custom,[61] the 'ought' has relinquished any transcendental power that it may have had to critique the 'is'. However, if, as Amy Gutmann has argued persuasively, 'cultural relativists agree that there can be standards for judging justice that are independent of social consensus, then they give up the distinctive premise of cultural relativism.'[62] I would argue that they must. The argument for any practice must be more than that the practice exists. A culture which permits child marriage or female circumcision must be able to support these practices by a stronger argument, or series of arguments, than that there is – if, indeed, this is the case – social consensus. An examination of the social understandings within the culture may reveal that there is no social understanding at all or that there are conflicting understandings, misunderstandings or inconsistencies. Often, it will reveal that the so-called dominant understanding is in reality the understanding of the dominant.[63] Many cultural practices when critically examined turn on the interpretation of a male élite, with a consensus having been engineered to cloak the interests of a section of the society.[64]

Both monists and pluralists disagree. Monists because they believe that a practice can be judged by an overriding value; pluralists because they claim that there are values independent of the context of the culture in question to which we can reasonably appeal in settling conflicts. There is surely no dispute that there are certain needs which do not vary either temporally – they are historically constant – or culturally – they are the requirement of people everywhere. This does not mean that there are not differences in the ways in which these needs are met. There is a need for food but not a need for meat and two vegetables.[65] There is a need for shelter but it does not have to be a semi-detached house. Nor are these needs only physiological. There are psychological needs too, for comfort, affection, companionship. There are social needs, for order, security, dignity, respect, privacy. There are minimum requirements of human welfare. They must be met whatever the conception of what constitutes a good life and regardless of what other values are upheld in any particular culture.[66]

It is easy to distinguish this model of pluralism from one of relativism. Relativists do not acknowledge these primary values and therefore fail to see that there are

---

[61] J.S. MILL in ON LIBERTY wrote of the 'despotism of custom'.

[62] A. Gutmann, *The Challenge of Multiculturalism in Political Ethics*, 22 PHILOSOPHY AND PUBLIC AFFAIRS, 171, 177 (1993).

[63] *Ibid.*, at 176.

[64] S.A. James argues persuasively that this is the case with female circumcision in African societies *supra* note 34.

[65] And the need is for food as nutrition. Food may have secondary purposes such as the fulfilment of religious obligations. This is not addressed by M. WALZER, in SPHERES OF JUSTICE, (1983) at 8, '. . .if the religious uses of bread were to conflict with its nutritional uses . . . It is by no means clear which should be primary' . . . Only a relativist could say this: it is crystal clear that the religious use of bread is of secondary importance to its use as nutrition. Nutrition is a basic, primary value: religion is not. *See further* J. FINNIS, NATURAL LAW AND NATURAL RIGHTS, (1980).

[66] *See also* J. Kekes, *Pluralism and The Value of Life*, 11 (1) SOCIAL PHILOSOPHY AND POLICY, 44, 49 (1994).

standards, independent of a particular culture, by which it can be judged. It is less easy to distinguish it from monism but it is a different claim, for primary values may conflict with each other, in which case it may become necessary to put the conflict into its cultural context to determine which, if either, should prevail. The contribution that the achievement of the particular value makes to the life of the individual concerned may also be significant: which of two values, for example, enhances the goal of his or her 'good life'.

RESPONDING TO THE CASE STUDIES – RELATIVISM

We may return now to the case studies used at the beginning of this chapter: child marriages, corporal punishment practices, child labour and female circumcision. The relativist would situate each of the case studies into its cultural context and would, I would argue, be impotent to offer any real critique. It is surely one of the limitations of cultural relativism that it can lead us to conclude that 'anything goes'. A consequence of this is that we lack the ammunition to protect the individual against the group. The challenge of rights is easily snuffed out. We are forced to condone practices which we find repressive or intolerable because we are told that is only our opinion and had our enculturation been into the culture we are now criticising our opinion would be different. The relativist has little to offer the child either by way of protection or empowerment, any more I suggest than he could have offered Jews living in Nazi Germany or blacks in South Africa under apartheid.[67]

THE MONIST RESPONSE

The monist response is more positive. It points to there being an evaluative consideration, an overriding value, which trumps all other considerations. It may take the form of a categorical imperative,[68] a harm principle,[69] a principle of generic consistency[70] or many other forms. It may take the form of a convention, like the CRC.

The epistemic relevance of these principles may be questioned. Certainly, a relativist might observe the use here of conceptions of reason and rationality firmly rooted within Western Enlightenment culture; there are other conceptions of 'reason' to which other cultures appeal, including myth, religious faith, intuition

---

[67] *See* A.D. Renteln, *supra* note 51, at 67, she believes that relativism is 'out of favor' mainly because of this supposed impotence. J. Cook described relativism as 'nihilistic' *see Cultural Relativism as an Ethnocentric Notion*, in THE PHILOSOPHY OF SOCIETY, 289 (R. Beehler & A.R. Drengson eds., 1978).

[68] As with Immanuel Kant.

[69] As with John Stuart Mill *see supra* note 59.

[70] *See* A. GEWIRTH, REASON AND MORALITY, (1978). *See also The Epistemology of Human Rights*, 1 (2) SOCIAL PHILOSOPHY AND POLICY, 1 (1984), and, briefly, *supra* note 58. *See further* D. BEYLEVELD, THE DIALECTICAL NECESSITY OF MORALITY: AN ANALYSIS AND DEFENCE OF ALAN GEWIRTH'S ARGUMENT TO THE PRINCIPLE OF GENERIC CONSISTENCY (1991), a sustained defence.

and tradition. Why, it may be asked, should alien reasoning processes be admitted when cultural practices external to the culture are ruled irrelevant? This is not un-reminiscent of the debates about the relevance of human rights language to non-Western traditions.[71] And there are parallel debates about the meaning of childhood in different cultures and political economies.[72]

The response of the monist to our four examples would depend upon the over-riding value or values chosen. Abstracting values from international human rights norms[73] would lead to condemnation of female child circumcision,[74] would result in castigation of countries which permitted child labour and would give no unequi-vocal answers on the other two matters. The CRC has nothing to say on marriages of the very young and though it is probably opposed to corporal punishment, whether Article 19 actually proscribes it is not entirely clear, though there can be little real doubt that this is the effect of international jurisprudence generally.[75]

THE PLURALIST APPROACH

To the pluralist the practices found in the case studies at the beginning of this essay have to be looked at both in terms of primary values and the cultural context in which the individuals concerned lived. If one takes preservation of physical integrity to be a primary value then even situating this within relevant cultural contexts leads to a condemnation of child female circumcision. Apart from ritualistic circumci-sion, where the clitoris is merely nicked and there is little mutilation or long-term damage, the term 'female circumcision' is a euphemism which has only the remotest similarity with male circumcision in terms of its physical effects. The practice has been described by Alison Slack as follows:

> The practice can be broken down into four basic forms that vary in degrees of severity. The first, and least severe form, is ritualistic circumcision ... The second form is simply called circumcision or 'sunna' by the Muslims. This involves the removal of the clitoral prepuce – the outer layer of the skin over the clitoris, sometimes called the 'hood', gland and body of the clitoris remain intact. Occasionally, the tip of the clitoris itself is removed. Sunna has been

---

[71] *See e.g.*, J.A.M. Cobbah, *African Values and the Human Rights Debate: An African Perspective*, 9 HUM RTS Q., 309 (1987); D. E. Arzt, *The Application of International Human Rights Law in Islamic States*, 12 HUM. RTS. Q., 202 (1990); *see also* A.E. MAYER, ISLAM AND HUMAN RIGHTS TRADITION AND POLITICS, 3rd Ed. (1999).

[72] *See* P. ARIÈS, CENTURIES OF CHILDHOOD: A SOCIAL HISTORY OF THE FAMILY, (1962); BARBARA A. HANAWALT, GROWING UP IN MEDIEVAL LONDON: THE EXPERI-ENCE OF CHILDHOOD IN HISTORY, (1993); *See also* R. STAINTON ROGERS & W. STAIN-TON ROGERS, STORIES OF CHILDHOOD: SHIFTING AGENDAS OF CHILD CONCERN, (1992).

[73] *See* J. O'Manique, *Universal and Inalienable Rights: A Search for Foundations*, 12 HUM. RTS. Q., 465 (1990).

[74] Using the Universal Declaration of Human Rights, adopted December10 1948, G.A. Res. 217A (111) 3 UN GAOR (Part 1) UN Doc.A/810 (148), Article 25 (and 15). *See further* James, *supra* note 34, at 12–22.

[75] But a case can be put that it would proscribe it, as Sweden, amongst other countries, has done *see further* P. Newell, *Ending Corporal Punishment of Children*, in this volume at 116.

25

equated with male circumcision, because the clitoris itself is generally not damaged.

A third, and more harsh form of the practice, is called excision or clitoridectomy. This is the most common form and involves the removal of the gland of the clitoris – usually the entire clitoris – and often parts of the labia minora as well.

Finally, the most severe form of the practice is infibulation ... where virtually all of the external female genitalia are removed – removing the entire clitoris and labia minora – and, in addition, much or most the labia majora is cut or scraped away. The remaining raw edges of the labia majora are then sewn together with acacia tree thorns, and held in place with catgut or sewing thread. The entire area is closed up by this process leaving only a tiny opening roughly the size of a matchstick, to allow for the passing of urine and menstrual fluid. The girl's legs are then tied together – ankles, knees and thighs – and she is immobilised for an extended period varying from fifteen to forty days, while the wound heals.[76]

Often, one of the harsher forms of the practice occurs, even though a milder type was intended, because the girls struggle due to the blunt instruments used and the lack of anaesthesia. The instruments used range from kitchen knives, old razor blades, broken glass and sharp stones to scalpels. The wounds are frequently treated with animal dung and mud to stop the bleeding. The practice occurs most often on young girls between the ages of three and eight. It is primarily found in areas where there is considerable poverty, where hunger, insanitary conditions and illiteracy are rife, and where there is little in the way of health care facilities. It is also pertinent to note that the economic and social status of women characteristically is low where female child circumcision is prevalent.

The practices are supported by a number of arguments. The control of female sexuality is the central justification.[77] It is said to prevent wantonness and to preserve the virginity of a future bride.[78] Where infibulation has taken place, the girl has to be 're-opened' surgically so that her husband may have sexual intercourse with her, reassured that he is the first to have done this. The preservation of virginity is essential for determining a woman's social position in these societies and in some areas the value of a prospective bride is based on the size of the infibulated opening.[79] There is a belief also that female circumcision is a religious imperative:[80]

---

[76] A. Slack, Female Circumcision: A Critical Appraisal, supra note 34, at 441–442. See also Dorkenoo Elworthy, supra note 35; see further K. Brennan, *The Influence of Cultural Relativism on International Human Rights Law: Female Circumcision as a Case Study*, 3 LAW AND INEQUALITY, 367 (1989); K. Boulware-Miller, *Female Circumcision: Challenges To The Practice as a Human Rights Violation*, 8 HARV. WOMEN'S L. J., 155 (1985).

[77] L.P. Cutner, *Female Genital Mutilation*, 40 (7) OBSTETRICAL AND GYNECOLOGICAL SURVEY, 438 (1985).

[78] *See* A. Slack, *supra* note 76 at 445.

[79] *Ibid.* at 446.

[80] The practice does not exist in the teachings of any formal religion. Slack, *supra* note 76, at 446 notes it is practised amongst Jews in Africa, but this is not correct. The Falashas in Ethiopia may have practised circumcision.

the belief is widely held among Muslims that the practice is scripturally mandated by the Koran.[81] Although the practice is often supported by Muslim leaders, there is no mention of either excision or infibulation in the Koran. Female circumcision is supported by these leaders as being a positive 'sunna', or tradition, one that serves to attenuate sexual desire in women.[82]

Muslim men in Africa hold uncircumcised women in contempt. One of the worst insults in Muslim Africa is to be called 'Son of an uncircumcised mother'.[83]

Justification of the practice also finds support in a number of myths including the belief that the clitoris represents the male sexual organ and, if not cut, will grow to the size of a penis,[84] that females are sterile until excised, the operation being thought to increase fertility, and that the operation is a biologically cleansing process that improves the hygienic and/or aesthetic condition of female genitalia.[85] There is also the argument that the adherence to the tradition of female circumcision amounts to a right to cultural self-determination and that the pursuit of this right brings psychological benefits to women. Research in the Sudan, Egypt and Nigeria suggests that the importance of tradition[86] is the most significant of justificatory arguments for the practice, and that the support amongst women for the tradition is hardly less than that by men.[87]

These justifications can be examined using the cultural pluralist framework that I have offered. That there is a violation of physical integrity, at least in the case of clitoridectomy and infibulation, is incontestable. To the monist or universalist that is the end of the question. But the cultural pluralist must go on to ask how important a value physical integrity is to women in the Sudan or Somalia, particularly when its preservation may lead to their being social outcasts. If an analogy may be given, it is clear that life is a primary value, but we can all think of circumstances, being in a persistent vegetative state (PVS) for example, when we would not wish to continue to live. A PVS condition may constitute life but hardly a 'good life'.

What this overlooks is the age of those who undergo female circumcision. They are for the large part very young children in no position to give informed consent. And yet the operations carried out upon them may severely and irreversibly affect

---

[81] *See* A.A. EL DAREER, WOMAN, WHY DO YOU WEEP? 71 (1982).

[82] Directing it, so it is said, to 'the desirable moderation' *see* M. Bassili Assaad, '*Female Circumcision in Egypt: Social Implications, Current Research, and Prospects for Change*, 11 (1) STUDIES IN FAMILY PLANNING, 5 (1980). Hanny Lightfoot-Klein nevertheless found that sexual desire and pleasure were experienced by the majority of women subjected to the most extreme form of circumcision, in spite of their being culturally bound to hide these experiences, *see The Sexual Experience and Marital Adjustment of Genitally Circumcised and Infibulated Females In the Sudan*, 26 JOURNAL OF SEX RESEARCH, 375 (1989). *See also* her PRISONERS OF RITUAL, AN ODYSSEY INTO FEMALE GENITAL MUTILATION IN AFRICA, (1989).

[83] R.H. DUALEH ABDALLA, SISTERS IN AFFILIATION: CIRCUMCISION AND INFIBULATION OF WOMEN IN AFRICA, 84 (1982).

[84] N. ATIYA, KHUL-KHAAL: FIVE EGYPTIAN WOMEN TELL THEIR STORIES, 11 (1982).

[85] *Female Circumcision*, THE LANCET, March 12 1983, at 569.

[86] R.A. Myers et al, *Circumcision: Its Nature and Practice Among Some Ethnic Groups in Southern Nigeria*, 21 SOC. SC. & MEDICINE, 584 (1985); El Dareer, *supra* note 81, at 141 *et seq.*; Atiyo, *supra* note 84 at 11.

[87] El Dareer interviewed over 4,500 adults in Sudan: 82.6 percent of women approved of circumcision regardless of the type and 87.7 percent of men approved the practice.

their future sexual experience. It may lead to their having difficulty with childbirth. There is an increased risk of sterility. Many are afraid of sex or can experience little enjoyment from sexual relationships. These are potential harms and are years in the future. There are immediate harms too: severe pain, shock, infection, scarring, bleeding, even death.[88] According to an UNESCO report, emotional reactions 'may present themselves as chronic irritability, anxiety, depressive episodes, conversion reactions or frank psychosis'.[89] Circumcision is thus, within the understanding of the cultures which legitimate the practice, dysfunctional. Even so, were it practised on adult women with their full and informed consents, we might be inhibited from attacking it (though whether the House of Lords, the final court of appeal in the United Kingdom, would find similar hesitation, in the light of its condemnation in *R v Brown* case[90] of sado-masochism may be doubted). We allow breast implants and even gender reassignments,[91] and both are financed by the National Health Service. Were girls purportedly to consent to circumcision we might still employ what I have defended elsewhere as 'liberal paternalism' to protect them from the consequences of actions that will prevent them subsequently enjoying rationally autonomous adulthood.[92] Here we have a situation where many of the girls concerned cannot consent, though looking at their circumcision as adult women would have done so. There are real dilemmas here which cannot be avoided by resorting to relativism, for then there would be no debate, or by seeking the refuge of monism, for this would impose a decontextualised overriding value. It would be comforting to rest in the moral certitudes of monism but this study has shown the fragility of the moral determinacy for which it stands.

How is then the cultural pluralist to respond? The answer lies in subjecting the practice to an internal critique, in deconstructing the arguments that are used to support it. The arguments in the case of female circumcision are, it will be recalled, fourfold. It is claimed as a control on female sexuality. Whilst there can be little doubt that it reduces sensitivity and responses to stimulation, it offers no guarantee that a woman has not had sexual experiences and, indeed, even infibulation is no guarantee – an unmarried woman can have sexual intercourse and then be re-infibulated before her marriage to disguise this fact from her husband. It is supposedly based on religion, but there is no evidence for this and there is at least a suspicion that it is an elitist religious fraud perpetrated by a clerical oligarchy on vulnerable women. It rests also upon sexual myths and these – such as that the clitoris is a masculine feature and will grow to the size of a penis – need to be shown for what they are. If features of the other sex need to be removed is there any move in any of these societies to excise male nipples? And, as for the supposed benefits, it has

---

[88] A. Slack, *supra* note 76, discusses these at 450–455; Dorkenoo & Elworthy, *supra* note 35, do so at 8–10.

[89] DRAFT REPORT OF THE WORKING GROUP ON TRADITIONAL PRACTICE AFFECTING THE HEALTH OF WOMEN AND CHILDREN. UN Doc. E/CN.4/H.C.42/1985, Sept. 12 1985 at.13.

[90] [1993] 2 All E.R. 75.

[91] Though we do not grant much in the way of rights to transsexuals: *see* Corbett *v* Corbett [1971] P. 83, and Rees *v* UK, 9 EHRR 56 (1986).

[92] F. PINTER, THE RIGHTS AND WRONGS OF CHILDREN, (1983).

already been shown that, to the contrary, there are physical and psychological harms which surely outweigh any social or cultural benefits.

There is in addition a suspicion that the cultural values upheld by the practices depicted here are the values of a section of the society rather than the whole of it. Of what value are the norms of a community when they are directed at a group at best devalued but more likely excluded from it? It is concerns such as these which lead one to ask whether in a clash between the value of physical integrity and the value of cultural identity, the latter can possibly prevail.[93]

It also leads me to conclude – though it has not been necessary to discuss the question in this paper – that, using similar reasoning processes, it would not be difficult to show that in a similar clash over male circumcision it would be the latter value, namely cultural (or religious) identity that would prevail.

On the other case studies set out at the beginning of this paper, much briefer answers must be given. The cultural pluralist is likely to come to the same conclusion on child marriages as the Divisional Court did in *Mohamed v Knott*. But he would need a deeper understanding of the cultural context than it would seem the English courts had.

The cultural pluralist's response to child labour in the developing world would require greater tolerance of the problems attendant on poverty, a greater understanding of the global economy and a more sophisticated approach to the relationship between child labour and education questions than is often found, but a conclusion not dissimilar from that in the CRC is likely to result from these deliberations.[94] On punishment practices s/he could be more categorical: there can be no reason for tolerating excessive punishment in the name of cultural difference; there is no cultural tradition or identity at stake.

A CONCLUDING COMMENT

This chapter sets out three approaches that may be adopted towards cultural conflict and children's rights. I reject cultural relativism because it renounces normative judgement. The moral determinacy of monism offers blanket solutions but fails to address cultural difference. Cultural pluralism, a *via media* perhaps between two extremes, situates values within a cultural context and offers dialogue and an opportunity to negotiate change. Nothing can provide solutions to the difficult cases thrown up by the ways different societies treat children, but cultural pluralism does, I believe, offer a challenge. It is one that those concerned with children, their welfare and their rights, must take up.

---

[93] Attacks on the practice of male circumcision have been launched by eminent thinkers like Alice Miller. There is also an organisation called NOHARMM in the US (National Organization to Halt the Abuse and Routine Mutilation of Males). *See also* D. Winn, *A Campaign to Save the Foreskin*, THE INDEPENDENT, April 20 1993.

[94] *See further* M. WEINER, THE CHILD AND THE STATE IN INDIA: CHILD LABOR AND EDUCATION POLICY IN COMPARATIVE PERSPECTIVE (1991). And with Olga Nieuwenhuys, CHILDREN'S LIFEWORLDS: GENDER, WELFARE AND LABOUR IN THE DEVELOPING WORLD, (1994). *See also* her review of his book in 2 INT.L J. OF CHILDREN'S RIGHTS, 205 (1994) and his article *Child Labour in Developing Countries: The Indian Case* at 121 (1994).

M. Siraj Sait

3. ISLAMIC PERSPECTIVES ON THE RIGHTS OF THE CHILD

INTRODUCTION

In contemporary internal discourses as well as Western-based critiques of Islamic human rights, the child is rendered virtually invisible.[1] The inability of the child to attract attention is a manifestation of the general neglect of child rights within mainstream dialogues as much as the overcrowded agenda driving the universalist human rights debates critiquing Islam.[2] Contentious issues identified therein such as treatment of minorities, theories of punishment or freedom of religion resurface in the Islamic child rights debates but overshadow an analysis of the nature and scope of child rights under Islamic frameworks. This 'medieval religious system', then, like several other cultural and traditional systems, are problematised and could perforce hardly comprehend the sophistication and expanse of the modern child rights regime, as exemplified by the 1989 United Nations Convention on the Rights of the Child (CRC).[3] Provocation for such assumptions comes from several Muslim majority countries who invoke the *Shari'a*, the Islamic law, to justify treaty reservations to the CRC. This chapter looks at and beyond the child rights deprecating positions of Muslim governments and argues that revisiting original Islamic sources provides both the textual basis for an expansive child rights regime as well as interpretative opportunities offering possible reconciliation strategies with universal child rights postulates in important areas.

An appraisal of Islamic perspectives on child rights could not only explore the multiplicity of factors affecting childhood in a specific religious and socio-cultural context but also yield an insight into the internal thought processes that contribute

---

[1] *See e.g.*, E. A. MAYER, ISLAM AND HUMAN RIGHTS, (2d ed. 1999) which has only passing references to child rights. Specialist study programmes in the Western academy too mostly subsume child rights within the study of family law reform with little focus on the nature and scope of child rights under Islamic law and practice.

[2] For a critique of the Western grandstand review of Islamic human rights, the choice of subjects and the methodologies employed, *see* J. Strawson, *A Western Question to the Middle East: 'Is there a Human Rights Discourse in Islam?'*, 19 ARAB STUDIES Q. 33–44 (1997). *See* also by the same author, *Islamic Law and English Texts* 6 LAW & CRITIQUE 21–38 (1995) where he argues that English texts do not merely present Islamic law, they construct it. The idea of inherent conflict between Islam and contemporary human rights has been refuted by a large number of Muslim thinkers. *See e.g.* the comments of former judge of the International Court of Justice Zafarullah Khan that 'Islam lays down broad values and standards which clearly endorse the spirit and purpose of the Universal Declaration of Human Rights, (though) it does not pronounce verbatim on all the specific provisions of the Declaration', in Z. KHAN, ISLAM AND HUMAN RIGHTS (1967). *See further*, M. KHADDURI, THE ISLAMIC CONCEPTION OF JUSTICE 236–37 (1984).

[3] Adopted 20th November 1989, GA Res 44/25, UNGAOR, 44th Sess., Supp No. 49 at 165, UN Doc. A/44/79 (entered into force September 2, 1990).

Deirdre Fottrell (ed.), Revisiting Children's Rights, 31–50
© 2000 *Kluwer Law International. Printed in Great Britain.*

to the conditioning of a pluralist but in some way 'unified' Muslim consciousness. The framing of human rights controversies in the jargon of conflict of cultures or civilisations[4] without unravelling the dynamics of specific childhood experiences turns out to be a self-fulfilling prophecy where the children of the 'other', far from being alienated from their traditions, enter adulthood only to re-affirm an Islamic socio-political and cultural identity that is distinct from, even at odds with, Western liberal human rights conceptions. The CRC, however, despite encountering problems in constructing a 'universal childhood' and empowering children in generally disempowered societies proposes an interface between universal child rights and Islamic formulations that could have positive implications far beyond this particular child rights instrument.

The choice of the term 'Islamic' rather than 'Muslim' in the title is not intended to overstate the importance of religion in Muslim society for religion not only influences society but is influenced by it.[5] As Abdullahi An-Naim emphasises, Islam is not

> sole determinant of the public and the private behaviour of Muslims, nor is *Shari'a* the only cause of human rights violations or protection in countries where Muslims are the majority of the population ... (they are) conditioned by a wide variety of economic, social, political, cultural and external factors that impact on all human societies.[6]

Nor can there be one essentialised Islamic society for a multi-million population spread over forty Muslim majority countries and as significant minorities in many

---

[4] *See* S. HUNTINGTON, THE CLASH OF CIVILISATION AND THE REMAKING OF WORLD ORDER (1996) which was an expanded version of *The Clash of Civilisations?* 72 FOREIGN AFFAIRS 22–49 (1993) which triggered intense debate but some acceptance that Islam is the new post-Cold War enemy of the West. *See further*, the work of Bassam Tibi, who disagrees, noting that there being no one 'Islamic civilisation', it is really a clash between a global civilisations and a host of 'local cultures', *Islamic Law/ Shari'a, Human Rights, Universal Morality and International Relations* 16 HUM. RTS. Q. 277 (1994). At the 1993 Vienna Conference on Human Rights, several Muslim countries expressed their concerns over Western-driven human rights but were reconciled to the compromise that 'All human rights are universal, indivisible' (but) significance of national and regional particularities and various historical, cultural, and religious backgrounds must be borne in mind'. *See, Vienna Declaration and Programme of Action* of 25 June 1993 reprinted in 14 HUM. RTS. L. J. 353 (1993).

[5] Barakat argues that society and not sacred texts should be the starting point of an enquiry into Muslim societies otherwise our viewpoint is shaped by the perspective of the past rather than the future. *See* H. BARAKAT, THE ARAB WORLD: SOCIETY, CULTURE, AND STATE 141 (1993). Bulliet too considers it necessary to view Islamic history not from the 'centre' (the political discourse) but from the social structures and experiences *see* R. BULLIET, ISLAM: THE VIEW FROM THE EDGE (1994). *See also* M. GILSENAN, RECOGNISING ISLAM: RELGION AND SOCIETY IN THE MIDDLE EAST (1993) he demonstrates how Islam evolves in response to shifting political, economic and class structures.

[6] A. An-Naim, *Islamic Law and Human Rights Today* 10 INTERIGHTS BULLETIN 3 (1996). Both pre-Islamic practices and customary law or *urf* played a role to varying degrees and nor could Islam have been entirely immune from the influence of other cultures, secular reform or historical episodes such as colonialism. It is by no means only Muslim states who are arrayed as child rights violators, *see e.g.,* Amnesty International, CHILDHOOD STOLEN: GRAVE HUMAN RIGHTS VIOLATIONS AGAINST CHILDREN (1995).

parts of the world, including the West. Despite certain shared religious character-istics, there are a variety of Islamic jurisprudential schools (*maddhahib*), sub-cul-tures, languages, political structures, histories and a number of variables that differentiate Muslim communities from one another.[7] Though the *Shari'a* appears to be the formal primary validating force in Muslim societies, it is hardly settled by particular dominant conservative versions. Instead, beyond matters of faith, reli-gion continues to be a contested domain with a plurality of positions employing a host of interpretative strategies.[8]

THE POLITICS OF PARTICIPATION AND 'ISLAMIC' RESERVATIONS TO THE CRC

Even before the advent of the CRC, the Muslim majority countries were circum-scribed not only by their religious invocations but through a highly persuasive pre-existing body of child rights emerging from specific declarations, child rights guarantees in general human rights treaties, regional arrangements where applicable and customary human rights norms. The CRC not only created an elaborate child-centred manifesto but by its drafting politics of inclusion sought to repackage rights through pre-emption or redressal of claims of imposition of Western values.[9] Unlike the earlier 'universal' human rights instruments which offered limited opportunities for a cross-cultural debate over claims of universality of human rights,[10] the CRC is promoted as a product of the participation of countries from different regions and cultures. The global ownership of child rights, however, cannot be sustained exclusively on the participation as recorded in the *travaux pré-paratoires* of the CRC.[11] For most of the 10-year drafting process and the format-ting of the CRC blueprint, the engagement of Muslim countries was limited. It was the second reading of the CRC draft, 11 days (November 28 to December 9, 1988)

---

[7]   Dominic McGoldrick notes that the practical effects, assertions of Muslim States regarding the incompatibility of the CRC and the requirements of *Shari'a* 'are difficult to determine because there is considerable controversy within and between Islamic states as to the proper Islamic interpretation of many matters relating to family and personal life' associated with the concept of 'cultural relativism'. D. McGoldrick, *The United Nations Convention on the Rights of the Child* 5 INT. J. L & FAMILY. 132 (1991) at 137.

[8]   *See e.g.,* H. Bielefeldt, *Muslim Voices in the Human Rights Debate,* 17 HUM. RTS. Q 587 (1995); K. DWYER, ARAB VOICES: THE HUMAN RIGHTS DEBATE IN THE MIDDLE EAST (1991).

[9]   This endeavour was enriched by the significant contribution of the international civil society, which kept faith in child rights through periods of limited governmental engagement. *See further,* C. Price Cohen, *Role of Non-Governmental Organisations in the Drafting of the Convention on the Rights of the Child* 12 HUM. RTS. Q. 13 (1990).

[10]   *See* Universal Declaration on Human Rights, adopted 10 December 1948, GA Res. 217A (III), 3 UN GAOR (Resolutions, part 1), UN Doc. A/810 (1948). While the Saudi Arabian representa-tive abstained from voting on the UDHR on Islamic grounds, other Muslim countries did support the document. *See further,* D. Arzt, *The Application of International Human Rights Law in Islamic States* 12 HUM. RTS. Q 202–230 (1990) at 215–217. On the nature of human rights *see generally,* A. Pollis & P. Schwab, *Human Rights: A Western Construct with Limited Applic-ability,* in HUMAN RIGHTS: CULTURAL AND IDEOLOGICAL PERSPECTIVES 1–18 (1989).

[11]   *See further,* S. DETRICK, CONVENTION ON THE RIGHTS OF THE CHILD: A GUIDE TO THE TRAVAUX PREPARATOIRES (1992).

and 22 sessions where about 15 Muslim countries joined 42 others to launch the CRC.[12]

The Muslim countries attended only those sessions which were controversial from their viewpoint,[13] and this engagement turned out to be productive, as Lawrence LeBlanc[14] notes

> ...the main objective of the Islamic States was to push through last minute substantive changes in the norms of the Convention to make them more compatible with Islamic thought and practice ... The [resulting] alterations reflect the importance of cultural factors in drafting international human rights instruments and show that the increased participation by Islamic States towards the end of the negotiations worked to their advantage.

The credibility of the CRC as a universal instrument is predicated on the debating opportunities it offered and its final adoption by consensus. This expression of consensus in the CRC embracing to a greater degree the concerns of the non-Western States, may have diluted the original expectations of several constituencies, but was designed to remove potential obstacles to the eventual ratification of the CRC by all States.[15] The 15 Muslim countries present during the concluding sessions neither contested the general thrust of the Convention itself nor sought to veto compromises reached with regard to specific provisions.

The Convention on the Rights of the Child turned out to be the most widely ratified human rights instrument.[16] For several Muslim governments, it was to be an entry point into the international human rights system. At least 20 Muslim countries which had bypassed both the International Covenant on Civil and Political Rights and the International Covenant on Economic, Social and Cultural Rights had now become parties to the CRC.[17] In signing up to the CRC, the Muslim States were in fact recognising the civil and political rights alongside socio-

---

[12] The limited level of participation and engagement of Third World countries, particularly in the earlier stages, has been attributed to a variety of factors including lack of trained personnel, scarce resources, indifference, even opposition to norm creation in the field of child rights. See L. LEBLANC, THE CONVENTION ON THE RIGHTS OF THE CHILD: UNITED NATIONS LAWMAKING ON HUMAN RIGHTS (1995).

[13] This was the pattern of participation from other blocs of countries too. For example, the Islamic delegations were mostly present to discuss the provisions on freedom of thought, conscience and religion, Western delegations were present only to discuss the article on recruitment of children into the armed forces or Latin American delegations present mostly to discuss the article on adoption. *See* D. Johnson, *Cultural and Regional Pluralism in the Drafting of the UN Convention on the Rights of the Child* , in THE IDEOLOGIES OF CHILDREN'S RIGHTS 133 fn.1 (M. Freeman & P. Veerman, eds. 1992).

[14] LeBlanc *supra* note 12 at 35–36.

[15] Johnson, *supra* note 13 at 103.

[16] All States with the exception of the United States of America and Somalia have ratified the CRC.

[17] For the purposes of this article, the 51 States who are members of the Organisation of Islamic Conference (OIC) are referred to as 'Muslim countries' though it excludes several countries where Muslims are in significant minority. For a convenient chart on the ratification of major human rights treaties by the OIC members, *see, Status of Selected International Human Rights Instruments in relation to States Members of the Organisation of Islamic Conference* 10 INTERIGHTS BULLETIN 42 (1996).

economic and cultural rights which they had rejected through other treaties. They were, thus, privileging the child over the adult since the formal acknowledgement of corresponding rights for the adults had often been withheld.

It may be that the CRC is replete with compromises and generalisations but its real breakthrough was to involve all States, including Muslim States, in reporting obligations (through the periodic reports to the Committee on the Rights of the Child) in the supervision of their compliance with those broad obligations.

Muslim countries also registered a number of reservations or declarations while signing up to the CRC. William Schabas questions whether such 'offensive reservations are merely part of a more general strategy aimed at weakening and undermining the spread of universal human rights norms'.[18] Nearly half of the 54 Articles of the CRC have been subject to caveats by a large number of countries, a majority of which are non-Muslim countries. Such reservations to human rights treaties are not however restricted to the CRC, and similar notices have been placed by Muslim countries to the Convention on the Elimination of Discrimination of Women (CEDAW).[19] While nine Muslim countries have created blanket reservations related to the *Shari'a*, a majority among them have entered none at all, and with regard to specific provisions Muslim responses have been neither unified nor consistent. Some writers would argue that these religiously justified reservations are determined primarily by evolving political contingencies, not the *Shari'a*.[20] Elizabeth Ann Mayer's position that the 'various national formulations of *Shari'a* law obviously only constitute an obstacle to legal reforms as long as men in power choose to retain them as law of the land'[21] only partially explains the choice of conservative versions over the liberal without adequately dealing with the relationship between the religious legitimisation process and the mandate of international human rights norms. The inconsistent and selective treaty reservation pattern to the CRC does not establish the Islamic critique of the CRC but rather political preferences. The Muslim engagement with child rights may have been reluctant in the past but the widespread ratification of the treaty signals a potentially meaningful encounter of Islamic beliefs and practices with the universal expositions.

---

[18] *See* W. Schabas, *Reservations to the Convention on the Elimination of All Forms of Discrimination Against Women and the Convention on the Rights of the Child* 3 WILLIAM & MARY JOURNAL OF WOMEN AND THE LAW 79 (1997) at 111. The CRC under Article 51 permits the making of reservations provided these are compatible with the aims and purposes of the Convention.

[19] Convention on the Elimination of All Forms of Discrimination Against Women, adopted December 18, 1979 by GA Res. 34/180 (1979) 1249 U.N.T.S 13 (entered into force September 3, 1981). Bangladesh, Egypt, Iraq, Kuwait, Libya, Malaysia, Maldives and Morocco have entered blanket reservations making their compliance with CEDAW subject to *Shari'a*. *See generally* R. Cook, *Reservations to the Convention on the Elimination of All Forms of Discrimination Against Women* 30 VA. J. INT'L L 661 (1990).

[20] On Muslim reservations to the CEDAW *see further*, Mayer, *Religious Reservations to the Convention on the Elimination of All Forms of Discrimination against Women: What Do they Really Mean?* in Howland (eds), RELGIOUS FUNDAMENTALISM AND THE HUMAN RIGHTS OF WOMEN (C.W. Howland, ed. 1999) at 106.

[21] Mayer, *Rhetorical Strategies and Official Policies on Women's Rights: The Merits and Drawbacks of the New World Hypocrisy* in FAITH & FREEDOM: WOMEN'S HUMAN RIGHTS IN THE MUSLIM WORLD 115 (F. Afkhami ed. 1995).

THE UNIVERSAL CHILD AND ISLAM

The philosophical foundations of universal child rights as well as the CRC's substantive innovations have been under scrutiny. Norman Lewis, for example, argues that 'the Convention is based on two fundamental fallacies: the fallacy of children's rights, and the fallacy of a universal childhood'.[22] On the other hand, it has been argued that 'in cultural terms, the (CRC), while by no means perfect, is probably more sensitive to different approaches and perspectives than most of the principal human rights treaties adopted earlier'.[23] The 12th preambular paragraph of the CRC, as well as several articles in the Convention, realise the differential of culture in child rights[24] as exemplified by Article 24, which creates soft obligations to deter injurious traditional practices, indicating that traditional practices could in certain circumstances be beneficial.[25] Several Muslim countries in their blanket reservations or specific caveats invoke the *Shari'a* as well as traditional values blurring the roots of their qualification. Abdullahi An-Naim argues that the pragmatic way to achieve a normative consensus is through procedural universality where the dynamic interplay between changing Islamic folk models and international standards is heard through internal discourse and cross-cultural dialogue, while minimum safeguards protect the best interests of the child from the abuse of the cultural card.[26]

Michael Freeman, while noting that 'childhood, like adulthood or old age, is to a large extent a social construct ... a product of historical accidents and responses to particular pressures at particular times', refers to Philipe Aries' seminal work *Centuries of Childhood* to largely accept that the notion of childhood was not recognised in the medieval society and was invented in Europe in the seventeenth century.[27] If that were true, then the Islamic quest for classical dimensions of childhood may be futile. Further, Muslim countries preoccupied with notions of authenticity are faced with the awkward choice of either incorporating the Western product for its intrinsic value or rejecting child rights altogether as alien culture. Contemporary Muslim writers, however, provide sufficient basis for Islamic co-

---

[22] N. Lewis, *Human Rights, Law and Democracy in an Unfree World* in HUMAN RIGHTS FIFTY YEARS ON – A REAPPRAISAL 77–99 (T. Evans, ed., 1998) at 82. He finds that the Convention is not an extension of rights or a universalisation of rights but its opposite; 'a shattering of the shell of legal equality – the infantilisation of society and the degradation of democratic rights' *Id* at 83. On problems of empowering children with rights *see* C. WELLMAN, THE PROLIFERATION OF RIGHTS: MORAL PROGRESS OR EMPTY RHETORIC? (1992) at 5.

[23] P. Alston, *The Best Interests Principle: Towards a Reconciliation of Culture and Human Rights* in THE BEST INTERESTS OF THE CHILD: RECONCILING CULTURE AND HUMAN RIGHTS 7 (P. Alston, ed., 1994).

[24] The 12th preambular paragraph of the CRC refers to 'taking due account of the importance of the traditions and cultural values of each people for the protection and harmonious development of the child'. *See also* Articles 20(3), 29 and 30.

[25] For a critique of Article 24 particularly in casting the obligation to deal with injurious traditional practices as social and cultural rights rather than civil and political rights, therefore only a matter of progressive realisation, *see* McGoldrick, *supra* note 7 at 146.

[26] A. An-Naim, *Cultural Transformation and Normative Consensus on the Best Interests of the Child* in Alston (ed) *supra* note 23 at 62–81.

[27] MICHAEL D.A. FREEMAN, THE RIGHTS AND WRONGS OF CHILDREN 6–13 (1983).

ownership of a child-centered ethos. For example, Haytham Manna'a argues that in the second century of Islam itself the implications of childhood were furiously debated by classical Islamic philosophers and jurists. While the Khajirites argued that children were unlike adults because they could not experience suffering for God could not have intended it, the Mutazalite rationalists argued that children too are subject to physical pain and that it is in the making of nature, not the act of God. As it emerged, Muslim thought travelled beyond the resolution of the spiritual fate of children into locating temporal responsibility for child protection with society and determining the concept of justice demanded by childhood.[28] Arab medieval writings from philosophers, jurists and physicians exhibit a child-centred focus, far more advanced than the prevailing European attitudes towards the interests of the child. Classical formulations on the status of the child, its progression through centuries and its application in contemporary society may well be relevant to the project of a universal child rights code.

While the appeal of the universal child rights regime is not contingent on the approval of God, nature, morality or reason, Muslim countries appear to claim that their child rights formulations are derived primarily through scriptural methodologies with a little support from socio-cultural traditions. Western critiques of the source and therefore the content of such claims may be in 'danger of overlooking the range of ideas, beliefs, practices and institutions which constitute religion'[29] which can also have a positive impact on child rights. Instead of visualising the choice as between secularised human rights and religion, the latter being considered a broader framework for life by believers, religion could be used to further child empowerment. In Judge Weeramantry's analysis,[30] human rights enforcement in Islam is not about

> ... how man asserts his rights against man but how man discharges his duties towards God. It is not preoccupied with the horizontal relationship of man with his fellow man but with the vertical relationship that subsists between each man and his maker. If the vertical relationship is properly tended, all human rights problems fall automatically into place.

The Universal Islamic Declaration of Human Rights (UIDHR)[31] and the Cairo

---

[28] H. Manna'a, *Child Rights in Arab/Islamic Culture* ROWAQ ARABI 33 (1997).
[29] *See* C. Ramazanoglu, FEMINISMS AND THE CONTRADICTIONS OF OPPRESSION (1989) at 151. Similarly, White argues that religion is a natural and necessary source of law, democracy and human rights – particularly in religious societies, *see* J. White, *Law, Religion and Human Rights* 28 COL. HUM. RTS L. REV 1 (1996) at 30.
[30] C.G. Weeramantry, *Islam and Human Rights*, in ISLAMIC JURISPRUDENCE 116–17 (1988). For another view *see* D. Hollenbach, *Human Rights and Religious Faith in the Middle East: Reflections of a Christian Theologian*, HUM. RTS. Q 94 (1992).
[31] The Universal Islamic Declaration of Human Rights, 19 September 1981 (UNESCO document, Paris) adopted by the Islamic Council of Europe, which is an influential think-tank. Weeramantry remarks 'It is remarkable that every one of the principles set out (in the UIDHR), with its great similarity to the most modern formulations, can be supported on the basis of specific Islamic texts'. *Supra* note 30 at 113.

Declaration on Human Rights in Islam,[32] are notable for the Islamic cultural relativist position being argued through the *Shari'a* as the exclusive source of legitimation. In real terms, the Cairo Declaration in Article 7 deals with the rights of the Child thus:

7(a) As from the moment of birth, every child has rights due from the parents, society and the State to be accorded proper nursing, education and material, hygienic and moral care. Both the foetus and the mother must be protected and accorded special care.

7(b) Parents and those in like capacity have the right to choose the type of education they desire for their children, provided they take into consideration the interest and future of the children in accordance with ethical values and principles of the *Shari'a*.

7(c) Both parents are entitled to certain rights from their children, and relatives are entitled to rights from their kin, in accordance with the tenets of the *Shari'a*...

The Declaration, while embracing child rights, suggests several departures from the CRC, particularly with regard to the relationship between the child and her parents. Yet the Islamic declarations as an alternative human rights framework are problematic not merely because they are non-binding and without enforcement mechanisms but because, far from consulting the various human rights constituencies or reflecting the vibrant internal Islamic discourses on human rights, they recycle conservative and reactionary views as the settled readings of sacred texts. There are significant differences between the universal child rights paradigm and Islamic interpretations but these can be addressed only by revisiting original Islamic sources.

An example of the changes brought about by Muslim lobbying during the drafting of the CRC is in the area of adoption. Article 21 now applies only to States that recognise and/or permit adoption, which effectively excludes countries that implement Islamic law.[33] Further, in a bid 'to incorporate the principal features of all legal systems'[34] the Islamic alternative *kafalah* (bonding relationship) was introduced into Article 20(3) in the concluding sessions. The most contentious issue as far as Muslim countries were concerned was Article 14, which dealt with the

---

[32] The Cairo Declaration on Human Rights in Islam, 5 August 1990 (adopted by member States of the Organisation of the Islamic Conference) and presented before the 1993 Vienna Conference. See UN Doc. A/CONF.157/PC/62/Add.18 (9 June 1993). Article 25 of the Cairo Declaration makes it clear that 'The Islamic *Shari'a* is the only source of reference for the explanation or clarification of any of the articles of this Declaration'. The International Commission of Jurists finds this Declaration 'gravely threatening the inter-cultural consensus on which the international human rights instruments are based' (and) 'that certain provisions are below the legal standards in effect in a number of Muslim countries'. *See* M. Rismawi. *The Arab Charter on Human Rights: A Comment*, 10 INTERIGHTS BULLETIN 8 (1996).

[33] *See* the *Qur'an* 33:4–5 on adoption.

[34] *See* LeBlanc, *supra* note 12 at 119.

freedom of thought, conscience and religion. It had been identified on the first day of the second reading as one of the five areas eluding consensus (others being inter-country adoption, rights of the unborn child, traditional practices and duties of children). Ultimately, a compromise was reached with neither the guarantee against coercion in exercise of thought, conscience and religion (as demanded by the Western and Latin American countries) nor the restriction or removal of the right (as Islamic States had wanted) being adopted.[35]

The relationship between child rights and religion is complex and has wide ramifications, involving other religions and Western societies too.[36] The CRC not only reasserts the right to education (Article 28) but proposes the objectives of universal education (Article 29) and, in establishing participatory rights for the child, calls for access to information from 'diverse' sources (Article 16). The conflict between parental prerogative to instil their religious values and the 'best interests of the child' principle showcases the dilemma for the believing Muslim, particularly where there is resistance to equal opportunity for the girl child.[37] Muslim conservatives see an obvious conflict between their understanding of Islamic and Western education: 'We want our children to be good Muslims, whereas this (Western) society wants children to be independent in their thinking.'[38] Far from resisting the beneficial effects of education, Muslim parents express their concern over Western proposals such as sex education in schools and the different orientation which, they say, has a tendency to corrupt their children.[39] The Western educational model may be projected as improving the quality of childhood but Muslims could be concerned that Islamic features of family life, care for children, respect for elders and concepts of modesty may be under threat from the liberal philosophy of the post-modern age.[40] The child's right to education is best served with the advantages and reconciliation of both models, which could be harmonised. The sources of Islamic law on children would provide an assessment of the gap between the CRC and Islam.

---

[35] *See* Article 10 of the Cairo Declaration which provides 'It is prohibited to exercise any form of compulsion on man or to exploit his poverty or ignorance in order to convert him to another religion or to atheism'. For a treatment of the debates G. VAN BUEREN, THE INTERNATIONAL LAW ON THE RIGHTS OF THE CHILD 156–162 (1995).

[36] *See e.g.*, a review of recent case-law in the United Kingdom, United States, Canada and the European Court of Human Rights. S.E. Mumford, *The Judicial Resolution of Disputes Involving Children and Religion* 47 ICLQ 117 (1998).

[37] *See generally* G. Van Bueren & D. Fottrell, *The Potential of International Law to Combat Discrimination Against Girls* in RELIGIOUS FUNDAMENTALISMS AND WOMEN'S HUMAN RIGHTS 129 (C.W. Howland, ed., 1999).

[38] The President of Bradford Council of Mosques quoted in P. Lewis, ISLAMIC BRITAIN: RELIGION, POLITICS AND IDENTITY AMONG BRITISH MUSLIMS 191 (1994).

[39] *See* C. MALLAT & J. CONNORS, ISLAMIC FAMILY LAW (1990). The manner in which the Western 'secular and multi-cultural' education omits reference to the history and contributions of Islam on several fields has also been under fire. *See e.g.*, M. Parker-Jenkins, *Muslim Matters: An Examination of the Educational Needs of Muslim Children in Contemporary Britain* 9 AM. J. ISLAMIC SOC. SCIENCES 359 (1992).

[40] *See e.g.*, A.S. AHMED, POSTMODERNISM AND ISLAM: PROMISE AND PREDICAMENT 5 (1993).

THE CHILD IN *SHARI'A* FORMULATIONS

The primary source of the *Shari'a* is the *Qur'an*[41] with its 114 *Surahs* (chapters), though only a fraction of the estimated 500 law verses deal with the rights of the child. The *Qur'an* recognises child rights in several dimensions. It assumes divine responsibility for the creation of every child '...God creates what He wills (and plans). He bestows children female or male according to his will ... and He leaves childless whom He pleases' (*Qur'an* 42:49–50).[42]

The *Qur'an* recognises the life of the unborn and is categorical about the physical integrity of every infant by stating in *Surah* (verse) 17:31 '...Kill not your children for fear of want (poverty). We shall provide sustenance for them as well as for you. Verily the killing of them is a great sin.'

It emphasises the equal preference of both sexes by criminalising the practice of *wa'd al-banat* (female infanticide) by raising the question of justice '...And the (female) buried alive shall be asked for what reason was she killed when the scrolls are laid open'... (*Qur'an* 81:8–9) – God would hear evidence on the crime against the child from the victim herself.[43] Castigating those who grieve over the birth of a female child instead of a male (as was the pre-Islamic *jahaliya* attitude), the *Qur'an* warns that ... 'indeed, wrongful is their judgement' (*Qur'an* 16: 58–59). Every child is born blemishless without any carryover sin and childhood is considered a state of purity. All children who die are considered to belong to *ala' l fitrah* (state of nature) and are guaranteed Paradise irrespective of the religion of their parents.[44] The *Qur'an* not only confers the basic rights of name, identity and paternity[45] but reiterates a broad framework for the physical, material (such as the right to property), emotional and spiritual rights of the child.

An example of the importance attached to child rights is reflected in *Surah* 107 titled *Al Ma'un* (Assistance). It reads

> ... Have you seen the one who refuses the Day of Judgement. For that is the one who thrust the orphan child away and does not urge the feeding of the needy. So unfortunate are those praying. The ones who are careless about their prayers and those who do good to be seen. And those who prevent common necessities ...

---

[41] The *Qur'an* is considered to be the direct revealed word of God and the *mushaf* standard Arabic copy transmitted through generations leaves little doubt about its accuracy. There are, however, several English translations and commentaries (*tafasir*), some of which provide more liberal interpretations of the classical Arabic text or contexts.

[42] Manna'a points out that because the female is mentioned before the male, some Muslims regard the birth of the female child before the male as a 'good omen' *supra* note 28 at 38.

[43] Y. Ali, THE HOLY QUR'AN: TRANSLATION AND COMMENTARY 1694 (1934).

[44] Ali cites the canonical *Sunnah* text of Imam Bukhari in support of this commonly held view. *See* M. ALI, THE RELIGION OF ISLAM 333 (1994).

[45] The issue is controversial but a Muslim child is legitimate (*jaez*) under Islamic law on acknowledgement (*ikrah*) of paternity, see L. Ali Siddiqui, *The Legal Status of a Child Under Muslim Law* 5 DHAKA UNIVERSITY STUDIES 87 (1994).

The *asbab al nuzul* (circumstances of this revelation) is that an orphan is left unclothed and hungry by Abu Jahl, the Prophet's bitterest enemy.[46] The child is advised by the community leaders to lodge a complaint with the Prophet since Abu Jahl had a duty to part with the child's father's property in his possession. The Prophet immediately accompanied the child and presented the child's case to Abu Jahl, who despite his opposition to the Prophet, relents without protest. The resulting *Qur'anic* verse above indicates the broad spiritual framework of child rights as a religious duty. Denial of the rights of the child is referred to in the context of meaningless prayer and denial of the day of reckoning – powerful *Qur'anic* metaphors. Moreover, the verse reiterates the general duty to provide for the needy and ensuring the basic necessities for children. Beyond the concept of *Wakf* (trust), the Islamic State is a welfare state which through its *baitul maal* (state fund) is responsible for catering to the economic and social protection of the child.

It has been suggested that since childhood under Islamic jurisprudence is characterised by lack of formed reasoning ability (*akl*), the child has no legal personality and on attaining *akl*, ceases to be a child. However, Islamic theory relies on both mental maturity (*rushd*) and physical development in determining the various stages of childhood. As David Pearl notes, citing the classical scholar Al-Misri, childhood is understood to be the inter-relationship between capacity of the child and power that can be exercised over her by the parent or *wali* (guardian).[47]

Islamic law, as a general proposition, creates a system of steps. Below a certain age (in Hanafi law seven years) the child is totally incapable. Above that age, when of '"perfect understanding" (s)he can participate in legal acts, but these are the subjects by the guardian or *wali* , if this is in the "interests of the minor"'.

During the prediscernment phase the child has no responsibilities, but has a right to have her interests, particularly of property, administered. From the age of seven to the period of puberty, her increasing judgement also creates expectations to conform to religious performance and social codes or otherwise face sanctions. But rather than the *Qur'an*, it is the secondary source of the *Shari'a*, the *Sunnah* (practice of the Prophet through individual reports, *hadith*) which are selectively used by conservatives to determine a stricter discipline regime. For example 'Order your children to pray when they are seven, and beat them for it when they are ten' or 'When the boy reaches six, he should be disciplined, and when he reaches seven his bed should be separated. At thirteen he should be beaten for prayer and fasting, and at sixteen his father should have him married and help him settle'. Such prescriptions, often contradicting themselves, certainly violate the CRC prohibition against all forms of corporal punishment and physical and mental violence (Articles 19, 28 and 37). Nowhere in the *Qur'an* is there any suggestion that children should be disciplined by force. On the contrary, such practices would violate the *Qur'anic* principle in *Surah* 2:256, 'Let there be no compulsion in religion'.

---

[46] For details *see e.g*, J. UN NISA BINT RAFAI, THE QUR'AN: TRANSLATION & STUDY (Volume Juz 30). 128 (1995).

[47] D. Pearl, *A Note on Children's Rights in Islamic Law* in CHILDREN'S RIGHTS AND TRADITIONAL VALUES 88 (G. Douglas & L. Sebba, eds. 1995).

While the authenticity of these particular sayings offending child rights are to be critically reviewed, the Islamist position on the spiritual obligations of the child provides an opening for child rights in general. If children are capable of comprehending the divine message with increasing age, so too must they be competent to participate in worldly affairs. The dualism of *akhira* (hereafter) and the *dunya* (worldly affairs) is well accepted in Islam. There is no set opinion on when a child attains majority (*baligh*), with the different Islamic schools of thought mostly relying on empirical assessment of child development. The *Qur'an*, on one occasion, does refer to the beginning of puberty as the stage when the child must be expected to begin respecting the privacy of adults.[48] Generally, under classical Islamic formulations childhood ends with the first signs of puberty while in Western conception childhood continues until the end of puberty.[49] In case of doubt over the physical signs of puberty, the age of 15 is recognised as the age for manhood, though several influential classical jurists such as Imam Hanifa and some Malikis preferred the threshold of 18.[50] The *Qur'an* itself does not specifically prescribe an age, or even the onset of puberty itself for the host of rights it conceives. Arguably, adopting a universal age (though the CRC does not require it) which remedies the problems such as marriageable age to doctrines like *doli incapax* (incapacity to commit crime) would appear to hardly offend the spirit of Islam. In any case, under Islamic legal reasoning, it is the State that emerges as the ultimate guardian or *parens patriae* responsible for promoting child rights despite the private domain regulated by the family or society and the spiritual dimension of the relationship between child and God.

The 'best interests of the child' principle is explicitly recognised in the *Qur'an* in several verses with regard to guardianship relating to property of the child held in trust. For example, in *Surah* 2:220 the *Qur'an* advises the guardians that 'the best thing to do is what is for their (orphans') good' by keeping their interests separate from that of the children. This fundamental principle in guardianship of property (*al wilayatu alal maal*) could equally well apply to not just the guardianship of the infant (*hadana*) but in diverse areas such as guardianship regarding education (*wilayat al tabiyya*)[51] or responsibility for arranging marriage (*wilayat al nikah*).[52]

---

[48] *See Qur'an* 24:58 stating that those who have attained puberty must seek permission before they enter the private quarters in others' houses. Yusuf Ali notes that he employs the term 'coming of age' instead of 'attainment of puberty'. Y. Ali, *supra* note 43 at 916.

[49] H. Motzki, *Child Marriage in Seventeenth-Century Palestine* in ISLAMIC LEGAL INTERPRETATION: MUFTIS AND THEIR FATWAS (M. Khalid Masud et al eds., 1996) at 130.

[50] *See* the Orientalist work of Reuben Levy, THE SOCIAL STRUCTURE OF ISLAM 142 (1965). In cases, the arrival of sexual maturity could be deemed 17 years for girls and 18 years for boys. Harald Motski points out that this age was higher than that of the law prescribed by the other societies and the Roman Church which continued to be followed by European States through the Middle ages. *See* Motzki, *supra* note 49 at 347, fn.4.

[51] For a discussion of these concepts *see* J. NASIR, THE STATUS OF WOMEN UNDER ISLAMIC LAW AND UNDER MODERN LEGISLATION 122 (1990).

[52] *See e.g.,* the limitations of the guardian with respect to giving consent in marriage where the child attains majority. S. Sardar Ali, *Is an Adult Muslim Woman 'Sui Juris'? Some Reflections on the Concept of 'Consent in Marriage' Without a Wali (With Particular Reference to the Saima Waheed Case)* 3 YR. BK. MIDDLE EASTERN L. 156 (1996).

At the same time, the *Qur'an* does not assume the infallibility of parents or that their decisions are always in the best interests of the child. The *Qur'an* calls upon children (and adults) to respect and show kindness towards their parents as a measure of their gratitude (reverence the 'wombs')[53] and in deference to their experience and affection.[54] However, if parents misguide their children (for example in matters of faith), there is no obligation to follow them;[55] in fact Yusuf Ali in his translation adds that in such contexts 'disobedience becomes the highest duty'.[56] Repudiating the notion of blind allegiance to parents or the legitimacy of all kinds of parental control, the *Qur'an* repeatedly emphasises that every individual searches for truth herself. Thereby, the *Qur'an* recognises the individuality of the child as one who could be influenced by parents in matters '... where (she) has no knowledge'. She has the duty to discern and the right to demand her best interests. The dozen odd references to the right of the child in the CRC to express herself may appear an unlikely aspiration in Muslim societies ruled by authoritarian or conservative governments but are entirely consistent with the *Qur'anic* emphasis on every individual's right and duty to participate in the pursuit of knowledge and truth.

A large majority of the child rights principles only recently codified through the CRC have pre-existed in some form or other in the *Qur'an*. There is also considerable scope for using general *Qur'anic* principles to counter practices detrimental to the interests of the child. For example, on the complex issue of child labour, it helps to point out that the *Qur'an* specifies that the family has sole responsibility as the breadwinner[57] and does not contemplate a child working. In protecting children during armed conflict, the *Shari'a* prohibition against harming children in any manner[58] and the exclusion of children from war campaigns during the Prophet's era may be instructive. However, despite the *Qur'anic* prohibition against sex discrimination of children (CRC Article 2) or the guarantee of right to life (Article 6), practices such as female genital mutilation[59] and honour killings, nowhere sanctioned in the *Qur'an*, continue to be justified in some Muslim societies. Even where

---

[53] *See Qur'an* 4:1 'O mankind, reverence Your Guardian Lord, who created you from a single person, created of like nature, his mate, and from them scattered countless men and women (like seeds) – Reverence God, through Whom you demand mutual (rights) and reverence the wombs (that bore you).'

[54] *See Qur'an* 17:23–24 'And be kind to your parents whether one or both of them attain old age in your life and say not a word of contempt, nor repel them. But address them in terms of honour ... and (ask God to) bestow on them mercy as they have cherished (you) in childhood.'

[55] *See Qur'an* 31:15 'If they strive to make you join in worship with God things of which you have no knowledge; obey them not.'

[56] *See Qur'an* 29:8. *See further*, Ali, *supra* note 43 at 1083.

[57] However, child labour being a practice founded on socio-economic grounds, it could not be wished away by a purely religious argument. *See* UNICEF, THE STATE OF THE WORLD'S CHILDREN (1997) focusing on child labour and providing statistical tables.

[58] *See* M. Ali, *supra* note 44 at 424, 432.

[59] Though there is no *Qur'anic* injunction (and none in the Prophet's household were circumcised), supporters of female circumcision rely on one *hadith* suggesting a mild modification 'just touch, do not obliterate' but the authenticity of this source is disputed. *See further*, H. AL KHATTAB, BENT RIB: A JOURNEY THROUGH WOMEN'S ISSUES IN ISLAM 92–93 (1997). *See also*, N. EL SADAAWI, THE HIDDEN FACE OF EVE: WOMEN IN THE ARAB WORLD (1990).

the strict moral code in the *Qur'an* prohibits sexual exploitation and trafficking or drugs (corresponding to CRC Articles 33–35) such abuse continues in several Muslim countries, despite the existence of deterrents.[60] With the appropriation of the interpretation of the sacred texts by conservative forces, the domestic application of Islamic and international standards stands constantly frustrated. Just as there are gaps between international standards and realities, the gulf between the Islamic ideal and its practice by Muslims is stark.

IJTIHAD FOR GREATER CHILD RIGHTS

While setting high standards for child care, the *Qur'an* appears both flexible and practical on how the child's needs can be met, as demonstrated by the suckling (*rada*)[61] advice. The *Qur'an* (*Surah* 2:233) recommends that the mother breast-feed her infant for two years, but adds that 'no one shall have a burden more than can be borne' and states that 'no mother or father be treated unfairly on account of the child'. If the mother is unable to breast-feed the baby for any reason, a wet nurse may be chosen by mutual consent. The woman who breast-feeds the infant is hardly viewed under *Qur'anic* law as hired help (though the father has an obligation to pay her) and instead is legally recognised as foster mother through whom relationships are established almost the same way as through normal parents.[62] In establishing this relationship between the child and the foster mother, a dynamic interpretation is again in evidence. Even though 10 feedings of a suckling child were considered necessary to establish the relationship, arguably on a *Qur'anic* revelation, this was subsequently reduced to five feedings.[63] The institution of foster mother, in the interest of the child, is not the only exemplary feature of the extended family concept – relatives too can be held legally responsible to take care of their needy.[64]

Though there is little available record of the Prophet's own childhood, the treatment of children during his generation is a pointer towards enhanced rights. In a conscious break from the pre-Islamic period, emphasis is placed on the child as 'the ornament of life', their care, education and individuality. The life of one central

---

[60] See e.g., A. Hussain, *The Sexual Exploitation and Sexual Abuse of Children in Pakistan* in WOMEN'S LAW IN LEGAL EDUCATION AND PRACTICE IN PAKISTAN: NORTH SOUTH CO-OPERATION 233–244 (R. Mehdi & F. Shaheed eds., 1997). For a similar attempt to use religion to stamp out child prostitution, *see* S. Satha Anand, *Looking To Buddhism To Turn Back Prostitution In Thailand* in THE EAST ASIAN CHALLENGE FOR HUMAN RIGHTS 193 (J. Bauer & D. Bell eds., 1999).

[61] 'Suckling is the first feeding of the infant after it is born and for this reason it is one of the infant's primary rights. It is the mother's duty to suckle him, while it is his father's duty to provide for the mother.' *See* M. Abu Zahra, *Family Law* in LAW IN THE MIDDLE EAST 153 (M. & H. Liebesney, eds., 1955).

[62] The concept of milk relationship differs from the 'Godmother' concept in the West in that Muslims are prohibited from marrying persons of several categories of suckling kin. *See* Zahra *supra* note 61 at 135.

[63] A. HASAN, THE EARLY DEVELOPMENT OF ISLAMIC JURISPRUDENCE 72 (1994). *See also* Y. DUTTON, THE ORIGINS OF ISLAMIC LAW: THE QUR'AN, THE MUWATTA AND MADINAN 'AMAL 125–26 (1999).

[64] *See e.g.,* Zahra, *supra* note 61 at 159–60.

Islamic personality, the wife of the Prophet, A'isha, tells us a great deal about child rights. Though the age of A'isha is disputed,[65] she certainly would have been considered a child at the time of marriage by the CRC threshold and, arguably, was in her teens when the Prophet died. According to one *hadith*, the Prophet treated her tenderly and even played with her and her dolls. However, despite her age, she not only participated in religious and political debates and accompanied the Prophet on the crucial flight from religious persecution (*hijra*) but when faced with rumours about her infidelity led a spirited defence to clear her name, which resulted in divine intervention in her favour.[66] A'isha's legacy, which is invoked by Muslim feminists, could equally be a strong talking point in calling for greater participation and right of expression for children.

As the corporal punishment debate within Islamic literature indicates, the limited *Qur'anic* verses substantially promote child rights but the copious traditions of *Sunnah* appear restrictive. Though the *Qur'an* overrides the *Sunnah*, the latter is binding where the *Qur'an* is silent on details. However, when the *Sunnah* began to be compiled in written form, only a hundred and fifty years after the Prophet's demise, a crisis of authenticity led to the science of *Asma al Rijala* (history of narrators)[67] and later the recognition of canonical *ahadith* (plural of *hadith*) texts. However, the debate over the accuracy or credibility of particular *hadith* continues to be debated. Recognising this challenge, Fazlur Rahman does not contemplate the abandonment of the *hadith*, which apart from being unacceptable to Muslims would leave little detail for the *Shari'a*. He states

> The studies of the *Qur'an* and *Hadith* are far from adequate, and it is hoped that a breakthrough in these all important subjects will come, a breakthrough that will at once be scientific and creative – that is, that will adequately meet the criteria of objective research and will, at the same time, reformulate and reinterpret the bases of Islamic thought and practice.[68]

Rather than being static, autonomous or rigid, the *Usul al-fiqh* (Islamic jurisprudence) itself provides for several juristic tools which reconcile revelation with

---

[65] The age of A'isha at the time of marriage has been the subject of scholarly debate. *For e.g.*, F. RAHMAN SHEIKH, FOOTPRINTS OF MUHAMMAD: LOCATING THE EVENTS IN THE LIFE TIME OF THE PROPHET 124–5 (1996). *See also*, N. ABBOT A'ISHAH, THE BELOVED OF MOHAMMED xvii (1942). Abbot's book though appearing favourable to A'isha was banned in Pakistan and several other Muslim countries because of her conclusion on A'isha's age at the time of marriage and some intimate details. It is generally agreed among commentators that consummation occurred some years after the marriage.

[66] *See generally*, D. SPELLBERG, POLITICS, GENDER AND THE ISLAMIC PAST: THE LEGACY OF AISHA BINT ABI BAKR 155–6 (1994).

[67] Developed in the second century of Islam, it initiated scrupulous verification of both the *isnad* (names and details of the chain of narrators traced to the Prophet) and the *matn* (the contents). *See* M. Zubayr Siddiqui, *The Ahadith and Orientalism* in HADITH LITERATURE: ITS ORIGIN, DEVELOPMENT & SPECIAL FEATURES 124–135 (1993).

[68] *See* F. RAHMAN, ISLAM AND MODERNITY: TRANSFORMATION OF AN INTELLECTUAL TRADITION 147 (1982), where he calls for a 'critique of *Hadith* that should not only remove mental blocks but promote fresh thinking'.

reason. The two other sources of the Shari'a – *qiyas* (analogic reasoning) and *ijma* (consensus of opinion) – offer avenues for progressive development of Islamic law and other supplemental law-generating forces such as *istishan* (juristic preference or equitable solution), *istislah* and *maslaha mursala* (common good or public interest) and *darura* (necessity)[69] could be beneficial for creating a responsive child rights framework.

Islamic law also provides particularly potent and creative machinery in *ijtihad*, or individual interpretation.[70] Though the earliest period of development of Islamic jurisprudence was a golden period for *ijtihad*, the gates of *ijtihad* were supposed to have been shut in the seventh century of Islam.[71] Whether real or fictitious, this influential view did lead to stagnation and ossification of Islamic legal thought until the twentieth century when Islamic liberal orthodoxy and modernists have resurrected the interpretative methodology. The contributions of Indian-born Muhammad Iqbal, Egyptian Mohammad Abduh, Syrian-born Rashid Rida, Turkish Ziya Gokalp, Pakistan-born Fazlur Rahman and more recently Algerian-born Mohammed Arkoun, Sudanese born Abdullahi An-Naim, American Amina Wadud, Indian Asghar Ali Engineer or South African Farid Esack point to an emerging global Muslim enterprise which, though using a variety of approaches, does re-interpret the textual basis of human rights formulations. This endeavour, however, has almost bypassed Islamic child rights doctrines so far.[72]

A natural ally would appear to be the feminist *Mujtahids* (those exercising *ijtihad*) who could extend their enquiry into children's interests. Cynthia Price Cohen, for example, considers the CRC a 'feminist landmark' because it goes far beyond the CEDAW in protecting the rights of the girl child and ought to interest gender activists.[73] An example of overlap between child and gender rights is the concern over the upbringing of the child under Islamic law. Though the Muslim parents have joint primary responsibility in bringing up the child, on separation the physical custody of the younger child (*hadana*) is with the mother, while the

---

[69] For an overview *see* W. HALLAQ, A HISTORY OF ISLAMIC LEGAL THEORIES: AN INTRODUCTION TO SUNNI USUL AL FIQH (1997).

[70] Literally 'an effort to find' the right principle, *Ijtihad* is not a option but a *fard e kifaya* (sacred duty) and is based on verses such as Qur'anic *Surah* 17:15 'He who follows the right way shall do so to his own advantage: and he who strays shall incur his own loss. No one shall carry another's burden.' *See also* Qur'an 74:38, 6:165. *See further*, M. HAKIM KAMALI, PRINCIPLES OF ISLAMIC JURISPRUDENCE 366 (1991).

[71] Muhammad Iqbal says 'the closing of the door of *ijtihad* is pure fiction suggested partly by the crystallisation of legal thought in Islam, and partly by the intellectual laziness which, especially in the period of spiritual decay, turns great thinkers into statues'. M. IQBAL, RECONSTRUCTION OF RELIGIOUS THOUGHT IN ISLAM 178 (1980). Several writers are of the opinion that no universal consensus was reached on the cessation of *Ijtihad*, *see e.g.*, B. Weiss, *Interpretation in Islamic Law: The Theory of Ijtihad* 38 AM. J. COMP. L. 199 (1978); W. Hallaq, *Was the Gate of Ijtihad Closed?* 16 INT. J. MIDDLE EAST STUD (1984).

[72] However, *ijtihad* has already been the basis of family law reforms in several countries. *See e.g.*, R. A. Codd, *A Critical Analysis of the Role of Ijtihad in Legal Reforms in the Muslim World* ARAB L. Q. 112–31 (1999).

[73] C. Price Cohen, *The United Nations Convention on the Rights of the Child: a Feminist Landmark* 3 WILLIAM AND MARY JOURNAL OF WOMEN AND THE LAW 29 (1997).

father is considered the natural guardian of the older child (*wali*).[74] Such a demarcation of guardianship responsibilities depending on the age of a child has been seen, among other things, as an impediment to countering international child abduction.[75] Feminists, critiquing the sex-based roles and biological stereotypes, have demanded parity for parents in the custody of children. Their rationale, in resisting patriarchal structures, however, has not been the 'best interests of the child'[76] (though this may well be a factor), but is cast as a gender right. Such replication of the gender viewpoint into their discourse may address some facets of child rights but could easily neglect the male child and even misconstrue the interests of the girl child to serve gender rights. Feminists revisiting Islamic sources to establish equal rights with male adults strive to break the link between gender rights and child concerns because they fear the infantilisation of their rights or being saddled with traditional mothering roles. However, if feminists critiquing polygamy, male custody or their exclusion from public life or political participation were to pause and consider what effect these practices have on children, a valuable contribution to child rights may be made.

Muslim children, initiated early into learning (at least memorising, if not understanding) the *Qur'an* and living under the *Sunnah*, do engage with the traditional rules that apply to them. The extent to which their opinions are sought or accepted depends on the nature of education available as well as the recognition by governments that children have transformed over the past 1,400 years – both in opportunities, as well as the problems they face and need to identify.[77] Since the doctrine of *tajzi'at al-ijtihad* (qualifications to exercise *ijtihad*) is restrictive, it would appear that the children could only be prepared for a future role that could augment the child rights of the next generation, not their own. The incorporation of a child rights perspective into general *ijtihad* efforts is the only real way forward in challenging dominant interpretations. Further, since most child rights issues in Islam have emerged from *ijma* (consensus of the community), initiative from *ijtihad* needs to be followed up politically. The community of laypersons, scholars and politicians

---

[74] The specific age at which this transfer of responsibility takes place is higher for girls and varies among the Islamic schools and in the practice of States. *See* Nasir, *supra* note 50 at 121–126 comparing the practice of North African Muslim States. Debates on this issue rage in several countries, for example in Egypt where an amendment to the Personal Status Law has been proposed to raise the maternal custody of children to 12 years for boys and 15 years for girls, *see* A. KARAM, WOMEN, ISLAMISMS AND THE STATE: CONTEMPORARY FEMINISMS AND THE STATE 150 (1998). *See also* how several Muslim countries have modified classical law by raising the age at which the father can claim guardianship. J.N.D ANDERSON, LAW REFORM IN THE MUSLIM WORLD 141 (1976).

[75] *See* David Pearl, *supra* note 46 at 87; LeBlanc *supra* note 12 at 139–40. Note that no Muslim country has ratified the 1983 Hague Convention on the Civil Aspects of International Child Abduction.

[76] Goonesekere points out that the 'best interests of the child' has been built through judicial *ijtihad* in South Asia in custody matters where Islamic law is silent. *See* S. GOONASEKERE, CHILDREN, LAW AND JUSTICE: A SOUTH ASIAN PERSPECTIVE 124–27 (1998). For a review of the case-law from Muslim countries on guardianship of minors indicating that the 'best interests of the child' as applied under Islamic law could lead to either parent being granted *see* D. PEARL & W. MENSKI, MUSLIM FAMILY LAW (1998).

[77] For the importance of participatory rights of children *see generally* M. FLEKKOY & N. KAUFMAN, THE PARTICIPATION RIGHTS OF THE CHILD: RIGHTS AND RESPONSIBILITIES IN FAMILY AND SOCIETY (1997).

needs to be persuaded that the time is right for a radical rethinking on the place of children in Islamic societies, fully consistent with *Qur'anic* principles. An example of a dynamic *ijma Shari'a* is provided by Bernard Freamon in a recent article[78] where he argues that even though the practice of slavery was not explicitly prohibited, it can be declared as violative of the *Shari'a* by the community at large. It is not contended that *ijtihad-ijima* could magically transform the child rights scenario or create a mirror image of CRC rights located in the *Shari'a* – significant differences will persist. Yet the failure to determine the nature and scope of child rights under Islamic law has understated the enormous potential to rework the substantive textual basis of these rights.

Conclusion

Review of the impact of the first decade of the CRC has been restricted to largely Western jurisdictions where case-law and legislative amendments are easier to monitor.[79] The primary basis of evaluating the response of Muslim countries has been the 'constructive dialogue' as part of the reporting obligations assumed by all Muslim countries.[80] Article 43 of the CRC stipulates that in the election of the 10 member expert monitoring committee, consideration is to be given to 'equitable geographical distribution as well as principal legal systems'[81] and representatives from Muslim countries have played an active role on the Committee. The record of Muslim countries in presenting their periodic reports does not compare unfavourably to the delays in the reports from other countries.[82] The CRC Committee has received a wealth of information on the status of children in Muslim countries and identified obstacles as well as progress in the implementation of the Convention. In particular, it has interrogated Muslim States on their *Shari'a* reservations and has called upon States such as Egypt, Iraq, Pakistan, Morocco, Tunisia and Indonesia to reconsider them. As the reporting system gathers momentum and the Muslim States become familiar with the expectations of the CRC, it is hoped that the CRC will begin yielding greater dividends.

A radical improvement in child rights in the Muslim world would depend on numerous factors – social, economic and political. Socio-cultural and certain religiously justified practices do undermine the standard treatment of children in Muslim societies. Sima Wali, for example, recounts the impact on refugee

---

[78] B. Freamon, *Slavery, Freedom, and the Doctrine of Consensus in Islamic Jurisprudence* 11 HARV. HUM. RTS. J. 1 (1998). *See also* A. HASAN, THE DOCTRINE OF IJIMA IN ISLAM: A STUDY OF THE JURIDICAL PRINCIPLE OF CONSENSUS (1992).

[79] *See e.g.,* J. Todres, *Emerging Limitations on the Rights of the Child: The UN Convention on the Rights of the Child and its Early Case-Law* 30 COLUM. HUM. RTS. L. R. 159 (1998).

[80] No country has entered reservations to the procedural monitoring provisions crucial to the Convention's success. See A. Bissett-Johson, *Qualifications of Signatories to the United Nations Convention on the Rights of the Child – What Did State Parties Really Agree To?* in FAMILIES ACROSS FRONTIERS 115–131 (N. Lowe & G. Douglas eds., 1996).

[81] *See* G. MOWER, THE CONVENTION ON THE RIGHTS OF THE CHILD: INTERNATIONAL LAW SUPPORT FOR CHILDREN 125 (1997).

[82] *See* the *Note by the Secretary General, Provisional Agenda of the Committee on the Rights of the Child* CRC/C/88 26 July, 1999, listing the countries with delayed reports.

children.[83] This chapter suggests that religion, rather than seen as an obstacle to child rights, could be harnessed to counter harmful practices. On the other hand, limited economic resources and their prioritisation too determine the conditions in which children live in. As Haytham Manna'a points out[84]

> Can we not be affected by the great discrepancy between Arab children in the countries of the 'black gold' and their siblings in the Arab shanty towns? How can we deal with the rights of the children without touching on the absence of opportunities for food, medical care, and education, and of adult crimes as familial and social domination, discrimination according to gender, and economic sanctions which affect children most of all and rarely affect the rulers?

However, the implementation of child rights – both civil and political rights as well as socio-economic and cultural rights – remains largely a matter of political will. Muslim States may say that they are apprehensive of Western values infiltrating their societies but their fear is really the prospect of an independent thinking new generation well positioned to challenge their authoritarian policies. On its own, even the optimist cannot hope that domestic application of international child rights standards can materialise, particularly when the CRC often reflects generalised aspirations without stipulating domestic remedies nor providing an individual petition mechanism for vindication of the Convention rights. The State is obliged to undertake both positive obligations (Article 2), and progressive realisation of economic, social and cultural rights (Article 4), but the limited international naming and shaming process works less perfectly than reconditioning of child rights in the very jargon of the Muslim governments – moral, ethical and spiritual basis of child rights through their articulation as *Shari'a* obligations. Child rights under the *Shari'a* then emerge as a useful promotional tool rather than an obstacle to the realisation of the CRC objectives.

The CRC does not present a straightforward dichotomous choice (compliance/ non-compliance) but rather serves as a guidance in building a new personhood of children and a catalyst for a worldwide revolution in children's policy.[85] As Stewart Asquith and Malcolm Hill note, abuse of the spirit of the Convention – using it as a platform to launch monthly condemnations of particular Third World countries as somehow evil because of the reality check – only serves as an instrument for creating outcasts in the global society. The importance of the CRC lies in its framework for cross-cultural dialogue which potentially creates future world citizens on the basis of certain shared perceptions, aspirations and experiences. Geraldine Van Buren argues that 'the Convention promotes an ethos of both cultural plurality and

---

[83] *See* the case study on Afghan Refugee Women and Children in S. Wali, *Muslim Refugee, Returnee, and Displaced Women: Challenges and Dilemmas* in Afkhami (ed) *supra* note 21 at 177.

[84] Manna'a, *supra* note 28 at 33. *See also* the UN Committee on the Rights of the Child's recognition of such factors as 'obstacles to implementation of the Convention'. *See further*, UNICEF, STATE OF THE WORLD'S CHILDREN 10 (1999) which notes the impact of armed conflicts and structural adjustments on educational development in regions such as Africa and the Middle East.

[85] S. ASQUITH & M. HILL, JUSTICE FOR CHILDREN 41 (1994).

universalism ... It does not want to promote a single fixed universal image of child-hood. Yet it does want to promote universal opportunities for children.'[86] The CRC and Islamic formulations may have distinctive features and several points of divergence but they could be different approaches to child rights. An endeavour to engage with internal Islamic discourses could only strengthen the battle for inter-national child rights standards under the CRC for Muslim children or those living under Muslim laws.

---

[86] G. Van Bueren, *Children's Rights: Balancing Traditional Values and Cultural Plurality* in Douglas and Leslie & Sebba (eds), *supra* note 47 at 19.

Hilary Lim and Jeremy Roche

4. FEMINISM AND CHILDREN'S RIGHTS: THE POLITICS OF VOICE

INTRODUCTION

In the 10 years since the United Nations Convention on the Rights of the Child (CRC) has been adopted by the UN the debates surrounding children's rights have become more complex, sophisticated and, appropriately, more global.[1] In this chapter we consider the contribution of feminist scholarship to these debates concluding that feminist engagement with children's rights has been partial. We argue that children's rights and feminist scholarship have much to gain from a more sustained dialogue, sharing as they do a number of common concerns. The first part of this chapter examines the 'participation rights' of the CRC, noting the radical potential of these provisions, and the contribution to date of feminism to the children's rights literature. We then consider feminist scepticism about rights in general and children's rights in particular before examining alternative feminist approaches to rights, including children's rights. In the third section we return to a direct consideration of the radical potential of children's rights. Inspired by the work of Drucilla Cornell we suggest a need to re-imagine children's rights, together with associated ideas of dependency and vulnerability.[2] We conclude by setting out some of the shared intellectual ground of feminist and children's rights scholars, speculating on how this scholarship might develop in the future.

PARTICIPATION RIGHTS AND FEMINIST PERSPECTIVES

The participation rights contained in Articles 12–16 of the CRC can be seen as constituting a 'dangerous centre' within the idea of children's rights with which few commentators have fully engaged.[3] Until the CRC all international children's rights texts fell within a conventional welfare rights framework. As such these instruments were exhortations to treat the child better and the State was required to take some steps to secure that better treatment. What is distinctive about the CRC is its opening up of a new territory which while linked to questions of welfare and devel-

---

[1] *See* P.A. ALSTON, THE BEST INTERESTS OF THE CHILD (1994) and S. K. GOONESEKERE, CHILDREN, LAW AND JUSTICE (1998).

[2] *See* D. CORNELL, AT THE HEART OF THE MATTER, (1998).

[3] There are notable exceptions, *see e.g.*, M.D.A. FREEMAN, THE MORAL STATUS OF THE CHILD (1997); CHILDREN'S RIGHTS OFFICE ALL RIGHT AT HOME? PROMOTING RESPECT FOR THE HUMAN RIGHTS OF CHILDREN IN FAMILY LIFE (2000); *see also* V. Morrow, *'We are people too': Children's and young people's perspectives on children's rights and decision-making in England*, 7 INT'L J. of CHILDREN'S RTS. 149–170 (1999).

Deirdre Fottrell (ed.), Revisiting Children's Rights, 51–72
© 2000 *Kluwer Law International. Printed in Great Britain.*

opment, is also concerned with the 'civil liberties' of the child. Thus it recognises the child as a social actor and gives the child a bundle of rights more commonly associated with citizenship in liberal democracies.[4]

These 'participation rights' are widely viewed as central to the children's rights agenda set by the CRC.[5] Goonesekere, for instance, sees these rights themselves as key and the concept of a child's right to be treated as a 'person' as crucial to the recognition of the child's identity, survival and development. She argues 'it is this linkage with personality and identity that gives participation rights a special dimension and makes them vital for the realisation of all child rights'.[6] However, participation rights also hold out the threat of fundamentally disrupting adult-child relations[7] and herein lies their 'dangerous centre'. The idea of the child having a right to express an opinion, or a right of access to information, goes to the heart of 'private' life, making demands which challenge the very nature of intimate human relationships within the family. Lucker-Babel sees Article 12 of the CRC as requiring that the child be consulted only when and where a decision exists concretely for the child or a group of children, not on everything. She argues:

> Apart from the fact that this interpretation limits the field of application for Article 12, it also gives the Article its full impact since it establishes a link with the daily life of every child. Consequently, the situations where Article 12 is implemented are found mainly in circumstances close to the child such as family ties, family life and education, place of residence, the school, the company (for apprentices and minor workers), hobbies, health care, institutional life or measures of child welfare, if the need arises. One will not exclude matters associated with road traffic or the protection of the environment, but one will ascertain that they have a real and specific bearing on the life of young citizens. The viewpoint is reinforced by a comparison with Article 3.1, which refers to the 'best interests of the child' and applies in 'all actions concerning children'.[8]

---

[4]   *See* B. Hafen and J. Hafen, *Abandoning Children to their Autonomy: The UN Convention on the Rights of the Child*, 37 HARV. INT'L L.J. 449, 452–53 (1996). The authors provide a critical analysis of autonomy rights in the CRC and argue that the 'early approach to rights for children centered on the child's special need for protection and development, not on the child's autonomous right to make his or her own choices'.

[5]   *See* B. Rwezaura, *Competing 'Images' of Childhood in the Social and Legal Systems of Contemporary Sub-Saharan Africa*, 12 INT'L J. OF LAW, POLICY & FAM. 253–278 (1998).

[6]   *See further,* Alston, *supra,* note 1, at 310. *See also* Freeman, *supra,* note 3, 56 where he writes that Article 12 of the CRC is 'the most significant ... because it recognizes the child as a full human being, with integrity and personality, and with the ability to participate fully in society'.

[7]   *See* K. Gale, S.L. Hills, D. Moulds and K. Stacey, *Breaking ground in inclusive conference practices with young people*, 7 INT'L J. OF CHILDREN'S RTS 259, 274–75 (1999) where the authors argue, for instance, that 'youth participation is neither a benign nor a neutral term'. The participatory rights gave rise to such a concern at the time of drafting, *see further,* L. LEBLANC, THE CONVENTION ON THE RIGHTS OF THE CHILD: UNITED NATIONS LAWMAKING ON HUMAN RIGHTS (1995), particularly the first chapter and 112–117.

[8]   M.F. Lucker-Babel, *The right of the child to express views and to be heard: An attempt to interpret Article 12 of the UN Convention on the Rights of the Child* 3 INT'L J. OF CHILDREN'S RTS. 391, 396–97 (1995). She continues: 'Even the "infans" (literally the one who does not speak) may participate. To be useful to the decision, the child's feeling must be interpreted by specialists trained

For children it is the family that represents the most significant space within which they act in society. However, the right to self-determination is perhaps less disruptive and more easily realised in the public, specifically the legislative, arena. Freeman has commented in the context of English law, for example, that: '[a] child has a greater "say" in care than in school or for that matter at home',[9] although he acknowledges that there are examples of domestic legislation which seek, at least at a symbolic level, to concretise the child's right to autonomy inside the private sphere.[10] This focus on linking the provisions of the CRC to the child's place within the family was evident in the deliberations of the Scottish Law Commission, which eventually led to section 6 of the Children (Scotland) Act 1995. The Commission noted that:

> The question as we saw it was whether a parent or other person exercising parental rights should be under a similar obligation to ascertain and have regard to the child's wishes and feelings as a local authority was in relation to a child in its care ... There are great attractions in such an approach. It emphasises that the child is a person in his or her own right and that his or her views are entitled to respect and consideration ... On consultation there was majority support for a provision requiring parents, in reaching any major decision relating to a child, to ascertain the child's wishes and feelings so far as practicable and give due consideration to them having regard to their age and understanding ... Many respondents clearly regarded such a provision as an important declaration of principle.[11]

Academics may agree on the centrality of the child's views to the ideology of the CRC, but responses to this aspect of the treaty are not always positive; indeed there is a tendency towards the ambiguous, sceptical or downright hostile.[12] Hafen and Hafen, for instance, take a distinctly less sanguine view than Freeman to the participation provisions and identify a possible threat to adult-child relations:

> Since 1989, the CRC has exported throughout the global community a new concept of presuming the autonomy of the individual child. This ... dimension of the CRC seems related to the UN's general contemporary interest in the

---

footnote continued
> to this effect. Moreover, an extensive attitude on the child's capacity to give his or her opinion is required if we want to maintain the dynamics of Article 12 of the Convention and to avoid the exclusion of a whole category of minors.'
[9] *See* Freeman, *Supra*, note 3, at 57.
[10] Freeman mentions legislation in Finland and Sweden *supra*, note 3.
[11] SCOTTISH LAW COMMISSION, ¶ 2.62–2.64 (1992). S. 6 of the Children (Scotland) Act 1995 imposes such a duty on parents and provides that children over 12 years of age are presumed in law to be old enough to express a view.
[12] *See e.g.* L.M. Kohm and M.E. Lawrence, *Sex at Six: The Victimization of Innocence and Other Concerns Over Children's Rights* 36 J. OF FAM. L. 361, 368-69-406 (1997–8), where the authors argue that 'lurking' in the CRC is the message that 'rights have become contraverted into capacity and emancipation, even if that emancipation is from one's own age, nature and incompetence'. Kohm and Lawrence identify Articles 12 and 14 as carrying this message 'subliminally' with 'legal culture' blurring 'the line between adulthood and childhood', when '[we] should, instead, actively recognize the unique qualities and characteristics of the very nature of a child'.

'concept of the radically autonomous individual' – a concept that obscures 'the importance of families rooted in stable marriages for the well being of children'.[13]

In their overt opposition to what they regard as the ideological victory of Western children's rights advocates in the drafting of these articles in the CRC, Hafen and Hafen highlight the real possibilities for change in adult-child relations that are inherent in participation rights. Others, more sympathetic to this particular aspect of the Convention, have not always followed through its potential for destabilising traditional ways of seeing children.[14] In any event the re-imagining of relationships in the context of the child's radical autonomy is not well developed. It is almost as if adults eager to carry on business as usual, in both their intellectual practice and their private lives, have decided to continue with established categories of thinking and familiar arguments.

In focusing upon autonomy rights we are not, of course, arguing that debates surrounding the welfare rights of children are straightforward. On the contrary, they give rise to highly complex intellectual, political and policy issues. For example, the question of child labour, together with the development of more positive and inclusive strategies to deal with it, are highly contentious. Intense discussions surround issues about whose interests are being protected when the threat of sanctions is deployed in the name of eradicating child labour, as do claims for recognition of the economic contribution such labour makes to households already struggling to survive.[15] The literature also reflects one of the truths about children's rights; they can only be imagined and contested locally. The CRC provides a text for thinking and debate, but the detail of the practical and symbolic meaning of arguments around children's rights of necessity is linked to time and space. When the focus is on an area like child labour the detailed analysis, including the political and economic calculations that go into deciding what action to take, differ enormously from place to place.[16]

---

[13] *Supra* note 4, at 457. Hafen and Hafen also claim that the CRC's autonomy model ironically undermines the very autonomy-building process of education and nurturing that every child needs ... 'To serve the interests of both society and its children, therefore, society has limited children's legal autonomy in the short run precisely in order to maximise their actual autonomy in the long run' at 476.

[14] *See e.g.* C. BARTON AND G. DOUGLAS, LAW AND PARENTHOOD (1995). *See also* J. Eekelaar, *The Importance of Thinking that Children Have Rights* in CHILDREN'S RIGHTS AND THE LAW 221, (P. Alston, S. Parker and J. Seymour eds., 1992).

[15] *See e.g.*, the debate in the United States on the Harkin Bill. The Bill was designed to limit the import of goods made with child labour and used the rhetoric of welfare, but for some it looked as if its purpose was trade protection. *See, Labelling: Will Goods Marked to Show that Goods Have Been Made by Children benefit Children* DCI UK Newsletter No. 4, June 1(1994). On a more general level, *see* E. Burman, *Local, Global or Globalized? Child development and international child rights legislation*, 3 CHILDHOOD 45, 46 (1996) where the author reviews the tension between global and local conceptions of childhood and the consequences for the success of the CRC, arguing that 'in seeking to promote children's well-being and welfare across the world, there is no escape from the difficult path between cultural imperialism and cultural relativism'.

[16] *Id.* at 47 where Burman suggests that global concepts such as rights 'by their very nature cannot specify the conditions and precise interventions called for in each domain of application ... it is a matter of interpreting what these general precepts mean in particular contexts'.

It is arguable that feminist approaches to children's rights are peculiarly appropriate to the challenges posed by children's participation rights. Some feminist writing, which has engaged with children's rights, particularly in the context of the CRC, has done so from a basis that assumes a commonality of interest between mother/woman and child, focusing on interrelations between their welfare rights. In human rights analyses one may also find a relatively unselfconscious linking of the rights of women and children. Kawewe and Dibie argue for example that '[a]lthough the UN is set in its patriarchal mode, recent developments in Beijing indicate a willingness to make radical statements regarding children, women, and various forms of oppression and exploitation'.[17] The reference appears to be to what Chinkin has described as women's NGOs' success at the World Conference on Human Rights in Vienna (1993) and UN Conference on Women in Beijing (1995), both in terms of the 'reaffirmation in the Beijing Declaration that "women's rights are human rights" and of the commitment to "the full implementation of the human rights of women and the girl-child as an inalienable, integral and indivisible part of all human rights and fundamental freedoms"'.[18] Writing on the girl–child Goonesekere argues that governments have initiated programmes for women 'without considering linkages to children'.[19] She goes on to argue in the South Asian context that 'the separation of women and girl-children's issues has ... turned out to be a disadvantage for both groups' and that 'laws and policy ... need to address the area of discrimination against girls and women on the basis that these interventions are two aspects of a single issue'.[20]

Olsen, reviewing the CRC in the early 1990s, remarked upon the ambiguous, sceptical and complex relationships that many feminists have with both legal rights and the legal protection of children.[21] Olsen's exploration of four feminist perspectives on children's rights[22] is as much concerned with predicting how these feminist theories *might* approach the rights of the child in general, and the CRC in particular, as it is with engaging with actual feminist writings on children's rights. In fact there is a relative absence of Western feminist work focusing upon children's rights. Olsen provides some indication as to why the rights of the child are not a fertile area for feminist study in pointing out that, while a society which tries to protect children from abuse and neglect is likely to create a climate which is beneficial to women as their primary caretakers, it is the case that '[l]egal protection of children

---

[17] S. Kawewe & R. Dibie, *United Nations and the Problem of Women and Children Abuse in Third World Nations*, 26 SOCIAL JUSTICE, 78–98 (1999).

[18] C. Chinkin, *Torture of the Girl-Child*, in CHILDHOOD ABUSED (G. Van Bueren, ed., 1998) at 86.

[19] *See* GOONESKERE, *Supra*, note 1, at 153.

[20] *Id.* at 154–155.

[21] F. Olsen, *Children's Rights: Some Feminist Approaches to the United Nations Convention on the Rights of the Child* 6 INT'L J. OF L. & FAM., 192 (1992). This stance is not one exclusive to feminist theorists and is shared with many writers beyond the feminist sphere who are engaged in developing a politics of transformation, including arguments about children and childhood. Scepticism about legal rights is one of the hallmarks of critical legal studies, *see e.g.*, A.D. Freeman, *Racism, Rights and the Quest for Equality of Opportunity: A Critical Legal Essay*, 23 HARV C.R-C.L L. REV. 295 (1988).

[22] These are 'legal reformist', 'law as patriarchy', 'feminist critical legal theory' and 'post-modern feminism'.

can be and has been used as a basis for controlling women'.[23] Minow also has written of the 'particular allegation of tension between women's rights and children's rights' and 'the charge that the feminist movement failed to fight hard enough for children's rights and needs'.[24] However, she warns against placing the blame for unmet children's needs at the door of the women's movement while acknowledging that there is an issue around the inadequacy of the coalition between the women's and children's movements, with both suffering as a consequence.

However, perhaps it is also the case that 'feminist ... analysis pertains not just to women but, equally, to other gendered subjects positioned at the margins of hegemonic discourses' and 'can help us to understand the construction of modernist discourses of childhood'.[25] Certainly, Federle has suggested that feminist legal methods have something particular to offer to any discussion of children's rights, although she believes that feminism needs to reconstruct its theories of rights to accommodate ideas about power. For her the problem is that while 'women have had some success in shifting the dialogue of rights beyond arguments about competence, when discussing the concept of children's rights, the debate invariably returns to the capacity of children'.[26] On the other hand as we will attempt to demonstrate, feminists have also disrupted the notion of the independent, autonomous rights-bearer. Thus there is a particularity in feminist engagement with children's rights, although within this particularity there are some curious silences.

Feminist scholarship has shown a dedication to revealing the realities of male, patriarchal power including male violence,[27] but is generally much quieter on the issue of the 'parental right to chastise'. As Schneider argues the issue of violence in the home has evolved from a 'private' to a more 'public' matter, but has not in this process become a more serious political issue. Schneider suggests that this is 'precisely because it has profound implications for all our lives ... [and] goes to our most fundamental assumptions about the nature of intimate relations and the safety of family life'.[28] Although this is not her particular concern, perhaps thereby she

---

[23] *Supra*, note 21, at 193. *See also* on this point Goonesekere, *supra* note 1, at 154.

[24] M. Minow, *Children's Rights: Where We've Been, and Where We're Going*, 68 TEMP. L. REV, 1581 (1995).

[25] P. Mankekar, *To Whom Does Ameena Belong? Towards a Feminist Analysis of Childhood and Nationhood in Contemporary India*, 56 FEMINIST REV 26–60 at 51(1997).

[26] K. Federle, *On the Road to Reconceiving Rights for Children: A Postfeminist Analysis of the Capacity Principle*, 42 DE PAUL L. REV. 983, 984–985 (1993).

[27] *See e.g.*, E. Schneider , *The Violence of Privacy* in THE PUBLIC NATURE OF PRIVATE VIOLENCE, 42 (M. Fineman & R. Mykitiuk eds., 1994) where she argues that the ideology of family privacy operates to permit, encourage and enforce violence against women.

[28] *See also*, A. Armstrong et al, *Towards a Cultural Understanding of the Interplay Between Children's and Women's Rights: An Eastern and Southern African Perspective*, 3 INT'L J. OF CHILDREN' RTS, 333, 359–60, (1995) where the authors see a link between women's rights and children's rights in the context of the violence of husband and fathers, which means that 'a similar cultural conflict is produced when attempting to enforce the child's right to be protected from violence and the woman's right to be protected from violence'. They argue that improving women's rights will operate to the benefit of children in two ways which may limit physical abuse of children: 'First, since the primary caretaker of the child is likely to be a woman, by empowering that woman, the child is protected indirectly ... Second, ... improving the legal, economic, social and psychological

also supplies a reason for the silence on the implications for children. Given the emphasis on 'voice' within feminist politics,[29] it is equally curious that there has been little take-up of the citizenship dimension of the CRC. It may be the case, as we will suggest later, that some part of the explanation lies in acknowledging how in the 1990s many feminists subjected the law, legal institutions and practices to a powerful critique involving a questioning of the value of rights talk both theoretically and politically. It is hardly surprising, therefore, that children's rights are fairly marginal to feminist discourse.

Strangely, however, these silences about both 'voice' and violence towards children in the home point to two interconnected inputs for feminism to the debate around children's participation rights. First, much feminist scholarship has made direct personal experience a priority and places a value, therefore, on women finding their voices. As Landes recently stated, '[f]eminism offered women a public language for their private despair [and] consciousness raising groups ... provided women with a route out of private isolation and into public activism',[30] although these aspects of feminism are implicated in the overarching tendency to essentialise. bell hooks for instance argues that while the 'emphasis on woman's silence may be an accurate remembering of what has taken place in the households of women from WASP backgrounds in the United States ... in black communities ... women have not been silent'. She argues that for black women, the 'struggle has not been to emerge from silence into speech but to change the nature and direction of our speech, to make a speech that compels listeners, one that is heard'.[31] Nevertheless, feminism should have an important role in challenging the 'politics of mutism' surrounding children.[32]

Second, various threads of feminist thought, as a consequence of the political focus upon the private, have concentrated upon the desanctification of the family and the destabilisation of the public/private border. Landes makes the point that 'among modern oppositional movements, feminism is unrivalled in its contribution to a deepening understanding of the historical, symbolic and practical effects of public and private life'.[33] Feminism has already analysed and challenged the

---

footnote continued

status of women should result in reduction of stress for women, with consequent reduction of abuse of children by women', at 359. As to whether parental chastisement should be equated with abuse, we would suggest that the issue is a social one and, in the context of the CRC, we would question the purpose behind any attempt to draw a distinction between the two. For a child's perspective on parental chastisement, *see* G. Willow & T. Hyde, *The Myth of the Loving Smack, Childright* No. 154, 18–20 (1999), who carried out research into how young children viewed 'smacking' and the clear message was that children found such chastisement to be both hurtful and embarrassing. A seven-year-old girl explained: 'A smack is parents trying to hit you but instead of calling it a hit they call it a smack'.

[29] Feminist theory has always valued personal experience, as is evident in the phrase 'the personal is political'. Feminist methodology is steeped in the idea of consciousness raising, which found concrete form most specifically in women's groups during the 1970s, and out of which theory develops. It begins with personal experience and is concerned with women 'finding a voice'.

[30] J. B. LANDES, FEMINISM, THE PUBLIC AND THE PRIVATE, 1 (1998).

[31] bell hooks, *Talking Back*, in MAKING FACE, MAKING SOUL, HACIENDO CARAS 207–208 (G. Anzaldua ed. 1999).

[32] J. O'Neill, *Is the Child a Political Subject?* 4(2) CHILDHOOD 241 (1997).

[33] *Supra*, note 30, 2.

public/private distinction and emphasised the importance of women's voice. If, as we suggest, it is necessary to rediscover the potential of children's participation rights within the private sphere of home and family, feminist discourse potentially provides a useful perspective.

Rwezaura observes that while the almost universal signing and ratification of the CRC could be taken as a sign of the world-wide acceptance of children's rights this should not deflect our attention from the fact, noted earlier, that the 'politics of children's rights' varies from region to region and from locality to locality.[34] These local variations impact on how the protection and provision rights of children are realised. For example practices in relation to child protection vary from State to State as do attitudes towards the parental 'right' to chastise their child. The country studies carried out as part of the Children's Rights Indicators Project, under the auspices of Childwatch International, recognise that the CRC must be read within particular localities and the project has 'established a framework and process through which country case study teams are able to develop protocols for data collection and indicator development that are relevant to regional, national and local situations'.[35]

The comments of the Zimbabwe Country Case Study team with respect to the participation rights in the CRC are apposite to our discussion. Workshops in Zimbabwe attended by welfare professionals to discuss both the CRC and the African Charter led to a regrouping of rights away from the three broad headings which dominate Northern-oriented commentaries of provision, protection and participation. As the team suggest 'the interpretation of the Convention in any social and cultural context will vary, just as ideas about children and childhood differ between cultures and societies'.[36] The team points out that data on children's participation rights in Zimbabwe are a 'central absence' and 'can only be understood in the relationships (ideal and real) that children have with adults'.[37] The team also argue that while children's participation rights are not visible in the Zimbabwean context, neither are they a well-developed subject globally. The subject, they assert, is only 'beginning to emerge as a result of the Convention on the Rights of the Child, as well as through programme experiences emanating from people who work with children in especially difficult circumstances, notably in Brazil, India and Senegal/West Africa, where children in difficulty have set up movements to articulate and defend their rights'.[38]

The more radical imagery associated with the participation rights of the CRC, as hinted at in the report from Zimbabwe, is potentially highly disruptive of estab-

---

[34] *Supra*, note 5; *see also*, LAW, CULTURE, TRADITION AND CHILDREN'S RIGHTS (W. Ncube ed. 1998); S.H. Hammad, *The CRC: 'Words on Paper' or a reality for children?*, 7 INT'L J. OF CHILDREN'S RTS., 215 (1999). *See also supra* note 15.

[35] RESEARCH REPORT: INDICATORS FOR CHILDREN'S RIGHTS (update: Nov. 1995), cited in C. Price-Cohen, S.N. Hart, & S.M. Kosloske, *Monitoring the United Nations Convention on the Rights of the Child: The Challenge of Information Management*, 18 H. RTS. Q., 464 (1996).

[36] I. CHINYANGARA et al, INDICATORS FOR CHILDREN'S RIGHTS: ZIMBABWE COUNTRY CASE STUDY, 6 (1997).

[37] *Id.*, 19.

[38] *Id.*, 19.

lished ways of viewing children and therefore, depending upon the particular place where it is being interpreted, may be highly contested, strangely absent or consciously ignored. A number of arguments are advanced for not taking participation rights seriously, including: the idea that children lack competence, especially younger children;[39] that they are properly dependent and what is required is not the abandonment of children to their rights but the imposing of appropriate obligations on parents/carers; and children's rights thus conceived undermine parental authority. This authority is put at risk anyway with State policies to protect children but it is even more the case when children are given the participation rights as contained in the CRC. It is in this context that we turn to look at the debate about children's rights within writings from broadly feminist perspectives, in order to explore new approaches to participation rights.

FEMINIST LEGAL SCEPTICISM AND FINDING THE RIGHT VOICE

Feminist scepticism about rights, like feminism itself, takes several forms, but it is tied to a more general feminist ambivalence about law and the legal system. Many feminist legal theorists in their discussions about the issue of rights, both in domestic contexts in terms of statutory or constitutional rights, and in the international domain, start from the position that engagement with law is dangerous for women. Far from leading to greater equality for women, or mitigating against the multiplicity of exclusions suffered by them, it is suggested that attempts to utilise rights rhetoric in legal fora serve only to empower the law and reinforce its empire.[40]

A number of feminist theoreticians also share the view that the use of rights rhetoric as a reform tactic is strategically unsound and liable to sap the strength of feminist politics. McColgan expresses the additional fear that women's organisations may be tempted into action to defend women's interests where entrenched rights are used to make countervailing claims against hard-won improvements in women's lives, including, for instance, control over their own bodies in pregnancy. She suggests that this may require 'the use of scarce resources on continual re-inventions of the wheel'.[41] Her recent conclusions from within a feminist per-

---

[39] *See e.g.* L. Purdy, *Why Children Shouldn't Have Equal Rights* 2 INT'L J. OF CHILDREN'S RTS 223. (1994), where she argues that there are differences between children and adults such that children are not able to take 'prudential and moral action'. However, recent scholarship questions such a presumption. Christiansen argues that children's competence is not fixed but variable, being determined through social processes of interaction and negotiation, P. Christiansen, *Difference and Similarity; How Children's Competence is Constituted in Illness and its Treatment* in CHILDREN AND SOCIAL COMPETENCE: ARENAS OF ACTION (I. Hutchby & J. Moran-Ellis eds., 1998). *See also* P. ALDERSON AND J. MONTGOMERY, HEALTH CARE CHOICES DECISION-MAKING WITH CHILDREN (1996); M. DE WINTER, CHILDREN AS FELLOW CITIZENS PARTICIPATION AND COMMITMENT 163, (1997) where he argues: 'What children can handle at a certain moment in their development is not a constant factor, but is partly the result of the space for learning and experiencing offered to them. By widening the field of development, for instance by involving children from a very early age in the organisation of the world in which they live, their repertoire of behavioural capabilities grows'.

[40] This point has been made forcefully by Carol Smart in a number of ways, most obviously in FEMINISM AND THE POWER OF LAW (1989).

[41] A. MCCOLGAN, WOMEN UNDER THE LAW 245 (2000).

spective on the provision of 'entrenched' or 'constitutional rights', such as those in the Human Rights Act 1998 in the United Kingdom[42] or the Canadian Charter of Rights, summarise effectively a prevalent standpoint:

> [E]ntrenched rights must not be regarded as a panacea against the ills of government. These rights ... are limited in their scope and their impact. They do not substitute for political action and, in addition to the dangers they pose, for example, to legislative action designed to safeguard women's autonomy or to secure substantive equality in the workplace, they can lull those who would otherwise engage in political action into taking their 'eye off the ball' and allowing reactionary politics to triumph ... One might argue that any rights are better than none at all ... But [there is] the danger of legitimation, whether as a result of judicial interpretation, or because of gaps in the content of human rights codes ... In the final analysis, entrenched rights are not the most effective mechanism for those who wish to pursue substantive equality.[43]

These warnings of the 'perils' and 'danger' of strategies incorporating rights rhetoric, or exhortations to take a path which avoids the 'the siren call' of law, are linked in some cases to a wider argument that legal discourse is phallocentric and rights discourse thoroughly imbued with male values.[44] However, it is not simply the link between law and rights which produces such warnings. Kiss, reviewing

---

[42] *Id.* at 2 where McColgan defines 'entrenched' or 'constitutional' rights both in terms of their level of abstraction, as compared to statutory rights, and that their application turns significantly upon judicial interpretation. She acknowledges that it can be argued that the rights in the United Kingdom's Human Rights Act 1998 should not be regarded as 'entrenched', because it does not provide the judiciary with a power to override the decisions of Parliament. However, she argues that the UK model will in practice share much in common with entrenched systems of rights. In addition McColgan makes the point that her conclusions relate only to the three areas which she considers, that is the spheres of reproduction and employment, together with the position of women as victims of violence. Moreover, her comments are confined to what she describes as the 'perils' of entrenched rights and do not have any bearing upon statutory rights, such as those in the Sex Discrimination Act 1975 which she believes have made 'very significant contributions to the position of women'.

[43] *Id.*, 304–310.

[44] Radical and post-modern theorists have argued that 'neutral' law and 'abstract rights' exclude discourses that run counter to the masculine world view, although often such views are accompanied by an appreciation of law as a site of struggle. Catherine MacKinnon writing from a radical feminist perspective argues that: 'The law like the hunt, warfare, and religion has been a male sphere. The values and qualities of these pursuits have defined both the male role and public life', C. MCKINNON, FEMINISM UNMODIFIED 26 (1987). However, she adds, in considering the future role of law in relation to women's rights, that although '[t]he law alone cannot change our condition... .[i]t can help'. Similarly, Tove Stang Dahl, who argues explicitly for women's law, indicates that law is 'an institution [that] to a large degree contributes to the maintenance of the traditional male hegemony in society' but '[a]t the same time law is fertile soil for the cultivation of rules which can provide a foundation for vast changes' [and] '[i]f the position of women is to be improved, this must also be done through law', see T.S. DAHL, WOMEN'S LAW, 14, (1987). *See further*, L. IRIGARAY, THINKING THE DIFFERENCE, 14 (1994) who writes from 'the reality of the difference between the sexes' and states that 'the order that lays down the law is male', but that law and justice have a sex only by default. She formulates a program of civil law for women consisting of a series of special rights, proceeding from an acceptance of natural and universal sexual difference. These include the right to human dignity, the right to human identity and the right to motherhood as a component of female identity, although it is questionable whether this programme should be taken at face value.

what she describes as 'feminism's uneasy relationship to rights', argues that different feminisms, which share little in common in theoretical terms, share doubts about rights.[45] Cultural feminists critique rights as 'abstract', 'impersonal' and contributing to a vision of society composed of isolated individuals, while 'feminist post-structuralists charge that rights language is bound up with socio-linguistic hierarchies of gender'.[46] Kiss also refers to those feminists for whom either an ethics of care is preferable to an ethics of rights or, more commonly, who view an ethics of rights as barren and alienating unless accompanied by an ethics of care.

Gilligan's analysis of women's moral development uncovered two mutually exclusive ethics: the ethics of rights or justice, which she associated with men, and the ethics of care, which she associated with woman's voice.[47] In setting up a dichotomy between these two ethics it appears that Gilligan did not seek to place them within a hierarchy, rather she was concerned, in the words of Kiss, that 'personal connections, and the care, attentiveness and responsibility that is the first virtue of central human relationships like those between parents ... and children, have not received the theoretical attention they deserve'.[48] Gilligan's writing has inspired a wealth of exploration into the moral concepts and values in an ethics of care, although rarely does this work abandon wholly the rhetoric of rights. Some endeavour to understand rights as relationships and discover the ways in which justice and care can, and do, knit together.[49]

At an international level different kinds of scepticism and uneasiness imbue feminist debates about rights. While some see in the Convention on the Elimination of All Forms of Discrimination Against Women (CEDAW), for instance, the framework for promoting women's rights as human rights, which with more active support could become a mechanism for producing fundamental changes in women's lives, others see the use of 'women's rights' as highly problematic. Cornell argues that the message from CEDAW is unequivocal, that the equivalent evaluation of women is a basic human right, although she recognises that the inclusion of women in rights talk is not without opposition.[50] At the heart of these attacks lies the critique of universalist conceptions of rights and 'the (impossible) object of international feminism'.[51] Ahmed raises this in the context of a discussion about the UN Conference for Women held in Beijing in 1995:

> We need to reflect upon how the setting up of an international feminist agenda could involve the authorising of the power of Western feminists to define the terms. The use of 'rights discourse' within the conference agenda hence marked

---

45 E. Kiss, *Alchemy or Fool's Gold? Assessing Feminist Doubts about Rights*, IN RECONSTRUCTING POLITICAL THEORY 1 (M. Lyndon Shanley & U. Narayan eds., 1997).

46 *Id.*, 2.

47 C. GILLIGAN, IN A DIFFERENT VOICE: PSYCHOLOGICAL THEORY AND WOMEN'S DEVELOPMENT (1982).

48 *Supra*, note 45, 9.

49 *See e.g.*, E.A. Bartlett, *Beyond Either/Or: Justice and Care in the Ethics of Albert Camus* in EXPLORATIONS IN FEMININIST ETHICS, (E. Browning Cole & S. Coultrap-McQuin, eds., 1992), 83–4. *See also* Kiss, *supra* note 45.

50 *See* D. CORNELL, AT THE HEART OF FREEDOM 151 (1998).

51 *See* S. AHMED, DIFFERENCES THAT MATTER 37 (1998).

out division and antagonism rather than a universal: who has the 'right' to authorise what constitutes 'women's rights' as 'human rights'? ... [T]he starting point must be the recognition of the incommensurability of feminist constructions for 'women's rights' ... [and] a more mutual engagement would require that one 'gives up' the power to authorise what are the 'proper objects' of feminist dialogue precisely by giving up one's power to authorise what constitutes women's rights.[52]

In part the ambiguous relationship that Western feminism has with the children's rights discourse lies perhaps in what Cornell has called, in a wide-ranging discussion about family law reform, 'an old argument ... that should be confronted'.[53] For 200 years she suggests 'numerous feminists have contended that naturalized motherhood is the enemy'. Shulamith Firestone made that argument in the 1970s. Other feminists like Simone de Beauvoir simply advocated the avoidance of motherhood in the name of freedom. Cultural feminists have responded strongly that this is just more of the same degradation of women and everything they stand for.[54] There is a strand of feminism which has sought to promote 'maternal thinking' and which draws some sustenance from Gilligan's identification of the ethics of care. In seeking to reclaim mothering as the crucial experience of women, it also views the family as having 'existential priority, and moral superiority over the public realm of politics'.[55] Maternal thinking, with its emphasis upon the mother-child dyad, seeks to create a new ethical polity, a 'moral imperative' for countering the prevailing liberal-individualist world view'.[56] This social feminism stands in stark contrast to earlier arguments in which the family and motherhood were regarded as reactionary and oppressive.

---

[52] *Id.*, 37–8.

[53] *Supra*, note 50, 130.

[54] *Id.*, 130. Cornell seems to be drawing quite heavily in these arguments upon Fineman's work in M. FINEMAN, THE NEUTERED MOTHER, THE SEXUAL FAMILY AND OTHER TWENTIETH-CENTURY TRAGEDIES (1995). Fineman identifies two Mother-negative discourses, which have been major contributors in the twentieth century to the constitution of negative images of the mother: (i) neo-Freudians; and (ii) contemporary liberal feminists. In both discourses Fineman suggests the Mother is 'marred by her burdens of obligation and intimacy in an era where personal liberation and individual autonomy are viewed as both mature and essential', at 72. Elsewhere in the preface to, MOTHERS IN LAW – FEMINIST THEORY AND THE LEGAL REGULATION OF MOTHERHOOD (M. Fineman & I. Karpin, eds., 1995) Fineman indicates that: 'to a large extent mothering has been perceived, and therefore theorized, as a "burden" or a problem for women' such that 'contemporary American feminist theory [typically casts] Mother as a problem-laden social and cultural institution, at ix. It is even suggested that many legal feminists regard the question of motherhood to be 'dangerous' and to engage with mothering in a positive way is 'to risk the dismissive label of "cultural feminist" and relegation "to the margins of feminist theory"', at x–xi. Like Cornell she cites in this context Simone de Beauvoir and a biography where the latter is quoted as saying that 'babies filled me with horror' and '[t]he sight of a mother with child sucking the life from her best ... all filled me with disgust'. De Beauvoir is reported as saying that she 'had no desire to be drained, to be a slave to such a creature' in D. BAIR, SIMONE DE BEAUVOIR: A BIOGRAPHY, 170 (1990).

[55] M.G. Dietz, *Citizenship with a Feminist Face: The Problem of Maternal Thinking*, in Landes, *supra* note 30, 47–48.

[56] *Id.*, Dietz names Sara Ruddick and Jean Bethke Elshtain as particularly important proponents of social feminism. *See e.g.*, S. Ruddick, *Maternal Thinking*, 6 FEMINIST STUDIES 34 (1980) and J. B. ELSHTAIN, PUBLIC MAN, PRIVATE WOMAN (1981).

Ramanazoglu assesses the Western feminist approach to motherhood as 'a major area of unresolved contradiction'[57] because women located in urban or industrialised societies are ideologically confined to the private, where children are also placed. Childrearing is, therefore, viewed as a private rather than a social issue. Women's responsibility for child care is inextricably connected with women's economic dependence upon men. Work outside the home does not resolve the situation but frequently does leave women 'torn and guilty at trying to operate conscientiously both at home and work'.[58] Motherhood combines 'an unparalleled experience of creativity' with for most women both 'limited control over their bodies' and 'a direct connection to economic and political subordination'.[59] However, this conception of motherhood should not feed essentialist notions of women's experiences. For instance, Ramanazoglu suggests that in rural areas the division between home and work may not be so clear-cut and motherhood may not be experienced as restriction. Her point is not that rural life is easy for women but she rejects any notion of motherhood as universally oppressive, rather each situation should be examined separately to establish specific mechanisms of domination.

There are other stories of motherhood. The Mothers of the Plaza de Mayo are perhaps the most well known of a number of groups for whom motherhood and politics are completely entwined. Hanan Mikhail Ashrawi describes her own experience in the context of activist Palestinian politics:

> A real mother goes beyond just the here and now of her children. She's not a captive of the daily routine but has a vision of what she wants for her children, and therefore she has to create that future and be part of it. She can't be passive. I'm extremely possessive about the future of my children: I have to be part of shaping it for them, not my moulding them as human beings, but by giving them their rights, doing whatever I can to ensure them a life of peace, dignity and freedom.[60]

At the general level there are also alternative feminist approaches to rights and uneasiness rarely amounts to outright rejection. Kiss names Martha Minow, Jennifer Nedelsky, Elizabeth Schneider and Patricia Williams[61] as being amongst those who

---

[57] C. RAMANAZOGLU, FEMINISM AND THE CONTRADICTIONS OF OPPRESSION 71 (1989). *See further*, our own discussion about motherhood in other articles, *infra*, note 61.

[58] *See* Ramanazoglu, *supra*, note 57, 72.

[59] *Id.*

[60] H.M. Ashrawi, quoted in M. GUZMAN BOUVARD, WOMEN RESHAPING HUMAN RIGHTS 117 (1996). Julia Wells has argued that the term 'maternal politics' is frequently used to describe those movements of women which are concerned both to protect their children and defend their role as mothers, J. Wells, *Maternal Politics in Organizing Black South African Women: The Historical Lessons* in SISTERHOOD, FEMINISMS & POWER: FROM AFRICA TO DIASPORA, (O. Nnaemeka, ed., 1998). Wells refers to a variety of well-documented movements including the mothers of the Plaza de Mayo and also the much earlier 'maternal movements' in South Africa and emphasises that this maternal politics should not be confused with feminism, particularly social feminism.

[61] The authors discuss Williams' and Minow's work with respect to children's rights in H. Lim & J. Roche *Feminism and Children's Rights* in FEMINIST PERSPECTIVES ON CHILD LAW, (J. Bridgeman & D. Monk, eds., 2000).

have 'constructed innovative arguments about rights'[62] from feminist perspectives. Schneider, for instance, challenges, through her discussion of 'rights in context', the notion that rights in legal discourse are always problematic and that using rights talk will lead to the sapping of strength in political, especially feminist, movements.

In a detailed analysis of women's self-defence work, and the case of *State v Wanrow*[63] in particular, Schneider tries to enter the intense 'dialogue on rights with a different voice'.[64] It is her view that this debate conceives of rights and politics in a static form which misses 'the dynamic interrelationship of rights and politics as well as the dual and contradictory potential of rights discourse to blunt and advance political development'.[65] For Schneider the different voice is one which expresses the idea that whether a rights claim inhibits or increases the potential of political struggle is dependent upon the time, place and environment in which the claim takes place. She argues that feminist critiques are partially accurate in their warning of the dangers of rights claims, including the contention that abstract rights carry with them a distance and objectivity which reflects a male outlook such that engagement with rights grants authority to the male norm. However, she also argues that such critiques are incomplete because they miss the political possibilities of rights.

Using her own personal construction of dialectics Schneider analyses the dual aspect of rights language: that it can both confine and enhance political struggles. It is a process by which she moves beyond a mere 'mechanical confrontation' between these two possibilities and places them inside the concept of rights itself and within political moments. Rights claims, she argues, grow out of political analysis and are then turned back into politics, therefore they may legitimise subordination or affirm the values of subordinated groups. If a political group becomes over-concerned with the legal forum and with winning legal cases to the exclusion of everything else this will inhibit the movement from moving beyond rights. However, rights discourse and lawmaking can also have a creative role independent of whether cases are won or lost. Deborah L. Rhode expresses the core to such innovative arguments thus: '...the most promising approach is both to acknowledge the indeterminate nature of rights rhetoric and to recognise that, in particular circumstances, such rhetoric can promote concrete objectives and social empowerment'.[66]

Feminist debates about women's problematic relations with law and the notion of liberal rights have an international dimension. As Olsen indicates 'feminist human rights lawyers have found ways to use the norms of international human rights' to enhance women's lives, but at the same time 'the human rights system not only tolerates but in significant ways perpetuates the international subordination of women'.[67] The uncritical linking of children's rights with women's rights, which we identified earlier as a problem, is deemed important in this pattern of oppression,[68]

---

[62] *Supra*, note 45, 8.

[63] 88 Wash. 2d 221, 559 P. 2d 548 (1a77).

[64] E. Schneider, *The Dialectic of Rights and Politics: Perspectives from the Women's Movement* (1986) 61 N.Y.U.L. REV. 589, 590 (1986).

[65] *Id.*

[66] F. Olsen, *Feminist Critical Theories*, 42 STAN. L. REV. 617, 635–36 (1990).

[67] *Supra*, note 21, 193.

[68] *See* Goonesekere *supra*, note 1, 23.

not least because of the way in which both childbearing and the family have often been seen as operating to the detriment of women in their struggles for equity and justice.[69]

As we have argued in detail elsewhere[70] the scepticism about legal rights has been less prevalent amongst feminists in their approaches to the CRC itself. Olsen in her analysis of the CRC indicated that despite certain misgivings she took a positive view of it and that 'overall it may stand to improve the status and lives of children'.[71] Price-Cohen is more enthusiastic, describing the Convention as 'a feminist landmark',[72] although she is concerned at the way 'women's issues' have dominated most feminist analysis and debate of the Convention. With reference to a dialogue between NGOs with interests in the CRC and those concerned with CEDAW, she identifies both an uneasiness 'about becoming associated with a children's treaty'[73] and an inability amongst supporters of the Women's Convention to view the CRC from the standpoint of the girl-child.

For Price-Cohen it is necessary to see the two Conventions in a sequential relationship and the CRC the 'precursor' to CEDAW, which protects the girl-child and is the 'starting point' for a 'broader definition of women's rights'.[74] Backstrom, on the other hand, suggests that the connection between women's rights and those of the girl-child is undeveloped, because there is a 'general notion that women's and children's rights are inherently incompatible and ... as such, human rights instruments must deal with them separately'.[75] She concludes with a plea for work to be undertaken to integrate provisions of the CRC, CEDAW and other human rights instruments, in order to more fully address the situation of the 'female child'.

Despite the relatively upbeat debate about the CRC from a number of feminist academics, scepticism about rights in general is also reflected in a seeming lack of interest in discussions concerning the rights of the child. This appearance of a relative lack of interest in child rights may be linked to the way in which the interests of academics in the United States dominate even Western feminism. Perhaps if the United States ratified the CRC this would stimulate Western feminist debate in this field. The dearth of writing on children's rights from a North American perspective may also be an effect of what Cornell describes as 'the appropriation of children's rights rhetoric in the father's movement'.[76]

---

[69] *Id.*, 27.
[70] *Supra*, note 61.
[71] *Supra*, note 21, 217.
[72] C. Price-Cohen, *The United Nations Convention on the Rights of the Child: A Feminist Landmark* 3 WM & MARY J. OF WOM. & L. 29 (1997).
[73] *Id.*, 71.
[74] *Id.*, 74.
[75] K. M. Backstrom, *The International Human Rights of the Child: Do They Protect the Female Child*, 30 GEO. WASH. J. OF INT'L L. & ECON., 541 (1996–7).
[76] *Supra*, note 50, 117. *See also*, M.A. FINEMAN, THE NEUTERED MOTHER, *supra*, note 54, where she refers to the mandatory paternity law of Wisconsin, written by Tom Loftus, which is designed to give the State the power to discover the paternity of a child where the name does not appear on the birth certificate. This legislation which is tied into the provision of AFDC to single mothers and the ideological construction of the 'bad mother' on welfare is supported through a rhetoric of individualised rights. Fineman quotes Tom Loftus arguing in support of this legislation

RE-IMAGINING CHILDREN'S RIGHTS AND DEPENDENCY

Cornell's own challenge confronts the argument that the maternal role is oppressive and consists of a plea for the legal protection of an imaginary domain in which 'the individual woman [will] be given the space to grapple with what motherhood means to her'.[77] The imaginary domain is a heuristic device, a prior moral space of 'dreams', a 'sanctuary' where it is possible to focus on what 'should be' and specifically in which women can be equivalently evaluated to discover what free persons should demand as a matter of justice.[78] In the course of a discussion about adoption she addresses indirectly, at a number of points, the issue of children's rights and in this she is relatively unusual amongst Western feminists. She argues for instance that 'Children should be recognized as persons with rights and responsibilities appropriate to their age ... [and] children should be recognized as persons and as members of the moral community from birth, with the scope of their rights increasing with maturity'.[79]

The prospect of privileging the mother-child dyad in the legal system, as suggested by social feminists because it is 'a metaphor for what loving care might be in a transformed society',[80] is repudiated by Cornell, on the basis that it exists only in fantasy and defeats the notion of a relationship between mother and child. She mounts a strong defence of children's rights, including autonomy rights. Rights on the other hand, or more specifically 'capability rights',[81] offer the child the possibi-

---

footnote continued

that: 'It [has] as its foundation that every child born in Wisconsin has a legal right to a father' (Tom Loftus, Remarks at the National Child Support Enforcement Association Annual Conference, New Orleans, LA (August 23, 1988), 427–28, in Fineman, 186.

[77] *Supra*, note 50, 130.

[78] *Id.*, 14. Cornell specifically rejects Irigaray's re-evaluation of civil law based upon sexed identity as a natural reality. Similarly, she disagrees with Fineman's conclusion that law reform should be based around the privileging in law of the mother-child dyad. Okin has argued for a theory of justice which would mean legislation and policies to end gender. Cornell on the other hand indicates that the defence of the imaginary domain, at the centre of her theory of justice, would mean legal reform to realise freedom. Cornell anticipates that her argument for a universal imaginary domain will raise the question of imperialism. She suggests that it is not necessarily a Western ideal but a social and moral right required by a human rights agenda addressing sex.

[79] *Id.*, 117.

[80] *Id.*, 118. Cornell is speaking directly in this context to such an argument raised by M. Fineman, *supra*, note 54.

[81] This term is derived from THE QUALITY OF LIFE, (M. Nussbaum & A. Sen eds., 1993). Nussbaum and Sen adopt a 'capabilities approach' to measuring quality of life. Rather than examining the actual distribution of social goods (e.g. health, education, housing, employment) in a society the capabilities approach requires an examination of what people in a given country are actually able to do and to be. The emphasis is thus on opportunity to realise one's potential and whether such opportunity is denied or restricted by poverty and oppressive and discriminatory ideas and practices. What needs to be focused on is the differing needs individuals have for resources to realise their potential. While their work does not address the human capabilities of children it seems to us that to include children in their category of persons is valuable. Sen argues that freedom is an essential component of quality of life. He argues that assessments of simply material life indices cannot explain the choices that people make in life. This is because people value the freedom to make decisions, to participate in the processes that lead to the making of decisions, and to changes in the choices that individuals make. This freedom, while important to the immediate life choices of individuals, is also important in another way. The exercise of freedom, with which comes a sense of responsibility, allows human

lity 'to become an individuated person … so that she can set out on life's way as her own person' and, presumably, develop the relationships made possible by the 'symbolic distance' of personhood.[82] In the context of adoption Cornell concludes with an unequivocal reference to the rights of the child and an understanding of the challenges inherent in such rights: 'We cannot lose our children because they are not ours to have. That children are not property is recognized by their inclusion in the moral community of persons from birth. Obviously, this idea of custodial responsibility and children's rights demands that we stretch our imaginations'.[83]

Cornell makes these comments within a brief analysis of dependency in intergenerational relationships. She rejects the use of the figure of the child as an analogy for all dependency and argues that: 'The dependency of an ill adult and that of a child should be differentiated in part to preserve the dignity of the adult, who needs to be recognised and respected for his maturity despite the fragility imposed by age.'[84] We have argued elsewhere[85] that dependency does not supply a justification for the denial of children's rights but draw an analogy between the dependency of children and other human dependencies. Young has suggested that the exclusion of women, children, the working class and the mentally disordered from the liberal order, which was explicit in early bourgeois liberalism, is now 'only barely hidden beneath the surface'.[86] It is dependency upon welfare bureaucracies which brings about the suspension of 'basic rights to privacy, respect and individual choice'.[87] She makes two further points with which we are in broad agreement. First, '[o]ne cannot imagine a society in which some people', including children, 'would not need to be dependent on others at least some of the time'.[88] Second, as Michael Freeman has also noted in the context of a discussion about

---

footnote continued
capabilities to form, develop and be enhanced. *See further*, M. Nussbaum, *Human Capabilities, Female Human Beings* in WOMEN, CULTURE AND DEVELOPMENT, 64 (M. Nussbaum and J. Glover eds., 1995), where the author notes that the term 'person' in the past has been withheld from certain groups of people, for example, women. Historically many others have been excluded from 'personhood' – most obviously slaves.

[82] *Supra*, note 50, 117–118. On the importance of 'distance' as an aspect of rights as relationships *see* P.J. WILLIAMS, THE ALCHEMY OF RACE AND RIGHTS (1991): *see also*, M. Minow *Interpreting Rights: An Essay for Robert Cover*, 96 YALE L. J. 1860 (1987).

[82] *Supra*, note 50, 127.

[84] *Id.*, 117. Cornell does not develop this point but presumably the argument being made here is the same as that offered by JAMES G. DWYER, RELIGIOUS SCHOOLS V CHILDREN'S RIGHTS (1998) who states: 'Of course, the situation of an adult who was competent but has become incompetent is distinguishable from that of a child who is not and has never been competent, since it is often possible in the first case, but not the latter, to refer to rational, informed preferences of the now incompetent person as a basis for decision (putting aside conceptual and practical difficulties in doing so)', at 75.

[85] *Supra*, note 61.

[86] I.M. YOUNG, JUSTICE AND THE POLITICS OF DIFFERENCE 54 (1990).

[87] *Id.*

[88] *Id., see also* Fineman, *supra*, note 54, where she makes a similar point when she states that 'dependency always has been and always will be with us', is 'natural and inevitable' and 'inherent in the status of infancy, illness, certain disabilities and, quite often, age'. Moreover, 'caretakers are dependent too – a derivative dependency flowing from their roles and the need for resources their caretaking generates', 162.

children's rights[89] '[a]n important contribution of feminist moral theory has been to question the deeply held assumption that moral agency and full citizenship require that a person be autonomous and independent'.[90] However, if we are to move from a simple recognition of dependency as a basic human condition and find the means for empowerment it is necessary also in Cornell's words to 'stretch our imaginations', specifically about the rights of the child.

It is perhaps pertinent at this stage to recall why that stretching of the imagination is so necessary and how important it is to disrupt those prevalent assumptions about moral agency and dependency. Waldron in a recent exploration of the discourses of rights and needs makes a powerful argument that claims posed in the language of rights imply that 'nothing short of full rights will do, for rights are rights of persons'.[91] He concedes that 'we talk of the rights of infants who cannot speak for themselves, and Amnesty International pursues rights on behalf of political prisoners everywhere' but argues that rights are 'claims made *naturally* (our emphasis) in the voice of the person who is the bearer' and that the 'rights-bearer is one who is self-aware and vigorously conscious of what one is entitled to demand from others and who is not embarrassed about advancing those demands'.[92] The implications of this 'natural' view of the association between capacity and rights is eloquently challenged by Federle who suggests that debates about children's rights always come down to questions of competency. She argues for a reconstruction of rights talk about children which 'repudiates the delimiting principle of capacity' and in a sense shares Cornell's desire to freely dream about what children's rights could become.

Freeman, aiming to think 'beyond' the CRC, argued for a 'cultural evolution' or a 'rethinking of the culture of childhood'. However, if we are to re-imagine children's rights, the notion of dependency deserves more exploration within a discussion which acknowledges, using Freeman's words, that 'childhood is not a decontextualised construct'.[93] We would argue that this also requires a recognition that age itself 'is as culturally constructed and personally negotiated as any other attribute'.[94] In an analysis of the chronological version of the life course Shurmer-Smith and Hannam, in their cultural geography, warn that familiarity with the bureaucratic management of age in Western societies, with such legal requirements as registration of birth within a specified number of days and its legal powers to do things following particular birthdays, whether applying for a driving licence at 17 or claiming an old age pension at 60 or 65, should not lead to the mistake of generalising such age structures into all spaces and all times. Drawing upon the work of Deleuze and Guattari and taking a critical approach to this

---

[89] M.D.A. Freeman, *The Sociology of Childhood and Children's Rights*, 6 INT'L J. OF CHILDREN'S RTS. 440 (1998).

[90] Young, *supra*, note 86, 55.

[91] J. Waldron, *Rights and Needs: The Myth of Disjunction*, in LEGAL RIGHTS, HISTORICAL AND PHILOSOPHICAL PERSPECTIVES 105 (A. Sarat & T. R. Kearns, eds., 1997).

[92] *Id.*, 103–4.

[93] *Supra*, note 3, 75.

[94] P. SHURMER-SMITH AND K. HANNAM, WORLDS OF DESIRE, REALMS OF POWER 150 (1994).

view of life and personhood, they argue further that: 'Age divisions serve few productive purposes in contemporary Western societies; they contribute to a system of unnecessarily rigid striations across the smoothness that life could be and, in doing so, they act as blocks to the communication of ideas and values; they set up false oppositions and they delay the young and debar the old from desire and power'.[95]

They advocate the acknowledgement of different perspectives, which disrupt, incidentally, the conventional familiarities of children in Western modernist social structures. Quoting a study of Hausa children in Kano, Nigeria, by Schildkrout, a number of questions are posed: 'What would happen to the adult world if there were no children?', '[I]n what ways are adults dependent upon children?', 'What is the significance of children in maintaining the relative status of men and women?' and 'Why do people want or need children?'.[96] Schildkrout noticed that the children in her study had a freedom of movement enabling them to trade in markets and information which was not available to adults, particularly urban women in purdah. According to Shurmer-Smith and Hannam, her analysis was that the children 'served as a conceptual category of asexual freedom in a society where gender-marking was absolute for adults'.[97] Schildkrout's conclusion was that 'it is important to take a perspective in which one views children and adults as complementary participants in the social system'.[98]

Similar kinds of disruptions to the rigid marking of age, and its categories of child, adult, youth, elderly and so on, may be encountered by Western, middle-class writers who confront working children. Shurmer-Smith and Hannam give the example of the nineteenth-century commentator, Mayhew, whose notion of childhood was shaken by the 'composure and self-reliance' of a young girl selling watercress who told him 'I ain't a child', 'I shan't be a woman till I'm 20', but that she was 'past eight'. His response was 'I did not know how to talk to her'.[99] In a way similar issues are raised in Neema's story at the beginning of Stainton-Rogers' *Stories of Childhood*.[100] Here the figure of Neema, a young women, is deployed to prise open our assumptions about age, sexuality and autonomy. Little is 'known' of Neema except that, aged somewhere between 14 and 20, she has had a baby. The question the Stainton-Rogers pose in relation to Neema is: 'How to do what's right in a situation of uncertainty?' In so doing they challenge our taken for granted assumptions about children and dispute the possibility of 'objective' knowledge about childhood.[101]

---

[95] *Id.*, 164.
[96] E. Schildkrout, *Roles of Children in Urban Kano*, in AGE AND SEX AS PRINCIPLES OF SOCIAL DIFFERENCE (J. La Fontaine ed., 1978), at 111, quoted in Shurmer-Smith and Hannam, *ibid*, 157.
[97] *Supra*, note 94, 157.
[98] *Id.*, 157.
[99] *Supra*, note 94, 151.
[100] R. STAINTON-ROGERS AND W. STAINTON-ROGERS, STORIES OF CHILDHOOD SHIFTING AGENDAS OF CHILD CONCERN (1992).
[101] *See also* N. Lee, *The Challenge of Childhood: distributions of childhood's ambiguity in adult institutions*, 6(4) *CHILDHOOD* 455 (1999).

CONCLUSION

While the law cannot unproblematically give rights to anyone, especially children, it can make symbolically important statements and can provide remedies for wrong-doing.[102] The participation rights of the CRC open up the possibility of an emergent social and legal subjectivity hitherto denied to children; indeed they may be seen as contradicting the very status of being a child. In other words the CRC 'welcomes' the child into the social community of 'persons', although it is not clear that the adult members of the community are prepared or welcoming. This links with the issue of the 'cultural evolution' referred to by Freeman and which we have termed the re-imagining of children and children's rights. There is now much emphasis on setting in place new mechanisms for permitting the child's voice to be heard and to require adults to think about the position of children. This is the context in which the enthusiasm for Children's Commissioners[103] and the production of 'child impact statements'[104] are to be understood. These are institutionally acceptable ways forward but if they are not to become implicated in the 'management' of the child's voice more needs to happen.[105] Such procedural and institutional initiatives might lead towards a radical rethink about the adult-child boundary, but we are concerned that by themselves they will not be sufficient. So how might feminist scholars assist in this project, and why? By way of conclusion we sketch out two areas where feminists are intellectually active and which have a direct bearing on the CRC 'rights agenda': the question of voice and the connected issue of the public-private boundary.

First, there is the question of the child's voice. What is required is a challenge to

---

[102] The submission of 'periodic reports' by States and the subsequent examination of the report by the Committee on the Rights of the Child is the only method of international supervision of the CRC.

[103] At the meeting to mark the anniversary of the adoption of the CRC, under the auspices of the Office of the High Commissioner for Human Rights and the Committee on the Rights of the Child 'Tenth Anniversary of the Convention on the Rights of the Child Commemorative Meeting: Achievements and Challenges', Palais des Nations, Geneva, 30 Sept–1 Oct. 1999 – Roundtable III was devoted to 'Building partnerships for the realization of rights', including discussion of children's participation and the creation of ombudspersons for children. The background papers of A. Vandekerckhove, *Quality Requirements for Ombudswork for Children,* and P. Newell, *Making Governments Work for Children,* record the extent to which special human rights institutions, especially ombudspeople and commissioners, have become an institutional feature at national level, notably in Europe; copies of both are on file with the authors. Newell comments that the challenge for the next decade is to get beyond the 'cosmetic phase'. The European Network of Ombudsmen for Children, which calls upon States to create societies which recognise children as rights-holders and not mere objects of concern and links together offices for children in 12 countries is further evidence of the extent to which ombudspersons for children have become established.

[104] Child impact statements are statements which indicate the impact of the proposed decision on the lives and well-being of children. Their existence can prompt decision-makers to see, perhaps for the first time, that what they are deliberating over might impact on the lives of children and this can lead to a commitment to consult and involve children in decisions which concern them, for example, about local transport policy. The introduction of child impact statements thus has the potential to open up new relations and public conversations between public authority, organisations concerned with the well-being of children and children themselves.

[105] Goonesekere, *supra,* note 1, concludes in her analysis of the work of the 'ombudsman' in the South Asian context that the office as presently constituted 'cannot be used to effectively monitor violations of child rights or create an environment for their realisation' at 361.

the 'politics of mutism' surrounding children.[106] Much feminist scholarship has been concerned to uncover the voices and experiences of women; this work is just beginning with children. Feminists have spoken for children and their rights in the context of male violence, especially sexual violence. However, as noted earlier, this is a limited engagement and much feminist scholarship, despite the place accorded to voice in women's movement politics, has treated children as an appendage to women's interests. Children's voices are now being heard in different ways. Children are more actively involved in the public sphere.[107] Much research is geared to finding out what children think, how they see the world, how they view issues ranging from transport policy to the politics of peace in Northern Ireland.[108] From this standpoint the language of children's rights is the beginning not the end.[109] It is about respecting and valuing the contribution children make to the world which children and adults share; a world hitherto defined and imagined primarily in adult terms. In order to be able to provide the kinds of support needed by children in different social locations adults will need to do things differently. Strategies will have to be thought through whereby children are empowered in a range of settings and this will require at the very outset a recognition of the relations of power at issue, alongside positive action to address these imbalances. Feminism's critique of patriarchy has been accompanied by an imagining of a better world for women. A similar project for children is permitted by the CRC and it is one in which, unlike women's liberation, both children and adults will have to participate.

Second, while one difference between women's continuing struggle for freedom and the struggle of children 'for their rights' is that women are able to speak for themselves, there is also a major similarity – the site of their oppression. For feminists traditional images of the public-private divide masked serious questions of injustice, abuse of power and inequality. Okin has argued that in her imagined 'genderless' society children, as well as men and women, would benefit:

It is undeniable that the family in which each of us grows up has a deeply formative influence on us ... This is one of the reasons why one cannot reasonably leave the family out of the 'basic structure of society,' to which the principles of justice are to apply ... the enhancement of justice that accom-

---

[106] J. O'Neill, *Supra* note 32.

[107] Respect for the voice of the child is an essential part of any project, that seeks to enhance the well-being of children. In Durham the community-wide 'Investing in Children' initiative is explicitly based on the participation of children. The initiative also acknowledges the impact and power of the problematising discourses that surround children today and it argues that 'Investing in Children' must challenge these negative images of children and publicise their positive achievements.

[108] B. Percy-Smith, *Marginalisation of children and youth in urban neighbourhoods: Implications for citizenship*, (paper presented to the Children and Social Exclusion Conference, Centre for the Social Study of Children, Hull University, March 1998, copy on file with the authors). *See also* A. Davis & L. Jones, *Children in the Urban Environment: an Issue for the New Public Health*, 22 HEALTH AND PLACE, 103 (1996). *See further*, M. DE WINTER, CHILDREN AS FELLOW CITIZENS PARTICIPATION AND COMMITMENT (1997), and DEMOCRATIC DIALOGUE, POLITICS: THE NEXT GENERATION (Report 6) (1997).

[109] A. McGillivray, *Why Children Do Have Equal Rights*, 2 INTERNATIONAL JOURNAL OF CHILDREN'S RIGHTS, 243, (1994).

panies the disappearance of gender will make the family a much better place for children to develop a sense of justice.[110]

Many children's rights scholars would be in whole-hearted agreement with this argument insofar as it raises the question of family justice as a central issue.[111] Interestingly, Goonesekere argues against the concern that the CRC will undermine the family. She suggests that the 'value base' of the CRC 'prevents children's rights from being used to launch an aggressive campaign for personal autonomy so as to undermine family privacy and the community and State's role in the care and development of children';[112] yet we are not sure this is what is at issue. It is not a question of undermining family privacy but of having a role to play and being involved in the development of one's own environment. Coles observes that 'we grow morally as a consequence of learning how to be with others, how to behave in this world, a learning prompted by taking to heart what we have seen and heard ... the child is an ever-attentive witness of grown-up morality or lack thereof'.[113] A better world for children will be a world in which questions of justice and respect are relevant within the home as well as the workplace.[114] Research carried out in the United Kingdom explored children's views about family life.[115] The research concluded that for many young people an 'ethic of respect' was central to family life and the right to participate, as opposed to the right to choose, in family life was taken for granted. For the young people concerned it was not a question of dependence versus independence but of an interdependence in which there was a reciprocity of concern, with respect for themselves and their voice.

There needs to be an acknowledgement that children in their own contexts can be competent and rational social actors. The participation and civil liberty rights of the CRC provide a practically and symbolically valuable resource for the contestations around children's rights at the local and international level; children's rights and feminist scholars have much to contribute to these debates which in the future will expose further abuses of power, advance the democratisation of family life and prompt new questions on what it is to be a child and an adult in modern society.

---

[110] MOLLER OKIN JUSTICE, GENDER AND THE FAMILY 184 (1989).

[111] *See e.g.*, CHILDREN'S RIGHTS OFFICE, BUILDING SMALL DEMOCRACIES. THE IMPLICATIONS OF THE UN CONVENTION ON THE RIGHTS OF THE CHILD FOR RESPECTING CHILDREN'S CIVIL RIGHTS WITHIN THE FAMILY (1995).

[112] *Supra*, note 3, 29.

[113] R. COLES, THE MORAL INTELLIGENCE OF CHILDREN, 5 (1997).

[114] This is not to claim that the distinction between the public and the private should be abolished. As Lister argues it needs to be re-articulated: *see*, R. LISTER, CITIZENSHIP FEMINIST PERSPECTIVES, (1997), although of course some feminists take a contrary position arguing for a defence of the private realm, *see e.g.*, J. Bethke Elsthain, *supra*, note 56.

[115] B. Neale, *Dialogues with Children: Participation and Choice in Family Decision Making*, CHILDHOOD (forthcoming, 2000).

Katherine O'Donovan

5. INTERPRETATIONS OF CHILDREN'S IDENTITY RIGHTS

INTRODUCTION

To talk of identity rights is to talk of all aspects of the human personality: birth, childhood, experiences and life in general. Nevertheless, identity rights have been included in the United Nations Convention on the Rights of the Child. The reasons for this can be found in specific historical episodes, explored below. And it may be that the protection of identity will found claims, as yet ignored.[1] Initially it is to national laws that the United Nations looks to implement this protection. It follows that interpretations of identity rights are made within jurisdictions with their own legal histories, institutions, concepts, legal methods and ways of doing law.

This chapter explores examples of historical episodes in which the identity rights of children appear to have been violated. The children involved did not know who their genetic parents were, or lost contact with them, or were denied the right to be brought up in their genetic families. Some were falsely registered at birth, or left without any means of knowing their origins. Today such denials to children are violations of the Convention on the Rights of the Child (CRC).[2] Nonetheless, within the CRC there are possibilities of varied interpretations. National jurisdictions fit the protections contained in the CRC into their own institutional structure. The chapter explores these variations. In so doing the argument is advanced that, however much States Parties to a CRC agree on a set of principles, the implementation of such principles takes places within national legal cultures. Plural interpretations inevitably result. Further, as the historical examples show, ideas of welfare or best interests of the child may be used to justify policies which do not protect identity rights.

HISTORIES OF IDENTITY LOSSES

The forcible removal of children from their families and communities is condemned today. So are falsifications of children's origins and identities, even where genetic parents are complicit in these lies. Yet during the past two centuries State policies

---

[1] *See generally,* Article 8 of the CRC which specifically protects a child's right to preserve his or her identity. The inclusion of this right was as a result of a proposal from the Argentinian delegate as a response to human rights abuses in that country at an earlier period. *See further,* J. Cerda, *The Draft Convention on the Rights of the Child,* 12 H. RTS Q. 115 (1990).

[2] The drafting of the Convention was completed in 1989. By December 31 1992 70 per cent of States had ratified. *See generally,* L. LEBLANC, THE CONVENTION ON THE RIGHTS OF THE CHILD, (1995).

Deirdre Fottrell (ed.), Revisiting Children's Rights, 73–85
© 2000 *Kluwer Law International. Printed in Great Britain.*

in many jurisdictions condoned, and in some places enforced, removals and lies. The stories told by the children and their families provide powerful arguments for the protection of identity as a human right.

Examinations of the histories of forcible removals in Australia, Canada and the United States[3] reveal some parallels with the export of children abroad from the British Isles. The personal histories involved are part of a wider history of colonisation and discrimination. The removed children in Australia and North America were from the indigenous peoples. Those who acted forcibly were the colonisers. Children 'exported' from Britain were to be part of the 'white' stock of the colonies,[4] whilst babies from Ireland were guaranteed to their American parents as of 'pure blood'.[5]

Identity in the discourses surrounding forcible removals is a source of shame if a child has the 'wrong' identity. Removals of indigenous children in Australia and North America were for purposes of absorption and assimilation into white society, whereas British and Irish children were prized for their racial origins. Looked at from a child's point of view, however, many elements of uprooting are shared. Loss of roots, anger about powerlessness, shock at official betrayal of the vulnerable, loss of contact with kin, a sense of being 'different' from others, damaged emotional lives – these elements are common. So is the sense of having been treated as inferior, for there were elements of the biographies of the Irish and British children, such as the circumstances of their births, or their parents' lack of power, which permitted their export.

Forcible Removals of Indigenous Children for 'Assimilation'

Experiences of children in Australia and North America subject to integration and assimilation through a legal form of kidnap are similar. Laws and policies authorised removals from home and placement in orphanages, boarding schools and foster homes. Australia will be used as the example here because the inquiry by the Australian Human Rights Commission documents these legal kidnaps so graphically.[6]

The Inquiry Report estimates that between one in three and one in ten indigenous children were forcibly removed from their families in the years 1910–70.[7] The policies started from the mid-nineteenth century and clearly legalise racial discrimination. From the 1850s in the eastern Australian states there was a policy of 'absorption' of children classified as 'half-caste', whereas the indigenous population classified as 'full-blood' were segregated for their 'protection'.[8] From 1937 an

---

[3] AUSTRALIAN HUMAN RIGHTS COMMISSION, BRINGING THEM HOME, 1997. *See also* ROYAL COMMISSION ON ABORIGINAL PEOPLES, REPORT 1996; *see further*, *Indian Child Welfare Program, Hearings of the US Senate*, 93rd Congress (1994).

[4] M. HUMPHRIES, EMPTY CRADLES (1994).

[5] M. MILOTTE, BANISHED BABIES (1997).

[6] *See further*, ROYAL COMMISSION ON ABORIGINAL PEOPLES, *supra*, note 3. The report is almost 700 pages long and evidence was taken from 535 indigenous people.

[7] *Id.*, at 37.

[8] *Id.*, at 30–35.

'assimilation' policy towards indigenous people was adopted nationally and legislation followed. From 1967 the language of 'integration' replaced that of assimilation.[9]

Although many aspects of these laws might be discussed, those aspects contrary to the subsequent Convention on the Rights of the Child will be highlighted. Articles 7 and 8 of the Convention protect identity and will be discussed in more detail below. The right, as far as possible, to know and be cared for by one's parents,[10] and the right to preserve one's identity, name and family relations[11] now protect children against such forcible removals. Understanding of why these rights are important can be gained from listening to the stories of those who underwent forced separations – the 'stolen generations' of Australia.

> When they went to mix in white society they found they were not accepted [because] they were Aboriginal. When they went and mixed with Aborigines, they found they couldn't identify with them either ... They were simply a lost generation of children. I know. I was one of them.[12]

The children suffered on various levels ranging from physical and sexual abuse in institutions and foster homes, through loss of roots, identity and language, to emotional and attachment disorders. One reason why the colonial policy of 'absorption' did not work in terms of identity change was that it did not appreciate how individuals identify themselves. 'The reality that indigenous people did not identify as Europeans, however much European 'blood' they had, was not taken into account.'[13] Many witnesses reported denigration of Aboriginality and their own consequent ignorance of their roots. So on the one hand 'it was drummed into our heads that we were white',[14] but on the other, it was precisely because they were classified as non-white that the children found themselves subjected to forced separations. And on an unspoken level, it was clear to them that their identities were stigmatised.

Genealogical bewilderment followed: 'that really buggered up my identity',[15] 'no identity with the land, no identity with a certain people.'[16] Effects of identity confusion have been documented as long term. Low self-esteem, loss of trust in others, inability to form intimate relationships, depression, anxiety, lack of parenting skills, have all been noted. Security about identity is the basis for self-confidence. And loss

---

[9] *Id.*

[10] Article 7(1) of the CRC provides:
The child shall be registered immediately after birth and shall have the right from birth to a name, the right to acquire a nationality and, as far as possible, the right to know and be cared for by his or her parents.

[11] Article 8 (1) provides:
States Parties undertake to respect the right of the child to preserve his or her identity, including nationality, name and family relations as recognised by law without unlawful interference.

[12] *Supra*, note 3, at 132.

[13] *Id.*, page 29.

[14] *Id.*, page 166.

[15] *Id.*, page 203.

[16] *Id.*

of identity with the land means material loss in that the stolen generations are deprived of claims to native title.[17]

The Australian Government submitted to the inquiry that, in judging laws, policies and practices of the past, regard must be paid to the standards and practices prevailing at the time. The Commission looked to common law, which had arrived with the colonists, and for the post-1948 period, to international legal obligations under human rights conventions.[18] The judgement is that, by colonial legal standards, there was a denial to indigenous people of liberty and equal treatment. Common law parental and guardianship rights were also breached. Under international law the Commission decided that 'absorption' and 'assimilation' policies after 1951 were in breach of article 11 of the Convention on the Prevention and Punishment of Genocide.[19]

The laws and policies which prevailed in Australia and North America were motivated not only by racism but also by beliefs about 'human nature' and how social engineering can be deployed. Behind these beliefs lay assumptions of cultural and racial hierarchies and superiorities.

EXPORTS OF CHILDREN

Emigration policies directed towards children from the British Isles exported to the colonies and to the United States can be distinguished from forcible removal policies for purposes of assimilation. The exported children, in general, were already separated from their parents, not necessarily forcibly. However the effects on the children were similar, despite the valuing of the European children for their 'white blood.' Beneath the racial distinctions lay a stigma in terms of birth and parenthood. The stories of abuse, unhappiness and identity-confusion share a common sense of loss.

Estimates of the exports of children from Britain to the colonies vary from 100,000 to 150,000.[20] Juvenile vagrancy provided the initial motive in the early part of the nineteenth century when 440 children were sent to South Africa by a voluntary society.[21] Public authorities were responsible for the export of 7,000 children to Canada between 1883–1908.[22] However, the great majority of children were emigrated by authorised voluntary bodies such as Barnardo's.[23] The official policy of emigration of lone children can be seen in s.17(2) of the Children Act 1948, which allowed local authorities to emigrate children, but required the consent of the Secretary of State. The Empire Settlement Acts 1922 and 1937 also reflected this

---

[17] *Kanak* Dominic Joseph [1995] NNTTA 12 (23 March 1995) 15 Aust. L. Rep. 329, *supra* note 3, at 205.
[18] *Supra*, note 3, 249–274.
[19] Article 11 of the Genocide Convention (1948) provides that the forcible transfer of children of a group 'with intent to destroy, in whole or in part, a national, ethnic, racial or religious group' is genocide.
[20] P. BEAN AND J. MELVILLE, LOST CHILDREN OF THE EMPIRE, 1 (1989).
[21] *Id.*
[22] HUMPHRIES, *supra*, note 4, 155.
[23] J. Eekelaar, *'The Chief Glory, The Export of Children from the United Kingdom'* in *FAMILIES ACROSS FRONTIERS*, (N. Lowe and G. Douglas, eds., 1996) at 539.

policy. However, as noted by Eekelaar, the sending abroad of children by local authorities was subject to legal control, whereas 'there were no restraints to curb the missionary zest of the philanthropic emigration societies'.[24]

Exports from Britain continued until 1967. From the perspectives of the child migrants their experiences were not dissimilar to those of the indigenous children of Australia: lack of consent by older children or their parents, loss of knowledge of geneology, parents, and roots, loss of contact with families, mistreatment and abuse in the new situation and uprooted emotional lives.

The export of babies from Ireland for adoption in North America might seem initially to be a different story. However there are common elements. Official figures are that about 2,100 infants were sent to the United States between 1949–73.[25] There is no way of establishing how many were sent unofficially, although individual stories confirm this practice. The life stories of the exported Irish babies bear witness to falsification of names, birth dates and consent signatures. Many mothers have recounted their lack of consent and some were told that their infants were dead. Irish adoption law does not contain a provision whereby adoptees can have access to their original birth certificates. In any case the adoption proceedings were carried out in the host country and American law is based on anonymity.[26]

CONSTRUCTIONS AND IDENTITIES

Examination of the histories briefly summarised above reveals that the actions undertaken by officials or voluntary agencies were based on constructions of indigenous peoples as 'savage' and of their children as 'neglected'. In the British Isles the children were constructed as in need of a 'better life', with an implied assumption that their birth parents were inadequate. At the time these policies were believed to be right and the actions taken were thus justified.

The examples given are of self-defined superiority, with the 'civilised' drawing together as race or nation, and defining others as 'savage'. Identity becomes not something to be protected but a source of stigma. Cure is via 'assimilation'. With the advent of the protection of identity as a human right, it is to be hoped that notions of hierarchies and stigmatisation of identities will disappear.

IDENTITY RIGHTS IN THE CONVENTION ON THE RIGHTS OF THE CHILD

Articles 7 and 8 of the CRC are designated the identity provisions. Article 7 provides for registration after birth, and rights to name, nationality, and 'as far as possible, the right to know and be cared for by his or her parents'.[27] Article 8 protects 'the right of the child to preserve his or her identity ... including family

---

[24] *Id.*, at 546.
[25] Milotte, *supra*, note 5.
[26] K. WEGAR, ADOPTION, IDENTITY AND KINSHIP: THE DEBATE OVER SEALED BIRTH RECORDS (1997).
[27] *See* text of Article 7 *supra*, note 10.

relations'.[28] Commentators on Article 7 take the view that it gives rights to know the identities of genetic parents. The United Kingdom made a declaration limiting the reference to 'parent' to those persons who, by national law, are treated as parents.[29] This means that 'parent' does not necessarily mean 'genetic parent' and that some children only have one parent. The Czech Republic, Luxembourg and Poland have also made declarations and reservations.[30] However, as Hodgkin and Newell observe, a reasonable assumption is that the child's right to know her or his parents includes genetic parents, birth parents, and psychological parents.[31]

English law takes an ambivalent attitude to children's rights to know their parents. On one hand adopted children have rights of access to their original birth certificates, and an adoption contact register has been established by law.[32] Official help is available to adopted children in attempting to establish the identities of their birth (but not necessarily genetic) parents. On the other hand, children conceived through donated gametes do not have rights to know the identities of their genetic parents, because it is believed that donors need protection.[33] In addition, there will always be a small number of children, abandoned at birth, who are unable to know their parents, and a further group whose fathers are unknown to them, if not to their mothers.

Issues about children who are abandoned or who are unable to know the identities of their genetic parents for other reasons provide an illustration of differing interpretations of Article 7. Clearly, contact with genetic parents is not possible if one does not know who they are. Children born as a result of donated gametes offer one illustration. Abandoned children provide the major illustration explored below.

CHILDREN BORN OF DONATED GAMETES

The Implementation Handbook for the Convention on the Rights of the Child notes that the United Kingdom Government entered a declaration and reservation to the Convention with regard to assisted conception.[34] This is the case also for the Czech Republic. The Committee on the Rights of the Child, charged with enforcement of the CRC, has noted that France, Norway and Denmark, amongst others, maintain secrecy of identity of sperm donors.[35] Practice, therefore, amongst State Parties to the Convention varies. Behind this lie a number of differing aspects ranging from legal rules to medical beliefs and practices.

Reasons given for the maintenance of secrecy in egg and sperm donation focus on two main arguments: best interests of the child and donor anxiety.[36] A stand-off

---

[28] *See* text of Article 8 *supra*, note 11.
[29] *See further*, UN Doc. CRC/C/2/Rev. 2, ¶ 33.
[30] *See further* UN Doc. CRC/C/2/Rev. 2, ¶ 16, 24 and 29.
[31] *See* R. HODGKIN AND P. NEWELL, IMPLEMENTATION HANDBOOK FOR THE CONVENTION ON THE RIGHTS OF THE CHILD 105 (1998).
[32] *See* Adoption Act 1976, § 51. *See also* Children Act 1989, Sch. 10, ¶ 21 inserting § 51A into the Adoption Act 1976.
[33] *See* Human Fertilization and Embryology Act, 1990, § 28(6).
[34] *Supra*, note 31.
[35] *Supra*, note 31, 105–106. Norway IRCO, Add. 23, § 10; Denmark IRCO, Add.33, ¶ 11.
[36] *Supra*, note 31, 106.

between deontological and utilitarian arguments is notable. Rights to know are said to conflict with best interests rights. Utilitarian points about the deterrence of future donors, the happiness of the future child, and the happiness of childless couples are made. In France, importance is attached to medical confidentiality which is justified by both deontological and utilitarian arguments.[37]

The Committee on the Rights of the Child notes the possible contradiction between 'the right of the child to know his or her origins' and the policies of State Parties 'in relation to artificial insemination, namely in keeping the identity of sperm donors secret'.[38] Not all jurisdictions maintain secrecy. Sweden provides a counter example whereby, subject to the child's best interests, she or he may 'obtain particulars concerning the donor, providing the child is sufficiently mature'.[39]

ABANDONED CHILDREN

'A newspaper delivery boy found a new-born girl abandoned in bushes. Police, began an immediate search for the baby's mother.'[40] The policy in Britain is to focus on the mother 'who may need medical attention ... Our aim is to reunite her with her child.'[41] In police statements and publicity about abandoned infants identity rights are not mentioned. Although silent assumptions may exist about identity as part of welfare, it is the mother's well-being which is made central. Whether or not a criminal charge is brought, for abandonment is a crime,[42] depends on the circumstances. Abandoning an older child is regarded very differently from abandoning an infant.[43]

Legal abandonment of infants at birth is possible in France, Luxembourg, Spain and Italy. Under the law of these jurisdictions a woman can enter a hospital or maternity clinic and give birth anonymously.[44] This means that, although the infant is registered after birth, the entry for 'mother' is 'X'. Through registration Article 7 of the CRC is observed in part, but the issue of knowing and being cared for by parents arises.

Luxembourg entered a declaration and reservation to the Convention in relation to Article 7, as follows:

> The government of Luxembourg believes that Article 7 of the Convention presents no obstacle to the legal process in respect of anonymous births, which is deemed to be in the interest of the child, as provided under Article 3 of the Convention.[45]

---

[37] *See* Code Civil, Article 341–1.
[38] Norway, IRCO, Add. 23, ¶ 10. *Supra*, note 31, 107.
[39] Sweden IR, ¶ 61, *Supra* note 31, 107.
[40] THE GUARDIAN, Dec. 27 1996, at.6.
[41] THE GUARDIAN, Jan. 2 1998, at.5.
[42] *See* Offences Against the Person Act 1861, § 27.
[43] A mother who left a three-year-old child in a wood was sentenced to five years imprisonment. THE GUARDIAN, May 22 1999, at 5.
[44] C. Neirinck, *L'acouchement sous X: le fait et le droit*, 329 LA SEMAINE JURIDIQUE, 143 (1993).
[45] *See* UN Doc. CRC/C/2/Rev. 2, ¶ 24.

The Committee on the Rights of the Child expressed doubts about French law:

> Regarding the right of the child to know his or her origins, including in cases of a mother requesting that her identity remain secret during the birth and declaration of the birth, adoption and medically assisted procreation, the Committee is concerned that the legislative measures being taken by the State Party might not fully reflect the provisions of the Convention, particularly its general principals.[46]

The short answer given to these criticisms by French commentators is that the words 'as far as possible' qualify the right to know and be cared for by one's parents contained in Article 7.[47] However, closer examination supports the thesis advanced at the beginning of this chapter, namely that interpretations of international conventions take place within national legal cultures, institutional ways of doing law, and understandings of concepts such as 'family' and 'best interests of the child'.

A serious debate took place in France in 1993 on amendments to French family law in accordance with the CRC.[48] Many changes resulted, including the amelioration of the status of a child born outside marriage. However, the issue of the right of a woman to give birth anonymously was not resolved. As will be discussed in detail, not only was this right strengthened, but it remains hotly disputed. In France this right is known as 'accouchement sous X'.

In the course of the debate on Article 7 of the Child Convention in the Assemblée Nationale members were divided into two opposing groups. There were those who wished to implement Article 7 fully, by repealing the right to give birth anonymously, contained at that time in the Family Code but not in the Civil Code. Those opposed pointed to the words 'as far as possible' qualifying the child's rights to know and be cared for by her or his parents. The outcome was the strengthening of the right to give birth anonymously through the insertion of a new article into the Civil Code. Under Article 341 not only may a woman demand anonymity and confidentiality on delivery, but also no filiation links can be established by the child, should the woman's identity be discovered.

Official figures estimate the numbers of children born annually to anonymous women as a minimum of 600;[49] scholars of family law put the figure nearer 1,000.[50] This can be compared to 65 infants abandoned in England and Wales of whom 52 were traced to their mothers.[51] The interest of comparison between French and English law lies in the adherence of both to the CRC, but with differing interpretation of the best interests provision in Article 3 and the identity provisions of

---

[46] France IRCO, Add. 20, ¶ 14.
[47] F. Dreifuss-Netter, L'accouchement sous X, *Liber amicorum à la memoire de Daniele Huet-Weiler* (Paris: PUS/LGDJ, 1994).
[48] J. Rubellin-Devichi, *Le principe de l'intérêt de l'enfant dans la loi française*, LE SEMAINE JURIDIQUE, I, 3739 (1999).
[49] F. DEKEUWER-DEFOSSEZ, RENOVER LE DROIT DE LA FAMILLE, 43–44 (1999).
[50] Information received by the author from Professor J. Rubellin-Devichi, November 1999.
[51] *See* Hall, THE GUARDIAN, Jan. 2 1998 at 5.

Articles 7 and 8. The explanations for these differences lie in legal history, legal cultures and ways of seeing families.

French law permits the woman who gives birth to remain anonymous and protects her right to do so. There is a distinction between maternity and motherhood. This is understood socially and the law reflects this. Furthermore, entry into a family is not by birth alone, but by the choice of the parents. In popular understanding in England giving birth makes a woman 'the real mother'. Law reflects this, and the identity of the mother must be recorded on the birth certificate in accordance with law. The infant is part of the mother's family, if only for a period between birth and legal adoption. Maternity and motherhood are conflates.

LEGAL HISTORIES, LEGAL CULTURES

History and tradition play a part in the interpretation and integration of the CRC in a domestic legal system. To acquire some understanding of why English and French law differ in their approaches to the abandonment of infants, we must look to the past. In France, and in the other jurisdictions which permit anonymous birthing, an institutional method of abandonment has existed since the Middle Ages.

In France the *tour* consisted of a hole in a wall (usually of a convent) with a wheel and a door. In Italy this was called the *ruota*. From the outside of the wall the door could be opened, and the infant placed on the wheel, which was then turned inward. From the interior the child could be collected without the identity of the user being seen. A bell could be rung to alert those inside the wall of the infant's arrival. Notes were sometimes attached to the child and could be used later for identification. Examples of the *tour* and of the notes can be seen at the Museum of Public Assistance in Paris. The *tour* was abolished in 1904.[52] However, the new millennium has seen its importation into Germany and the United States.

Accouchement sous X was first introduced in France in 1793. At the National Convention of the French Revolution a law was passed 'where the pregnant girl might go in secret to give birth'.[53] Although this law was not observed once Robespierre's dominance was established, nevertheless the idea was subsequently revived during the 1870s. Popular sentiment favoured protection of young women and infants, particularly where the latters' fates were likely to be infanticide or exposure.[54] A hospital circular issued in December 1899 reminds women about to give birth that they may choose to place their identity documents in a sealed envelope to be returned on leaving hospital. Subsequently refuges for secret delivery were established. These were legalised between 1914 and 1924.[55]

The Vichy Government of occupied France in the 1940s followed a pro-natalist policy. A law of 2 September 1941 was adopted for the protection of birth. This

---

[52] Dreifuss-Netter, *supra*, note 47, 100.
[53] C. Bonnet, *La loi de l'accouchement secret*, LES DOSSIERS DE L'OBSTETRIQUE, Mai, (1995) at 20.
[54] Rubellin-Devichi, *Droits de la mère et droits de l'enfant: reflexions sur les formes de l'abandon* REVUE TRIMES FRIELLE DE DROIT CIVIL, 90 (1990).
[55] Bonnet, *supra*, note 53.

permitted anonymous birthing in public hospitals without cost to the woman involved, for two months, if necessary. This law was repealed in 1953 but the protection of secret maternity continued. Sympathy for maternity in distress, allied to the idea of choice between maternity and motherhood, has a long history in France.

Similar provisions to those passed by the Vichy Government were enacted in 1953 as part of the Family Code. In addition, Article 47 of the Social Services Code, passed on 6 January 1986 and still in force, provides that the expenses of accommodation and delivery of women who have requested anonymity shall be borne by the social services of the local *département*. This presupposes the possibility of anonymity without stating it directly as a right. Further, the general principle of medical confidentiality is interpreted as applying to maternity cases who ask for secrecy.

Until the debate in the French Parliament in 1993 on legal reforms to implement the CRC, the Family Code and the Social Services Code provisions created the legal right to give birth anonymously. Paradoxically, the parliamentary debate led to the strengthening of the woman's rights. The protection of anonymous birthing in Article 341 of the Civil Code, and the absolute bar to the establishment of a filiation link with the mother by the child, gives unprecedented prominence to the woman's rights. This debate is not over in France, despite the entry of the X right into the Civil Code. The next section will consider this. The final section will discuss the importation of the *tour* into Germany and certain states of the United States.

Debates on Accouchement Sous X

Since the strengthening of the right to give birth anonymously a debate has ensued in France. Supporters of the women's right call on a major empirical study containing interviews with 'X' women.[56] Catherine Bonnet, the author, argues that the choice to give birth anonymously protects children from abuse and infanticide, and in some communities may also preserve the life of the woman. Further, she argues, anonymity is a fundamental freedom, and can also be justified as a privacy right, and as an autonomous choice to renounce the motherhood of a particular child. Given that legal parentage is treated as a juridical concept in France, rather than as a 'natural' fact as in England, such an argument is possible.

Pressure groups exist in France representing both the 'X' children and the 'X' women. Their rights are constructed as in conflict. The children, now adults, argue that the current law does not protect their identity in accordance with Articles 7 and 8 of the CRC. They are not necessarily seeking a filiation tie but genetic and social identity information. Since a filiation tie automatically creates inheritance rights, a renunciation might ease the conflicts.[57] However, the 'X' woman is likely to have been young at the time of maternity, to have rejected motherhood of the 'X' child, and not to wish to establish contact now. Complicating the picture are the adoption pressure groups which favour retention of the law of 1993 and the abortion law which restricts termination after twelve weeks of pregnancy.[58]

---

[56] C. BONNET, GESTE D'AMOUR (1991).

[57] Interview by the author with Nadine Lefourcheur, Paris, November 1998.

[58] Law of 17 January 1975 limiting elective abortion to the first twelve weeks of pregnancy.

The right of accouchement sous X has been put in question by two recent reports. The sociologist Irene Thery has prepared a report entitled *Couple Filiation and Parenthood Today* for the Ministries of Justice and Employment.[59] Thery sees the entry of the right to give birth as 'X' into the Civil Code as symbolically reinforcing the absolute character of the right of secret maternity. She argues that this negates the objective fact of parturition, and clashes with the rights of children to know their origins. The focus of this argument is on the pain caused to X children. 'Perhaps it is worse to know that the effacement of one's origins was organised by society, than to be faced with the silence of the unknown, as with lost children.'[60] Admitting that the debate is passionate and controversial Thery advocates the repeal of Article 341-1 of the Civil Code. The effect would be to abolish accouchement sous X.

Thery's report has added to the controversy, but a compromise proposal has emerged. Françoise Dekeuwer-Defossez has chaired a committee of experts appointed by the Justice Ministry on the renewal of family law. Her report proposes that the right of accouchement sous X be retained, but that the bar on the establishment of filiation links be abolished.[61] In other words, should the child discover the identity of 'X', a legal tie, effectively forcing recognition and legal motherhood on the woman, could be established. French filiation law is traditionally based on a voluntary parental acceptance, so this would be a significant change.[62] However, it does not meet the desire of some 'X' children to lift the veil of secrecy over their births.

Entry into understanding of another legal culture and legal system requires caution. This writer's tentative conclusion about the French response to the CRC is that genuine efforts have been made to amend family law. The debate in the French parliament was motivated by a desire to incorporate the principles of the Convention into domestic law. If these efforts seem to the outsider, or to the Committee on the Rights of the Child, to have been incomplete, the explanation lies in the conception of the family at the heart of the Civil Code. Although the notion of admission to a family on birth as dependent on the will of the patriarch has given way gradually to a recognition of the rights of both parents, permission to enter a family still holds sway.[63]

Filiation is central not only to family law but also to the law of property, because it gives rise to automatic rights, including those of inheritance. The gradual change of French family law will continue. The rights of children to family membership, already much augmented since 1993, will grow. What is curious, however, is that the anonymous abandonment of infants is now to be permitted in jurisdictions without the long traditions existing in France, and to a degree in Luxembourg, Italy and Spain. The final section considers these developments.

---

[59] I. THERY, COUPLE FILIATION ET PARENTE AUJOURD'HUI (1998).
[60] *Id.*, 179. (Author's translation).
[61] MINISTRY OF JUSTICE, F. DEKEUWER-DEFOSSEZ, RENOVER LE DROIT DE LA FAMILLE (1999).
[62] *Id.*, at 36.
[63] *Id.*, at 35–40.

'Letter Box Babies'

The German city of Hamburg has recently instituted a system whereby infants can be deposited anonymously in a letter box.[64] The states of California, Texas, Florida, Pennsylvania and Minnesota in the United States are considering legislation to introduce similar systems.[65] It seems that the French *tour* of the Middle Ages is to be revived for a new age. In discussions of these proposals the languages of the 'disposable baby' or 'dump and run' have been used. A distinction must be drawn between the officially organised secret maternity of France, legal under the law, and the new *tour*. The 'X' child in France is registered at birth but without identified parentage. The *tour* child of today may have a birth certificate recording the mother's identity, but the connection between child and certificate will not be made if the parents are guaranteed the freedom to leave the child with no questions asked.

The United States is not a party to the Child Convention, but Germany is. The concern amongst American law makers is that 108 infants were abandoned in public places in 1998, up from 65 in 1991.[66] The Hamburg facility is justified by similar concerns and the main justification that is given is the saving of the life of the child. Quite why full anonymity is to be guaranteed to the parents is not clear. It should be possible to keep the parents' identities secret whilst preserving the child's birth certificate.

Conclusion

This chapter sets out to examine the possibilities of varied interpretations of the CRC. The fitting of the Convention into existing legal cultures and structures inevitably produces plural interpretations. The right of a woman to give birth in France has been shown to be the result of legal history and a particular way of seeing the family which permeates many aspects of law. This can be distinguished from a new method of dealing with abandoned babies, such as the import of the *tour* into Germany. In the latter example the protection of identity rights of the child must surely be carefully discussed.

Investigating institutions and practices in a legal system to which one comes as an outsider must be undertaken with caution. Intervening as an interpreter in another legal culture requires sensitivity to structures, meanings, ways of doing law, and to the means one uses in reporting one's findings. As Pierre Legrand points out

> Scholars who engage in comparative work about law face an exigent challenge. First, having been prepared for another legal culture, they need to amplify their appreciation for different structures of meaning, to the point where they

---

[64] SUNDAY TIMES, Mar. 3 2000, at 6.
[65] SAN JOSE MERCURY NEWS, Jan. 16 2000.
[66] *Id.*, quoting the US Department of Health and Human Services.

will ultimately be in a position to report on discrepant cognitive processes in an apperceptive mode. Secondly, comparatists, acting as cultural intermediaries, must determine how to convey their acquired understanding of another legal culture within the inconsonant parameters of their own.[67]

Although the possibilities of comparative work may be doubted, the shared adherence to a particular international convention, particularly where domestic law is put in question, raises issues of comparison. Convergence of laws on children's rights may be gradual but eventual.

---

[67] P. Legrand, *Comparative Legal Studies and Commitment to Theory*, 38 MOD. L. REV. 262 (1993).

Ursula Kilkelly

6. THE IMPACT OF THE CONVENTION ON THE CASE-LAW OF THE EUROPEAN COURT OF HUMAN RIGHTS

INTRODUCTION

In its short 10-year history, the UN Convention on the Rights of the Child (CRC)[1] has achieved more than enough to warrant its celebration. One of its distinguished features is the comprehensive nature of its provisions, which set out the rights to be secured to children and young people in many aspects of their lives and in a variety of circumstances. The CRC's provisions are both numerous and detailed and they combine, historically, civil and political rights, such as the right to liberty and the right to a fair trial,[2] and social, economic and cultural rights, such as the right to education, the right to an adequate standard of living and health care, and the right to play.[3] Many CRC provisions reflect those of other, more general human rights instruments,[4] but there are also new provisions which recognise, *inter alia,* the right to identity[5] and the rights of vulnerable children to special protection.[6] Further-more, the Convention breaks fresh ground by providing for child-specific versions of existing rights, like the freedom of expression,[7] and it establishes new standards by codifying for the first time the right of the child to be heard, both in general and more specifically, in all proceedings which affect her.[8] This latter provision, toge-ther with the principles of non-discrimination and best interests,[9] form the guiding principles of the CRC, which, symbolically and practically, reflect the ethos of respect and autonomy, which the Convention aims to create for the child.

---

[1] *See* United Nations Convention on the Rights of the Child, UN Doc A/44/25 (1989), reprinted in 28 I.L.M. 1457 (1989).

[2] *See further* Articles 37 and 40, *ibid.*

[3] *See further* the Convention on the Rights of the Child, *supra* note 1, the rights are contained in Arti-cles 28 and 29, 24 and 27 and 30, respectively.

[4] *See e.g.,* Article 40 of the Convention on the Rights of the Child, *supra,* note 1 and its similarity to Article 14 of the International Covenant on Civil and Political Rights, 999 UNTS 171, opened for signature Dec. 16 1966 999 UNTS 171, on rights of the defendants in criminal proceedings. There are similarities also between Article 28 of the Children's Convention and Article 13 of the International Covenant on Economic, Social and Cultural Rights opened for signature Dec. 16 1966, 993 UNTS at 3.

[5] *See further*, Articles 7 and 8 of the Convention on the Rights of the Child, *supra*, note 1.

[6] *See e.g.,* Convention on the Rights of the Child, Article 20 concerning children deprived of a family environment, Article 22 concerning refugee children and Article 23 concerning children with dis-abilities, *ibid.*

[7] *See* Convention on the Rights of the Child, Article 13, *ibid.*

[8] *See* Convention on the Rights of the Child, Article 12, *ibid.*

[9] *See further*, Convention on the Rights of the Child, *ibid*, where these principles are set out in Articles 2 and 3, respectively.

Deirdre Fottrell (ed.), Revisiting Children's Rights, 87–100
© 2000 *Kluwer Law International. Printed in Great Britain.*

Although it is a binding instrument of international law, the CRC lacks a powerful system of enforcement, which would allow for the adjudication of complaints of individual children.[10] The mechanism by which States' implementation of the CRC's principles and provisions is monitored is now well established, however, and initial evidence shows that the work of the Committee on the Rights of the Child is being carried out effectively and comprehensively in this regard.[11] Although its advisory and non-adversarial approach to the promotion and protection of children's rights is beginning to take effect,[12] it involves necessarily meeting long-, rather than short-term goals. In addition to its legally binding nature, the CRC carries certain moral force which is derived from its original, unanimous approval by the General Assembly in 1990 and the status it has subsequently acquired as the most widely ratified instrument in international law.[13] Thus, while the merits of using the CRC as a blueprint for government action are clear, and its effective employment to educate and create an awareness of children's rights is integral to its complete implementation, these methods alone have rather limited potential to remedy serious violations of children's rights. It is important, therefore, to look for alternative methods to enforce the CRC's standards and it is submitted that one such approach is to use its principles and provisions in the interpretation and application of the European Convention on Human Rights (ECHR). Although children's rights are essentially absent from the ECHR,[14] nevertheless it boasts a highly successful system of individual petition and an influential base which, with 41 States now party to the ECHR, is truly pan-European. Consequently, by using the detailed and comprehensive child-specific provisions of the CRC to interpret the ECHR in accordance with its highly successful system of individual petition, it is possible to maximise the potential of both treaties to protect and promote children's rights.

With regard to the practice of the European Court of Human Rights, while the Court and, up to its abolishment, the Commission, do not adopt this strategy in all children's cases, nevertheless, references to the CRC are being made with increasing frequency in Strasbourg. The purpose of this chapter is to examine the use of this

---

[10] *See e.g.*, D.A. Balton, *The Convention on the Rights of the Child: Prospects for International Enforcement* 12 HUM. RTS. Q. 120–129 (1990).

[11] *See further*, U. Kilkelly, *The UN Committee on the Rights of the Child: An Evaluation in the Light of Recent UK Experience*, 105 CH. & FAM. L.Q.. *See also*, by the same author, *In the Best Interests of the Child? An evaluation of Ireland's performance before the UN Committee on the Rights of the Child* 19 IRISH LAW TIMES 293 (1998).

[12] In Ireland, for example, the government is committed to establishing an office of Ombudsman for Children; drawing up a national children strategy and raising the age of criminal responsibility to 12 years. While domestic pressures also played a significant part in securing these changes, they were strongly recommended by the Committee on the Rights of the Child. *See further*, the concluding observations of the Committee on the Rights of the Child on the initial report of Ireland, UN Doc. CRC/C/15/Add.85, 23 January 1998.

[13] The Convention on the Rights of the Child has been ratified by 191 States. Only the United States and Somalia have not ratified the Convention, although the United States signed the Convention in 1995, *see further*, A.D. Renteln, *United States Ratification of Human Rights Treaties; Who's Afraid of the CRC?* 3 ILSA J. INT'L & COMP. L 629 (1997).

[14] *See further* KILKELLY, THE CHILD AND THE EUROPEAN CONVENTION ON HUMAN RIGHTS, 1999.

approach by the Commission and the Court of Human Rights in their consideration of children's cases and in doing so, to attempt to evaluate the influence which the CRC has had on the case-law of the ECHR. It will focus particularly on two areas in which the influence of the CRC is most strongly felt, i.e., physical punishment and juvenile justice. The contribution will conclude with some speculation as to the future potential for this approach in terms of protecting and promoting children's rights in Europe.

THE EUROPEAN CONVENTION ON HUMAN RIGHTS AND CHILDREN

Although the Strasbourg system of individual petition is sophisticated and has brought about change in a wide range of legal areas across the jurisdictions of Europe, the text of the ECHR contains few express references to either children or their rights. Minors or juveniles (the text is inconsistent in its use of relevant terminology) are mentioned only twice in the main body of the Convention, in Article 5 concerning the right to liberty and in Article 6 in relation to the right to a fair trial. Article 5 guarantees the right to liberty subject in paragraph 1 to various exceptions including following conviction by a court and on suspicion of having committed an offence. While it would appear that the grounds on which detention is permitted under 5(1) also apply to children, at the same time paragraph 5(1)(d) makes additional provision for the detention of a minor for the purpose of educational supervision.[15] Article 6 sets out the right to a fair trial, including a public hearing, and it goes on to provide for an exception to that principle in the case of minors, insofar as the press and public may be excluded from all or part of the trial where the interests of juveniles require. Clearly the emphasis is on offering minors protection but there is little mention of the parallel need to ensure that children involved in the criminal system are also guaranteed their rights of due process. The only provision which guarantees a right specifically to children is contained in Article 2 of the First Protocol,[16] which deals with the right to education. However, there is no express mention of the child here and moreover, this provision goes on to secure to parents, rather than to children, the right to ensure that the education conforms with their religious and philosophical convictions.[17] Similarly, the provision which holds the greatest significance for children – Article 8 which guarantees the right to respect for family life – does not refer expressly to children, their rights or their need for protection, either. Article 5 of the Seventh Protocol rectified this to an extent by recognising parental equality in relation to their children, and it introduces expressly for the first time the right of the State to take such measures as are necessary in the interests of the children.[18] While this is the only express reference to the

---

[15] *See* Bouamar *v* Belgium, Eur. Ct. H.R. Series A at 129, 11 EHRR at 1 (1988): On the interpretation of the provision *see also* KILKELLY, *supra*, note 14 at 42–46.
[16] *See* Protocol No 1 to the European Convention for the Protection of Human Rights and Fundamental Freedoms, 20 March 1952, ETS No 9.
[17] *See further* KILKELLY, *supra* note 14 at 62–87.
[18] *See* Protocol No 7 to the European Convention for the Protection of Human Rights and Fundamental Freedoms, 22 November 1984, ETS No 117.

best interests of the child in the ECHR, the principle has been found to be implicit in other areas, and it is, most notably, a prominent feature of the case-law on Article 8 in areas of custody, contact, adoption and alternative care.[19]

The ECHR is thus clearly short on substantive rights for children. However, there are a number of factors which make the use of the CRC as an interpretive guide both possible and highly useful. First, many of the ECHR's provisions are phrased in broad terms and this allows them to be interpreted in an expansive and imaginative way. A good example is Article 8 of the ECHR, which guarantees the right to respect for private and family life, which has been and continues to be very dynamically interpreted. For instance, among the rights found to fall within the scope of Article 8 are the right to physical integrity,[20] the right to a healthy environment[21] and the right to parental leave allowance.[22] In children's cases, the broad nature of Convention's provisions allows the Court to adapt them in a manner which takes account of the particular needs and rights of the child. This is made possible, *inter alia*, by the existence, in international law, of other more relevant and more specific standards, which can be relied upon as part of the process of dynamic interpretation. This approach to interpretation is compatible with the evolutive character of the Convention, which was recognised by the Court in the Tyrer case in 1978.[23] There, the Court established for the first time that the Convention is a living instrument, which must evolve so as to maintain relevance to current legal and social conditions. Thus it is well recognised that the Convention cannot operate in isolation from surrounding legal and social influences. Indeed, the Court has always drawn on factors outside of the Convention in applying its standards, and this is evident from its approach to the margin of appreciation. Here, States will enjoy less discretion where their approach is out of line with commonly accepted modes in the Council of Europe and beyond.[24] Further evidence of the compatibility of this approach with the Convention can be found in the practice of the Court, where among the sources of expertise upon which it frequently draws are the various legal instruments and treaties which make up both regional and international human rights law. While there is no specific provision for this approach in the Convention itself, as long as it does not lead to an interpretation of its provisions which goes beyond the Convention's spirit and purpose, then it must be seen as a valuable and useful tool.[25] This is particularly important in children's cases, where ECHR guidance is frequently absent, and where, consequently, the detailed and specific provisions of the CRC can be used to great effect.

---

[19] *See further* KILKELLY, *supra* note 14 at 201–203.

[20] *See* X & Y *v* the Netherlands Eur. Ct. H.R., Series A no 91, 8 EHRR 235 (1985).

[21] *See* Lopez Ostra *v* Spain, Eur. Ct. H.R., Series A no 303, 20 EHRR 277 (1994).

[22] *See* Petrovic *v* Austria, judgment of 27 March 1998, Reports 1998-II, no 67 (1998).

[23] *See* Tyrer *v* UK, Series A no 26, 2 EHRR 1(1978).

[24] *See further* N. Lavender, *The Problem of the Margin of Appreciation*, 4 EUR. HUM. RTS. L. REV. 380–390 (1997).

[25] The interpretation of the Convention should not be so dynamic as to lead to the creation of new rights, which would cause States to question the legitimacy of the Convention system. *See further* M. Pellonpää, *Economic, Social and Cultural Rights* in THE EUROPEAN SYSTEM FOR THE PROTECTION OF HUMAN RIGHTS, 855–874, 867 (N. St. J. Macdonald, F. Matscher & H. Petzold, eds., 1993).

A final important feature of the ECHR in this context relates to Article 1, which guarantees Convention rights and freedoms to 'everyone'. Despite its seemingly innocuous nature, this provision has a central role in the way in which the ECHR is interpreted and applied and it takes on added significance in children's cases. In particular, the fact that the ECHR makes few express references to the rights of the child means that any facility which reinforces the child's entitlement to enjoy all Convention rights is welcome. The child's equal entitlement under the ECHR is enforced further by Article 14, which prohibits discrimination in the enjoyment of Convention rights on numerous grounds, including age.[26] In theory, then, Convention rights are guaranteed to all, and there is little, other than the obvious practical difficulties, to prevent their application to children. Moreover, in practice, the Commission and Court of Human Rights have refrained from placing express or general limits on the application of the Convention in children's cases. Frequent reference to the standards of the CRC have encouraged this approach and generally raised the profile of children's rights in ECHR proceedings, as well as at domestic level where such cases necessarily originate.

INFLUENCE OF THE CRC ON THE ECHR: A HISTORY

The practice of referring to other, more detailed or more specific human rights instruments, where relevant, has emerged as one of the Court's methods of interpreting the ECHR. One of the first times it adopted this approach was in the first children's case to come before it. *Marckx v Belgium*[27] concerned the inferior legal status of an unmarried mother and her child born outside marriage, which, the Court found, constituted a lack of respect for the family life of both mother and child in violation of Article 8. In reaching this conclusion, the Court relied, controversially as it was not yet in force at the time, on the Council of Europe Convention on the Legal Status of Children Born Outside Wedlock 1975 as evidence of an increasing acceptance of equal treatment for children regardless of their parents' marital status.[28] In other children's cases, the institutions have referred to the Council of Europe's Convention on Adoption,[29] as well as the UNESCO Convention against Discrimination in Education and the 1959 Declaration on the Rights of the Child.[30]

---

[26] *See further* KILKELLY, *supra*, note 14 at 2–6.

[27] *See* Marckx *v* Belgium, Eur. Ct. H.R, Series A no 31, 2 EHRR 330 (1979).

[28] *See* European Convention on the Status of Children Born Out of Wedlock, 1975, ETS No 85. For criticism of the Court's approach see J. S. Davidson, *The European Convention on Human Rights and the 'Illegitimate' Child'*, in CHILDREN AND THE LAW: ESSAYS IN HONOUR OF PROFESSOR H.K. BEVAN, 75–106, at 95–96 (D. Freestone ed. 1990).

[29] *See* X & Y *v* UK, Application No. 7626/76, Decision of Eur. Comm. H.R., Decision Nov. 7 1977, 11 D & R 11, 160. *See also* Inze *v* Austria, Eur. Ct. H.R., Series A no 126, 10 EHRR 394, (1987) ¶ 32, both the Commission and Court referred expressly to provisions of the European Convention on Adoption, ETS No 58.

[30] In Application Nos *5095/71, 5920/72 & 5926/72* Kjeldsen, Busk Madsen & Pedersen *v* Denmark, Eur. Ct. H.R., Decision Mar. 21 1975, Series A no 23, ¶ 153, the Commission referred to the UNESCO Convention against Discrimination, 429 UNTS 93 (1960); *see also* the Declaration of the Rights of the Child, G.A. Res 1386 (XIV), 14 UN GAOR Supp. (No. 16), UN Doc.A/4354 (1959).

While the reference by the Strasbourg institutions to other regional and international treaties is noteworthy, the use of the CRC is a particularly important development, not least because its effect is often to maximise the potential of both treaties to protect children's rights. Both the Commission and the Court have referred to provisions of the CRC in children's cases since it came into force in 1990. Moreover, even though the youth of the CRC suggests that it is only in the last decade of case-law that its influence can be seen in Strasbourg, it would be inaccurate to say that it has had no effect on older case-law. For instance, in a recent case the Court revisited one of its well-established principles and added a reference to the CRC which gave it a further dimension. Thus, in the *Marckx* case, handed down in 1979, the Court established the principle that legal safeguards must enable the child born outside marriage to integrate into her family from the moment of birth.[31] The *Marckx* principle was later reiterated in the *Keegan* case in 1994, which concerned the placement for adoption without his consent or knowledge of the child of an unmarried father.[32] Here the Court went on to refer expressly in that context to Article 7 of the CRC, which provides for the child's right to know and be cared for by her parents.[33] It is possible to argue, therefore, that by making the link between the *Marckx* principle and Article 7 of the CRC, the Court was, in a way, updating its case-law, by giving it a more conventional, children-oriented slant. This is a particularly important trend because it allows the Court, not to rewrite its case-law, but to refocus and develop it further in children's cases to take account of other established international law in the area.

PHYSICAL PUNISHMENT AND ABUSE

An area of Strasbourg case-law in which the influence of the CRC is clearly evident is those cases of dealing with physical punishment and abuse. In fact, one of the first references to the CRC was made by the Court in the *Costello-Roberts* case, which concerned the physical punishment meted out to a 7-year-old boy in a private school in the UK.[34] The boy complained that his treatment violated both Article 3 of the ECHR, which prohibits treatment which is inhuman or degrading, as well as Article 8, which requires respect for private life, of which the right to physical integrity is an important part. Although both of the boy's substantive complaints failed before the Court, the Court established for the first time in this case that the State could be held responsible for breaches of the Convention which occur in the private sphere. In reaching this conclusion, particular regard was had to the educational context of the dispute and the Court recalled the State's obligation to secure to children their right to education under Article 2 of the First Protocol. In this regard, it was noted that the provisions of the ECHR must be read as a whole and the Court found that functions relating to the internal administration of

---

[31] *See* Marckx *supra* note 24.
[32] *See* Keegan *v* Ireland, Eur. Ct. H.R., Series A, No. 290, 18 EHRR 342 (1994).
[33] *Ibid*, ¶ 50.
[34] *See* Costello-Roberts *v* UK, Eur. Ct. H.R., Series A, No. 247-C, 19 EHRR 112 (1993). *See further* KILKELLY, *supra* note 14 at 160–170.

school, like discipline, cannot be said to be ancillary to the education process. Importantly, the Court found support for its proposition that the disciplinary system of a school falls within the ambit of the right to education in Article 28 of the CRC. The Court thus went on to cite paragraph 2 of that provision, which places an obligation on States to take all measures to ensure that school discipline is administered in a manner consistent with the child's human dignity and in conformity with the CRC, and relied on it to reach its conclusion that the State cannot absolve itself from responsibility by delegating its obligations to private individuals or bodies.

As is frequently the case, the Commission has led the way in terms of looking to the CRC for appropriate guidance when applying the ECHR provisions to children. Indeed, the Commission has gone further than the Court by making reference to the observations of the UN Committee on the Rights of the Child, where relevant.[35] It did for the first time in 1997 in the case of *A v UK*.[36] 'A' was a 9-year-old boy whose complaint was based on the fact that he had been beaten by his stepfather with a garden cane on two or three occasions within the period of one week. At least some of the strokes were inflicted directly onto the bare skin and they caused severe bruising which was visible several days later. The injuries were considered to be sufficiently serious to merit the initiation of criminal proceedings against the boy's stepfather, but he was acquitted when his defence that the punishment amounted to moderate and reasonable chastisement found favour with the jury. The boy complained to the Commission that this amounted to a breach of Article 3, which prohibits treatment which is inhuman or degrading. The Commission, in short, agreed and in reaching its conclusion it drew support both from the CRC and the UN Committee's application of it. Having found that the treatment in question fell within the scope of inhuman and degrading treatment under Article 3, the Commission went on to consider whether responsibility could be imposed on the State for treatment which was inflicted by one private individual on another. While it recognised that a State cannot guarantee through its legal system that inhuman and degrading treatment can never be inflicted by one individual on another, the Commission concluded that State responsibility will be incurred where it is shown that the domestic legal system, in particular the relevant criminal law, fails to provide practical and effective protection of the rights guaranteed by Article 3. In determining whether such protection was provided in this case, the Commission attached importance to the international recognition of the need to protect children from all forms of ill-treatment. Here it made particular reference to Article 19 of the CRC, which requires states to take all appropriate measures to 'protect the child from all forms of physical or mental violence, injury or abuse'.[37] In terms

---

[35] Application No. 25599/94 A *v* UK, Eur. Comm. H.R., Commission Reports, Sept. 18 1997, Reports 1998-VI no 90. *See also* Application No. 24724/94 T *v* UK, Comm Rep, and No. 24888/94 V *v* UK, Eur. Comm. H.R. Commission Reports, Dec. 12 1998/98, unreported.

[36] Application No. 25599/94 A *v* UK, *ibid.*

[37] *See* UN Convention on the Rights of the Child, *supra* note 1. *See also* Marckx judgment, *supra* note 24.

of the protection available to the applicant, then, the Commission noted that the relevant English law contains criminal sanctions for assault. However, it went on to find that

> the protection afforded in this area by the law to children within the home is significantly reduced by the defence open to parents ... that the acts in question were lawful, as involving the reasonable and moderate physical punishment of the child.[38]

Thus, it was the operation of this defence which caused the Commission most concern and in particular the fact that, in such cases, the burden lies on the prosecution to negate the defence by satisfying a jury beyond reasonable doubt that the punishment was not in all the circumstances reasonable or moderate. The defendant is thus not required to substantiate the reasonable and moderate value of the punishment applied. The fundamental problem in this case, however, was that the jury, which was required to consider this defence, was provided with little guidance as to the meaning of reasonable and moderate chastisement. This is significant because, as the Commission noted, 'the imprecise nature of the expression' had led the UN Committee on the Rights of the Child, when considering the first report of the UK in 1995, to express its concern about the possibility of it being interpreted in an 'arbitrary and subjective manner'.[39] The Commission thus referred directly to the concluding observations of the Committee on the Rights of the Child, not simply to support its own position, but in pointing to further evidence of the problem which it identified. The Commission then went on to add its own concern about the application of the defence of moderate and reasonable chastisement and its compatibility with the test under Article 3 (of inhuman and degrading treatment) to that of the UN Committee. In particular, it noted that the jury did not receive direction on the relevance of such factors as the age or state of health of the applicant, the appropriateness of the instrument used in his chastisement, the suffering experienced or the relevance, if any, of the defence claim that the punishment was 'necessary' and 'justified'. As a result, and unconvinced by the Government's reliance on reported cases where convictions had been obtained in cases involving excessive physical punishment, the Commission concluded that domestic law had failed to provide the applicant with adequate and effective protection against corporal punishment which was, in the circumstances, degrading within the meaning of Article 3.

While the Court reached the same conclusion as the Commission in the *A* case,

---

[38] *See* Application No. 25599/94 A v UK, *supra* note 35. *See also* Application No. 24724/94 T v UK, and No. 24888/94 V v UK, *supra* note 35.

[39] *See* concluding observations of the UN Committee on the Rights of the Child on the initial report of the United Kingdom, UN Doc CRC/C/15/Add.34, ¶ 16. *See further* Kilkelly, *The UN Committee on the Rights of the Child: An Evaluation in the Light of Recent UK Experience, supra* note 11 at 114–115.

its judgment is phrased in more general terms.[40] The Court confined its references to the CRC to the question of State responsibility where it recalled that children are entitled to State protection against serious breaches of personal integrity apropos Articles 19 and 37 of the CRC.[41] Thus, although the Court failed to make the same specific reference to the UN Committee's criticism of the defence of 'moderate and reasonable chastisement', it nonetheless made the all important link between the general prohibition in Article 3 of the ECHR and the equivalent, but more detailed, child-specific provisions of the CRC.

JUVENILE JUSTICE

Juvenile justice is one area of Strasbourg jurisprudence which is ripe for development given that the application of Article 6, the ECHR's fair trial provision, to children in conflict with the law is at a relatively early stage. Although the equivalent provision in the CRC, Article 40, is little different in content from Article 6 of the ECHR, the former provision makes the important statement that children in conflict with the law must be treated in a way which promotes the child's sense of dignity and worth and which takes into account his/her age.[42] Moreover, Article 6 has also been found to include other rights which are an inherent part of the fair trial process, such as the right to access and participate adequately in proceedings, which have obvious significance for minors. Until very recently, however, only a minority of the Commission and Court had referred to the importance of treating children in the juvenile justice system in an appropriate manner and, in doing so, have made reference to the CRC. In the *Nortier* case for example, the applicant, a minor, complained that he had not received a fair hearing by an independent tribunal, in contravention of Article 6, due to the fact that the same judge took decisions on his case both at the pre-trial and trial stages.[43] Although neither the Commission nor the Court found any evidence of bias in this particular case, dissenting members of both institutions stated clearly their belief that the juvenile justice system in question was designed to take the particular needs and circumstances of the young accused into account.[44] Moreover, Mr Judge Morenilla in the Court agreed with Mr Trechsel and his like-minded colleagues in the Commission that while minors are entitled to the same protection of their fundamental rights as adults, the application of Article 6 to such cases should involve taking into account the developing state of their personality and the limited social responsibility which they incur as a consequence. The Judge quoted from the Preamble of the CRC that States should afford young people the 'necessary protection and assistance so that

---

[40] *See* A *v* UK, Eur. Ct. H.R. Reports 1998-VI no 90 (1998).

[41] *Ibid* ¶ 21.

[42] *See* UN Convention on the Right of the Child, *supra* note 1, Article 40(1).

[43] Application No. 13924/88 Nortier *v* the Netherlands, Eur. Comm. H.R, Commission Reports, July 9 1992, unpublished and Eur. Ct. H.R, Series A, No 267, 17 EHRR 273 (1993).

[44] *See* the dissenting opinion of Mr Trechsel, joined by Mr Schermers, Mr Frowein and Sir Basil Hall, in the Commission Report, *ibid* and the dissenting opinion of Judge Morenilla in the Court judgment, *ibid*.

they can fully assume their responsibilities within the community', and to prepare them 'to live an individual life in society'. In particular, he referred to Article 40(3) of the CRC which requires States to promote the

> establishment of laws, procedures, authorities and institutions applicable to children alleged as, accused of, or recognised as having infringed the penal law.[45]

Despite the fact that this was not the view expressed by the majority of the Court, it is encouraging that this opinion was expressed just three years after the CRC came into force, and more importantly, that it was not a view which contradicted with the majority, *per se*, but rather presented a more children's rights-friendly version of it. Equally, the dissenting views expressed throughout the *Nortier* case as a whole illustrate the delicate balance to be achieved between guaranteeing to young accused the right to a fair trial, while at the same time ensuring that they receive special protection as a result of their vulnerable state.

The ECHR organs have rarely been faced with issues as to the application of Article 6 to juveniles, and the search for balance between applying special considerations to young persons in conflict with the law and refraining from any dilution of the fundamental guarantees of Article 6 in their criminal trial continues. The Commission was the first institution to deal with this issue head on in the case of *T & V v UK*, which involved the trial for murder of two 11-year-old boys in an adult court. According to the facts, the accused were provided with defence counsel and the assistance of a social worker and the court sittings were shortened to take their limited concentration span into account. Despite these 'not inconsiderable safeguards', however, the boys were nevertheless subjected to the full rigours of the adult, public court in their trial for the murder of a two-year-old boy. The trial process in an adult court with attendant publicity was regarded by the Commission as a severely intimidating procedure for a child and consequently it held that these conditions must have seriously impinged on their ability to participate in the proceedings in any meaningful way. The end result was a violation of their right to a fair trial under Article 6.[46] While the Commission did not refer expressly to the CRC in its application of Article 6 (nor, incidentally, did it refer to the special provision in Article 6 itself which allows for excluding the press or public from a trial in the interests of juveniles), its opinion clearly reflects both its principles – the best interests principle under Article 3 as well as the child's right to participate in proceedings concerning her under Article 12, and its provisions on juvenile justice, particularly Article 40. Indeed, Mr Bratza, in his separate opinion agreeing with the majority, made express reference not only to the importance of the best interests principle in Article 40 of the CRC, but also to Article 14(4) of the International Covenant on Civil and Political Rights[47] as well as the Beijing Rules (UN Standard

---

[45] *Id.*
[46] *See* Application No. 24888/94 V v UK, *supra* note 35 ¶ 98–108.
[47] *See* International Covenant on Civil and Political Rights, *supra* note 2.

Minimum Rules for the Administration of Juvenile Justice)[48] to drive the point home.

The Court, in its judgment in December 1999, agreed with the Commission in its conclusion that the accused were unable to participate effectively in their criminal trial and that that gave rise to a violation of Article 6.[49] In particular, it reiterated the Commission's view that

> it is essential that a child charged with an offence is dealt with in a manner which takes full account of his age, level of maturity and intellectual and emotional capacities, and that steps are taken to promote his ability to understand and participate in the proceedings.[50]

For the Court this involved two factors: the question of the children's ability to participate in the proceedings and the related factor of publicity. In relation to the latter, the Court found that in respect of a young child charged with a grave offence attracting high levels of media and public interest, it is necessary to conduct the hearing in such a way as to reduce as far as possible his/her feelings of intimidation and inhibition. In this regard, it referred to a number of international instruments advocating the protection of the privacy of child defendants, including the Beijing Rules, the CRC and a recommendation adopted by the Committee of Ministers of the Council of Europe in 1987.[51] In light of this guidance, the Court observed that where it is considered appropriate in view of the age of the child and the surrounding circumstances, this need to protect the defendants' privacy could be balanced with the general interest in the open administration of justice by using a modified reporting procedure, including selected attendance rights and judicious reporting. As the trial in this case was conducted in a blaze of publicity, which led eventually to the release of the defendants' names following its conclusion, this raised a clear issue of its compatibility with Article 6. In relation to the boys' participation in the trial, the Court noted that it was highly unlikely in the charged atmosphere of the courtroom that they could have consulted with their lawyers. Moreover, their immaturity and disturbed psychological state also made it unlikely that they would have been able to co-operate with their lawyers outside the courtroom in the preparation of their defence.[52] The combination of these factors made it clear that the accused were unable to participate effectively in the criminal proceedings against them, giving rise to a breach of their right to a fair trial under Article 6(1).[53]

---

[48] The UN Standard Minimum Rules for the Administration of Juvenile Justice (the Beijing Rules) were adopted by GA Res 40/33 U.N. GAOR of 29 November 198, upon the recommendation of the Seventh United Nations Congress on the Prevention of Crime and Treatment of Offenders in Milan, 1985.

[49] *See* T *v* UK and V *v* UK, Eur. Ct. H.R., judgments of 16 Dec. 1999. Slight variations occur in the judgments. Reference will hitherto be made to the judgment in the *V* case.

[50] *Ibid*, ¶ 86.

[51] *See* Committee of Ministers of the Council of Europe Recommendation no. R (87) 20, *ibid* ¶ 87.

[52] *Ibid*, ¶ 90.

[53] The Court reached this conclusion by a majority of sixteen votes to one, *ibid.*

While the Court did not rely directly on the CRC in its judgment in this case, it is obvious from the wording and the context of its judgment that it was informed by its juvenile justice provisions and other, more general standards, including the best interests principle in Article 3. This is highly significant in the light of the fact that it is the first time that the Court has dealt squarely with the issue of what constitutes a fair trial for juveniles. It is clear from the judgment that certain modifications to the adult trial court and procedure are necessary in order to take into account the age, understanding and ability of the accused to participate in their trial to ensure compatibility with the ECHR. In particular, this suggests the Court's support for Article 40(3) of the CRC, which requires States to seek the promotion of legal procedures and authorities specifically designed for dealing with children in conflict with the law. However, the Court did not find that the attribution of criminal responsibility to the 11-year-old defendants breached the ECHR and was unconvinced by the guidance of the Beijing Rules,[54] and Article 40(3) of the CRC, which merely requires the establishment of a minimum age of criminal responsibility, in this respect.[55] Similarly, references to the CRC standard on privacy, which proved significant in the Court's consideration of the Article 6 issue, was not persuasive enough to determine whether the trial in public amounted to ill-treatment of the severity necessary to bring it under Article 3.[56] Nor was the boys' indeterminate sentence of detention during Her Majesty's pleasure severe enough to fall within the scope of inhuman punishment under Article 3.[57] However, in reaching this conclusion, the Court referred expressly to Article 37 of the CRC, which provides that the detention of a child should only be used as a measure of last resort and prohibits life imprisonment of minors without the possibility of release. In this context, it noted that a continued failure to fix a tariff, leaving a detainee in uncertainty as to his future over many years, may give rise to an issue under this provision.[58] Moreover, the Court went on to find that the tariff-fixing procedure, which was carried out by the Home Secretary rather than a court or tribunal independent of the executive, violated Article 6.[59] Finally, the applicants' inability to have the continued lawfulness of their detention determined by a judicial body was found to constitute a violation of Article 5(4).[60]

---

[54] Rule 4 of the Beijing Rules invites States not to fix the age of criminal responsibility too low, *see further* UN Standard Minimum Rules for the Administration of Juvenile Justice, *supra* note 48.

[55] *See* judgment of the Eur. Ct. H.R. in V *v* UK, *supra* note 49, ¶ 62–74. Judges Pastor Ridruejo, Ress, Makarczyk, Tulkens and Butkevych disagreed with the Court and found that the combination of (i) treating children of 10 years of age as criminally responsible, (ii) prosecuting them at the age of 11 in an adult court, and (iii) subjecting them to an indeterminate sentence, reached a substantial level of mental and physical suffering, which violated Article 3. In particular, they noted that only four Contracting States out of 41 are prepared to find criminal responsibility at an age as low as, or lower than, that applicable in England and Wales and had little trouble concluding that the existing standard amongst the member States of the Council of Europe was to find juveniles criminally responsible from the age of 13 or 14.

[56] *Ibid*, ¶ 62–80.

[57] *Ibid*, ¶ 93–101.

[58] *See* V *v* UK, Eur. Ct. H.R. judgment, *supra* note 49 ¶ 100.

[59] *Ibid*, ¶ 107–114.

[60] *Ibid*, ¶ 115–122.

It is clear from the above that the judgment of the Court in the case of *T & V v UK* is indeed a landmark judgment, which provides valuable and necessary guidance as to the compatibility of juvenile criminal proceedings and the sentencing of juveniles with Article 6 and other ECHR provisions. Direct references to the standards of the CRC are frequent and meaningful throughout the judgment. What is more significant, however, is that the judgment as a whole is informed by and consistent with the provisions and principles of the CRC. There is thus firm evidence that the CRC standards in the area of juvenile justice have been accepted by the Court, which, as an international tribunal, is in a position to enforce them.

TAKING THE APPROACH FORWARD

In addition to the areas of physical punishment and juvenile justice, there is evidence of this approach in other areas of the Strasbourg case-law also. For example, there is a strong link between much of the case-law on family life in relation to the alternative care of children and the principles and provisions of the CRC.[61] In particular, much of the ECHR case-law mirrors the reliance on the best interests principle in Article 3 as well as the importance of contact between parents and children in care recognised in Article 9(3) of the CRC.[62] Moreover, parental involvement in all aspects of alternative care proceedings, the importance of which is recognized in Article 9(2) of the CRC, is put into practice through the approach of the European Court, which has found adequate involvement to be implicit in respect for family life.[63] This notwithstanding, there are other areas within the context of respect for family life that would benefit from the guidance offered by the CRC. The question of independent representation for children is one such area, should such a complaint ever reach the Court. In particular, Article 12 of the CRC, which recognises the right of the child to be heard in all relevant administrative or judicial proceedings, could undoubtedly inform the Court's deliberations on the claim of a child or young person, who, although competent to do so, was unable to participate effectively in care or other proceedings concerning their welfare. Such a claim might arise either under Article 8, which guarantees respect for family life, or Article 6, which guarantees access to a court, and the appointment of a guardian *ad litem* would undoubtedly be central to such a case.

Another area in which reference to the provisions of the CRC may be influential is in relation to the child's right to identity, contained in Articles 7 and 8. The Court's consideration of this issue thus far has been hesitant. In *X, Y & Z v UK*, for example, the Court appeared to postpone consideration of whether it is in the child's interests to have the name of a person on her birth certificate who is not the

---

[61] *See e.g.*, Olsson *v* Sweden, Eur. Ct. H.R Series A no 130, 11 EHRR 259 (1988); Andersson *v* Sweden, Eur. Ct. H.R., Series A no 226-A, 14 EHRR 615 (1992): *see also* Johansen *v* Norway, Eur. Ct. H.R., Reports 1996-III no 12, at 979, 23 EHRR 78 (1996). *See generally*, KILKELLY, *supra* note 14 at 263–294.

[62] *See* UN Convention on the Rights of the Child, *supra* note 1.

[63] *See* W *v* UK, Eur. Ct. H.R., Series A no 121, 10 EHRR 29 (1987); *see also* McMichael *v* UK, Eur. Ct. H.R., Series A no 308, 20 EHRR 205 (1995).

biological father arguably due, *inter alia*, to concerns for the child's right to identity.[64] Were the Court to revisit this issue then reference to the CRC may play a positive role in the context of the entitlement to birth information. Useful guidance could be sought from its provisions, as well as the UN Committee's positive interpretation of them,[65] with respect to any future challenges to policies of anonymity in adoption and artificial reproduction systems and their compatibility with respect for private and family life.

CONCLUSION

The importance of using the CRC as a tool to interpret the European Convention cannot be underestimated, particularly in States, like the United Kingdom, where the latter Convention has been incorporated into domestic law, but the former has not. In this regard, there is plenty of scope for using the principles and provisions of the CRC in a positive and dynamic way to support use of an ECHR argument for persuasive value in the domestic courts, as well as in Strasbourg. However, it is essential for the integrity of the Strasbourg system that references to the CRC are limited to where they are appropriate to guide its interpretation, for example, where such guidance is lacking in either the ECHR or its case-law. Nevertheless, it is an important interpretive tool which can have a significant positive effect on the application of the ECHR to children, as existing case-law shows. Moreover, as States continue to implement the CRC and the treaty itself continues to grow in profile and status, the European Court of Human Rights will rely increasingly on its standards. While such reliance may not always be explicit in the judgments of the Court, there is little doubt that its standards are at last beginning to inform the process of decision-making at European level, where children are concerned. Thus, the use of the CRC to guide the interpretation of the ECHR in children's cases, either implicitly or expressly, holds real promise for maximising the potential of both treaties to protect and promote children's rights. As the century in which all of these human rights standards were finally codified at international level finally draws to a close, and as the history of the UN Convention on the Rights of the Child enters but its second decade, this is indeed a positive and a welcome development.

---

[64] *See* X, Y & Z *v* UK, Eur. Ct. H.R., Reports 1997-II no 35, p 619, 24 EHRR 143 (1997).

[65] In particular, the Committee has found that total anonymity in such procedures which prevented the child from obtaining vital birth information would be contrary to the Convention. *See* UN Doc. CRC/C/15.Add.20.

Jenny Kuper

7. CHILDREN AND ARMED CONFLICT: SOME ISSUES OF LAW AND POLICY

INTRODUCTION

Two decades ago the children's rights 'movement' was still in its infancy. A number of writers and others had publicly debated the position of children in society,[1] but the debate was confined within a fairly narrow circle. Since then, and particularly since the adoption on 20 November 1989 of the Convention on the Rights of the Child (CRC), the debate about children's rights, and awareness of this notion, have grown exponentially. What are the implications of this for specific categories of children, such as those caught up in situations of armed conflict? Are they better protected now that there is a greater awareness of their legal entitlements? Or does it make no difference at all?

This chapter will address these questions, and consider certain theoretical and practical problems relating to international law and children in armed conflict. It will start by outlining the main applicable legal rules in order to place the subsequent discussion in context. A detailed consideration of the relevant law will not be undertaken here, and can, in any event, be found elsewhere.[2] For the purposes of this chapter, it will suffice to outline only the key provisions of humanitarian treaty law regarding: child civilians, child soldiers, culpability, and the sources of this law.

KEY PROVISIONS

First, as regards the *child civilians*, these provisions include:

- The fundamental principle that children in armed conflict are entitled to special treatment.[3]

---

[1] For discussion of some of these, *see e.g.*, P. VEERMAN, THE RIGHTS OF THE CHILD AND THE CHANGING IMAGE OF CHILDHOOD, 75 (1992). *See also*, J. Holt, *Why not a Bill of Rights for Children?* in THE CHILDREN'S RIGHTS MOVEMENT 319 (B. Gross & R. Gross, eds., 1977); J. HOLT, ESCAPE FROM CHILDHOOD (1974); *see further*, FARSON, R. BIRTH-RIGHTS: A BILL OF RIGHTS FOR CHILDREN (1974).

[2] On child soldiers, *see generally*, G.S. GOODWIN-GILL, & I. COHN, CHILD SOLDIERS (1994). Regarding child civilians, *see generally*, J. KUPER, INTERNATIONAL LAW CONCERNING CHILD CIVILIANS IN ARMED CONFLICT (1997), Kuper explains that the relevant law includes international human rights law, humanitarian law (or the laws of war), and international children's law – as articulated both in treaties and in customary principles.

[3] *See* in particular Article 77(1) Additional Protocol to the Geneva Conventions of 1949 Relating to the Protection of Victims of International Armed Conflicts, adopted Geneva, June 8 1977, (hereafter 1977 Geneva Protocol 1); *see also* to lesser extent, Article 4(3) of the Additional Protocol to the

- More specific rules stating that children should not be arbitrarily killed, or tortured, or ill-treated in any way, and this includes a prohibition on the sexual abuse of children.[4]
- The rule that children should be granted priority in receiving necessities such as food and shelter.[5]
- The rule that children should be kept with their families and communities whenever possible, and given means of identification when separation is unavoidable. Any separation should be for the shortest possible time.[6]

These are the main rules on the treatment of child civilians in situations of armed conflict, most of which are to be found in the widely ratified 1949 Geneva Conventions, the 1977 Geneva Protocols, and in the 1989 CRC.

Second, as regards international humanitarian law on the treatment of *child soldiers*, these include the following rules:

- That children under 15 should never be used as combatants.[7]
- However, when, in contravention of the law, children under 15 do participate in hostilities and are then captured, they are entitled to special treatment in the same way as are child civilians.[8]
- Also, children under 15 should never be recruited as soldiers, and this includes voluntary recruitment.[9]
- When recruiting among persons between the ages of 15 and 18, priority should be given to those who are oldest.[10]

---

footnote continued

Geneva Conventions of 1949 Relating to Victims of Non-International Armed Conflicts, adopted Geneva, June 8 1977 (hereafter 1977 Geneva Protocol II). These provisions are both incorporated within Article 38, UN Convention on the Rights of the Child, UN Doc. A/44/736 (1989), reprinted in I.L.M. 1457 (1989).

[4] *See further*, Article 77(1) of 1977 Geneva Protocol I; *see also*, Art. 4(3) of 1977 Geneva Protocol II, and arguably certain provisions of the CRC are relevant, most particularly Article 6 which protects the child's right to life, survival and development, Article 19 which prohibits abuse or neglect of children, Article 34 which prohibits sexual exploitation and abuse, and Article 3 which requires that the best interest of the child be a primary consideration in all matters concerning the child.

[5] *See* The Declaration on the Rights of the Child passed by the League of Nations General Assembly, Records of the Fifth Assembly, Supp. No 23 League of Nations Official Journal, (1924) Principle 3. *See also*, Declaration of the Rights of the Child, G.A. Res 1386 (XIV), 14 GAOR Supp. (No. 16), UN Doc. A/4354 (1959), Principle 8, Article 23 of Geneva Convention IV(1949), and Article 70(1) of Geneva Protocol I (1977).

[6] *See e.g.*, Article 49 of Convention Relative to the Protection of Civilian Persons in Time of War, signed Geneva Aug. 12 1949, 75 UNTS 287 (hereinafter 1949 Geneva Convention IV 1949); Article 78 of Geneva Protocol I (1977), Article 4(3)(b) and (e) of Geneva Protocol II (1977) and, arguably, certain provisions in the CRC such as Article 10 and 20.

[7] Article 77(2) Geneva Protocol I (1977), Article 4(3) 1977 Geneva Protocol II (1977), and Article 38(2) CRC (1989).

[8] Article 77(3) Geneva Protocol I, Article 4(3)(d) Geneva Protocol II (1977).

[9] Article 77(2) Geneva Protocol I (1977), Article 4(3)(c) Geneva Protocol II (1977), and Article 38(3) 1 CRC (1989).

[10] Article 77(2) 1977 Geneva Protocol I and Article 38(3) CRC. Geneva Protocol II (1977), relating to non-international armed conflict, does not contain an analogous provision.

- Children should not be subject to the death penalty for offences related to the conflict which were committed when they were under 18.[11]

Again, these rules are to be found mainly in the 1977 Geneva Protocols, the CRC, and, to a lesser extent (i.e. only in relation to certain rules regarding the death penalty), in the 1949 Geneva Conventions.

Third, as regards both *child civilians* and *child soldiers*, the relevant treaties offer different levels of protection, depending on the intensity of the conflict. Thus, for example, there are more detailed rules regarding the treatment of children in situations of international armed conflict, and less detailed rules in relation to non-international armed conflict (i.e. internal disputes and civil wars).[12]

Finally, one last set of rules are important to note here: rules regarding *culpability*. These make it clear that government leaders, as well as soldiers and their commanders, may be personally liable for violations of the laws of armed conflict. Once again, many of the relevant rules can be found in the 1949 Geneva Conventions and in 1977 Geneva Protocol I.[13] Such rules are also set out in the statutes of war crimes tribunals, including early tribunals such as the Nuremberg tribunal, the tribunals on the former Yugoslavia and on Rwanda, and, most recently, the International Criminal Court.[14]

PROBLEMS ARISING

This chapter is written on the assumption that there is a consensus that the legal principles outlined above are conducive to the welfare of children, and that therefore there is value in encouraging compliance with these principles. However, there may be those who question the cultural assumptions behind some of these rules (e.g., as regards the age limits for child soldiers).[15] It must be acknowledged that to some extent these rules do represent a particular value system that has shaped conceptions of human rights and children's rights as represented in international law.

The various issues to be examined below can be analysed in both theoretical and practical terms. Having briefly summarised the main pertinent rules above, this

---

[11] Article 68 Geneva Convention IV (1949), Article 77(5) Geneva Protocol I, and Article 6(4) Geneva Protocol II (1977).

[12] For an outline of the different categories of conflict as defined in international humanitarian law, *see generally* KUPER, *supra*, note 2, 61–62.

[13] The Geneva Conventions (1949) contain rules concerning 'grave breaches' of their provisions, and oblige States Party to these Conventions to ensure such breaches are punished (*see e.g.*, Article 147 of 1949 Geneva Convention IV). Geneva Protocol I (1977) expands the 1949 Geneva Convention definitions of 'grave breaches', and sets out additional measures to address these (*see e.g.*, Articles 85, 86, 88 and 89). Geneva Protocol II (1977) makes no provision regarding the concept of 'grave breaches' in non-international armed conflict.

[14] *See* Charter of the International Military Tribunal, annexed to the Agreement for the Prosecution and Punishment of the Major War Criminals of the European Axis, London, August 8 1945, and UN Doc. S/RES/827, UN Doc. S/RES/955 and UN Doc.A/Conf.183/9* respectively.

[15] For a discussion of this issue, *see e.g.*, T.W. BENNETT, USING CHILDREN IN ARMED CONFLICT: A LEGITIMATE AFRICAN TRADITION? and CRIMINALISING RECRUITMENT OF CHILD SOLDIERS (1998).

chapter will initially consider some of the more theoretical problems that arise in relation to international law on children in armed conflict.

Why Special Rules for Children

First, why should there be a special body of rules regarding the protection of children in armed conflict? Surely the existing law of armed conflict applies equally to children and adults?[16] This question has a number of possible answers. As regards child civilians, it could be argued that children are indeed in the same position as all other civilians, and therefore entitled to the same treatment in situations of armed conflict. The relevant law does include all civilians, children and adults, within its scope, and it provides for their basic protection (e.g., that civilians should not be directly targeted,[17] that they should generally be treated with respect when in enemy hands,[18] and provided with necessities such as food and shelter[19]). Why should children be entitled to additional protection?

One reason for this additional protection seems rather obvious. Although children in armed conflict may have many similar experiences to those of adults, younger children, especially, are physically more vulnerable – and almost all children are economically, politically, and militarily powerless in such situations. It therefore seems self-evident that steps must be taken to address their particular needs. To take a simple example, an adult whose parents are killed in the conflict will generally still be able to take care of themselves, but young orphaned children may well find it difficult to do so. Hence, the law makes special provision for orphaned and unaccompanied children.[20]

There is another, more pragmatic reason for having and making use of laws particularly concerning child civilians in armed conflict. That is, interventions on behalf of children are sometimes more easily tolerated by parties to a conflict than other types of intervention, precisely because of the special status accorded to children in many countries and societies.[21] Such intervention may also be of benefit to the wider community, for example by providing a degree of protection and economic support to families as a whole.

---

[16] For fuller discussion of this question, *see further*, KUPER, *supra*, note 2, at 6–7.

[17] *See e.g.*, Articles 48 and 51 of Geneva Protocol I, and Article 13 of Geneva Protocol II (1977).

[18] *See e.g.*, Articles 27, 31, 32, 33 and 55 of Geneva Convention IV (1949), Art. 75 of Geneva Protocol I and Article 13 of Geneva Protocol II (1977).

[19] *See e.g.*, Articles 23 and 55 of 1949 Geneva Convention IV, and Articles 69 and 70 of Geneva Protocol I.

[20] *See e.g.*, Articles 24 and 50 of Geneva Convention IV and Article 78 of Geneva Protocol I. The particular vulnerability of children in armed conflict is also exemplified, *inter alia*, by the experiences of Kurdish children who were subject to chemical weapon attacks by Iraqi government forces in 1987–88. The young children were physically less able than adults to escape the effects of these attacks and therefore died in great numbers. P. GALBRAITH, & C. VAN HOLLEN, CHEMICAL WEAPONS USE IN KURDISTAN: IRAQ'S FINAL OFFENSIVE: A STAFF REPORT TO THE SENATE COMMITTEE ON FOREIGN RELATIONS 14–15 (Washington D.C. 1988).

[21] *See e.g.*, the short-term cease-fires, or 'days of tranquillity', that have been successfully established during a number of conflicts, (such as in El Salvador, the Lebanon, the Sudan) allowing, *inter alia*, for children to be immunised, and provided with necessities, see KUPER, *supra*, note 2 at 83.

In the case of child soldiers, the relevant law clearly does have to distinguish children from adults in order to establish the age at which children should be able to participate in armed conflict, and the level of their participation (i.e., 'direct' or 'indirect' participation).[22] Silence on this point would leave the use of child soldiers entirely unregulated, as was the case prior to the 1977 Geneva Protocols, which, surprisingly, are the first international humanitarian law treaties to specifically address the problem of child soldiers. However, there are those who may argue that it was better left unregulated.[23]

The Role of Law

Then, another question arises: is the role of the relevant law to empower children in situations of armed conflict, or simply to protect them?[24] This question goes back to the roots of the children's rights movement, which found on the one side the 'child savers', emphasising the child's need for nurture and protection, and calling for society to provide services for the child, and on the other the 'kiddy libbers', advocating self-determination for children over various aspects of their lives. Given the particular brutality and danger of situations of armed conflict, it is arguable that here the emphasis, particularly as regards young children, must generally be on 'child saving', in the positive sense of facilitating the entitlement of children to protection in situations of extreme danger. However, this does not preclude efforts to empower children in these situations in terms of, for example, encouraging them to participate in decisions being made about them, and facilitating their access to many other entitlements set out in the CRC, such as their right to education and to family life.

Those are some of the initial difficulties that need clarification in a discussion on international law relating to children in armed conflict. There are many other challenging issues, and some of these will be considered below, in particular the special situation of adolescents, the current controversies concerning child soldiers, and certain fundamental questions about the use or usefulness of this body of international law.

Adolescents

An issue that tends to be ignored is the experience of adolescents in situations of armed conflict. A key question here is how to find the balance between the approach of the 'child savers' and that of the 'kiddy libbers'. That is, should international law and policy aim primarily to protect adolescents from the particular

---

[22] 'Direct' participation, as prohibited in Article 77(2) of Geneva Protocol I (1977), refers to children participating in armed conflict as combatants. 'Indirect' participation (not prohibited under that Article, but prohibited under Article 4(3)(c) of Geneva Protocol II), includes activities such as carrying supplies for the armed forces.
[23] *See* the reference to these arguments in BENNETT *supra*, note 15, although he himself does not support such arguments.
[24] For a fuller discussion on this *see* KUPER, *supra*, note 2, at 11–13.

traumas that they may experience, or should it aim to empower them to act on their own behalf? Or can these two aims go hand in hand?

For example, it is undoubtedly the case that adolescents may suffer particular traumas in situations of armed conflict, including the sexual abuse of adolescent girls[25] and forced conscription, or targeting of adolescent boys by parties to disputes because they may be suspected of engaging in military activity.[26] Further, as was pointed out in a 1996 UN study on children in armed conflict (Machel Report),[27] despite the many hazards faced by adolescents in situations of armed conflict, 'adolescents, during or after wars, seldom receive any special attention or assistance. This is a matter of urgent concern.'[28] In that context, it is therefore clear that adolescents in conflict situations do require specific provision to address their particular needs and guard against violations.

However, young people generally, and perhaps adolescents in particular, may also be a source of considerable strength and resilience in conflict situations. Again, the Machel Report points out, 'All cultures recognize adolescence as a highly significant period in which young people learn future roles and incorporate the values and norms of their societies.'[29] Further, 'young people must not be seen as problems or victims, but as key contributors in the planning and implementation of long-term solutions.'[30] This point is confirmed, for example, in some interesting research recently carried out among the Teso people of eastern Uganda, who were engaged in armed conflict for a period of 12 years from 1979–91. The research showed that

> young people, despite the impact of the conflict on their childhoods, despite their suffering, have not emerged from their experiences as passive victims. They show resilience, strong strategies for coping and for effecting the processes of post-war recovery both for themselves and for their wider community. Indeed ... the strategies of young people and their initiatives for post-war recovery are relied upon and are central to everyone in the wider community.[31]

Child Soldiers

As regards international law and policy, it therefore seems appropriate both to place greater emphasis on the special protection required by adolescents, and also on ways of building on their strengths and their potential to contribute to their societies.[32]

---

[25] *See e.g.,* G. MACHEL, REPORT ON THE IMPACT OF ARMED CONFLICT ON CHILDREN, (Machel Report), UN Doc. A/51/306, 26 Aug. 1996, ¶ 91–110.

[26] *Id.,* ¶ 34–62.

[27] *Supra,* note 25.

[28] *Id.,* ¶ 170.

[29] *Id.*

[30] *Id.,* ¶ 242.

[31] *See,* J. de Berry. *Children in Conflict,* Seminar, London, 24 Sept. 1999, ¶ 4, unpublished, copy on file with the author.

[32] *See* recommendations made in Women's Commission for Refugee Women and Children, Untapped Potential: Adolescents Affected By Armed Conflict (2000).

Another problematic area in international law concerning children in armed conflict is the issue of child soldiers. The drafting of the relevant provision of the CRC, Article 38(b) and (c), proved to be among the most contentious in the entire Convention, and almost failed to achieve consensus.[33] That controversy has continued to date, and the arguments will not be rehearsed at length in this chapter. The most controversial issue concerns the age at which children should be eligible to become combatants. Since 1994 efforts have been under way within the UN to draft an Optional Protocol to the 1989 CRC,[34] with the aim of raising the relevant age limit for participation and recruitment from 15 years to a higher age limit. On 21 January 2000, after six years of negotiations, agreement was reached on a draft of this Optional Protocol,[35] which will come into force when it has been ratified by 10 States. Among other things, this document establishes 18 years as the minimum age for conscription and direct participation in hostilities. As regards the voluntary recruitment of children, it requires governments to raise the minimum age beyond the current minimum of 15 years, and to make a binding declaration stating the minimum age they will respect. In relation to non-governmental forces, it goes even further and prohibits *any* recruitment or use in hostilities of children under 18 years, requiring States to criminalise such practices.

Prior to this, the 1998 Statute of the International Criminal Court specifically made it a war crime to conscript or enlist children under 15 years into armed forces, or to use them to participate actively in hostilities.[36] This prohibition applies to both international and non-international conflict, but falls short of a ban on the involvement of those under 18. Moreover, a 1999 ILO Convention, the Convention Concerning the Prohibition and Immediate Elimination of the Worst Forms of Child Labour,[37] had included a prohibition on 'all forms of slavery or practices similar to slavery, such as … forced or compulsory labour, including forced or compulsory recruitment of children for use in armed conflict'.[38] Under this Convention, children are defined as those under 18 years.[39] It therefore incorporates a ban on forced recruitment of children under 18 years, although it fails to comprehensively ban the use of children under 18 years as soldiers, and their voluntary recruitment. However, with agreement having been reached on the draft Optional Protocol, it seems that progress is being made towards a comprehensive ban on the use of child soldiers under the age of 18.

Usefulness of the Relevant Law

Then there is another – and arguably central – problem. That is, can acts done in

---

[33] *See e.g.*, THE UNITED NATIONS CONVENTION ON THE RIGHTS OF THE CHILD: A GUIDE TO THE TRAVAUX PREPARATOIRES, 502–517 (S. Detrick, ed., 1992). *See also* KUPER, *supra*, note 2 at 105–106.

[34] *See e.g.*, UN Doc. E/CN.4/1998/102.

[35] UN Doc. A/54/L.84 (16 May 2000).

[36] *See* UN Doc. A/Conf.183/9* (Note 14 above), Article 8(2)(b)(xxvi) and Article 8(2)(e)(vii).

[37] ILO Convention No. 182.

[38] Article 3(a).

[39] Article 2.

compliance with international law, ostensibly for the protection of children in armed conflict, be counter-productive? Can they actually cause harm to such children? Indeed, there are certain extreme cases where such acts have proved very harmful to some children. For example, the UN intervention in the civil war in Somalia went horribly wrong in a number of ways, although ostensibly motivated at least in part by a desire to provide humanitarian aid to a suffering civilian population of adults and children. Among other things, it led to the notorious killings and torture of some young Somalis by Canadian, Belgian and Italian UN peacekeeping troops.[40] A further example is found in Iraq, where children have been dying in huge numbers largely as a result of the imposition of sanctions by the UN in the aftermath of the 1991 Gulf War.[41] This is a complex situation in that arguably the plight of the Iraqi children has been exacerbated by the intransigence of the Iraqi Government.[42] However, the irony is that children have been so drastically harmed by sanctions imposed to encourage Iraq to comply with international law.

The Machel Report, too, indicates a number of situations where intervention on behalf of children, in accordance with international law, has proved counter-productive. For example, in some conflicts the introduction of armies has resulted in widespread use of young girls as prostitutes for these armies, including peacekeeping forces. Thus, 'in Mozambique, after the signing of the peace treaty in 1992, soldiers of the United Nations Operation in Mozambique (ONUMOZ) recruited girls aged 12 to 18 years into prostitution ... In 6 out of 12 country studies ... prepared for the present report, the arrival of peacekeeping troops has been associated with a rapid rise in child prostitution.'[43] Further, this report points out as regards efforts to rehabilitate children affected by conflict, in accordance with Article 39 of the CRC, that

> experience with war trauma programmes has shown that even those designed with the best intentions can do harm. Some organizations, for example, put a great deal of emphasis on trauma therapy in residential treatment centres ... In-depth clinical interviews intended to awaken the memories and feelings associated with a child's worst moments risk leaving the child in more severe pain and agitation than before, especially if the interviews are conducted without ongoing support or follow-up.[44]

And there can also be harmful consequences from the work of human rights and other journalists and researchers, who may '... encourage children to relate horror stories. Such interviews can open up old wounds and tear down a child's defences.

---

[40] *See e.g.*, THE INDEPENDENT, July 15 1997, at 17. *See further*, THE GUARDIAN WEEKLY, June 7 1998.

[41] *See e.g.*, the Harvard and UNICEF research summarised in KUPER, *supra*, note 2 at 182–183.

[42] Certainly the sanctions do not seem to have affected the affluent life-styles of the Iraqi elite. *See e.g.*, M. O'Kane, *Iraqi Rich Make Mockery of Sanctions*, THE GUARDIAN, Nov. 21 1998.

[43] Machel Report, *supra*, note 25, at ¶ 98.

[44] *Id.*, ¶ 175.

Children who are photographed and identified by name can be exposed to additional problems and harassment'.[45] Thus, there clearly can be negative consequences from well-intentioned acts that are in compliance with international law.

However, the question posed above could be reframed. Instead of asking whether international law, or actions based on it, can be counter-productive, the key question now is: can international law regarding children in armed conflict be *productive*, or effective? Can it improve the treatment of children in armed conflict? Can it, or does it, actually work?

These are complex questions, which can only begin to be addressed in this chapter. The short answer to these questions seems to be 'No'. International law, or actions based on it, do not seem to be of much use to children in situations of armed conflict. It is, to use a cliché, honoured more in the breach than the observance. Accounts in the media record endless examples of children being killed, tortured, maimed, kidnapped, sexually abused, or otherwise maltreated in current armed conflicts. UNICEF statistics in 1995 estimated that, during the decade from 1985 to 1995, child victims of armed conflict included '... 2 million killed; 4 to 5 million disabled; 12 million left homeless; more than 1 million orphaned or separated from their parents; some 10 million psychologically traumatised'.[46]

Indeed, various commentators seem to feel that it is a feature of many modern conflicts (usually internal conflicts involving non-governmental forces) that civilians, including children, are particularly targeted.[47] From this perspective, the conclusion must be that international law has generally failed to protect children in situations of armed conflict or to create a climate in which they are better protected, and this is as true today as it ever was.

A difficulty here, though, is how to assess either: first, the extent to which children are or are not protected in situations or armed conflict or, second, improvements (or deterioration) in this protection. Clearly it is not feasible to conduct reliable empirical research, to stand in the midst of conflicts and count child soldiers and/or child casualties, or to observe the treatment of children generally. Nor could such observation be sufficiently objective and comprehensive to be useful. So, how is it possible to ascertain if the relevant international law has any effect? Perhaps the most that can be done, aside from a painstaking analysis of individual conflicts,[48] is to assess what seems likely to have any impact, and to take note of instances in which progress is made, for example when an army agrees to stop using soldiers under 18 years, or a rebel group agrees to release children it has captured.[49]

As regards initiatives that are likely to strengthen the impact of the relevant law, a number of factors have been identified. For example, there are the obvious strate-

---

[45] *Id.*, ¶ 176.
[46] UNICEF. THE STATE OF THE WORLD'S CHILDREN 13 (1995).
[47] *See e.g.*, GUARDIAN WEEKLY, Oct. 28–Nov. 3 1999 at 3. *See also*, KUPER (1997) 58–59 and 76–77.
[48] This is a difficult and inevitably impressionistic undertaking, as the author discovered. *See* KUPER *supra*, note 2, Chapter 7.
[49] In any event, it is arguable that the relevant law serves its purpose if it enables even one child to escape death or injury in armed conflict situations, and clearly it has succeeded in that respect in many instances (e.g., in creating 'zones of peace', in evacuating children, etc.). *Id.*, at 244.

gies of political pressure, both at the national and international level. There are economic sanctions, the threat of military intervention, and war crimes trials. There is the human rights work being done by many NGOs. Again, it is beyond the scope of this chapter to look at all these mechanisms,[50] but a few can be examined. Before doing so, however, it is necessary to emphasise the obvious point that law in itself cannot achieve much. Its effectiveness depends on the way in which it is implemented, and it is only one component (although an important one) in a complex web of political, economic and social factors that influence the conduct of conflicts.

Starting with war crimes trials, these clearly serve a purpose as part of a quest for justice and in challenging the impunity of perpetrators, including perpetrators of crimes against children.[51] In so doing, such trials may deter others from committing similar violations. Olara Otunnu, the UN Special Representative of the Secretary General for Children and Armed Conflict, had an interesting story to tell at a recent conference in London.[52] He described how, in discussions with one armed faction in Sierra Leone, he realised the combatants seemed very conscious of the various war crimes trials currently under way, and that they, too, might be subject to such trials one day. Although that awareness could not assist the children they had already harmed, it seemed possible that it might limit future violations. Certainly the existence of the Rwanda and Yugoslav tribunals, and the International Criminal Court (when established) does, in itself, challenge impunity, although an effective system also requires other mechanisms, including national tribunals.

In this context, another factor that is currently being prioritised is better training for soldiers and others on the law relating to children in armed conflict. Ideally such training should take place in times of peace, so that military personnel develop the appropriate reflexes to act in compliance with international law when in combat.[53] There are at the moment many initiatives in operation as regards such training, for example, initiatives of Olara Otunnu's office, of UN peacekeeping forces themselves, of Save the Children organisations, and of UNICEF. An important function of such training is precisely to make soldiers and others aware that they could be criminally liable for the ill-treatment of children in armed conflict, that there are limits and rules, and that individual soldiers bear individual responsibility for blatantly unlawful acts. Cynically, it could be argued that self-interest at least might then restrain the commission of such acts against children. Even more cynically, it could be argued that self-interest might only result in soldiers or others making a greater effort to conceal the evidence of their crimes.

---

[50] For more detailed information on such mechanisms in relation to children in armed conflict, see KUPER, *supra*, note 2, particularly Chapter 6.

[51] In fact one writer has argued for a specialised international tribunal to adjudicate on war crimes committed against children. See BENNETT, *supra*, note 15.

[52] Conference organised by Save the Children, *Innocent Victims: Protecting Children in Times of Conflict*, in London, October 1999.

[53] This point has been made by, among others, A. Segal, Legal Adviser to the International Committee of the Red Cross (ICRC) in a paper on, *National Implementation*, at a British Red Cross Conference *The Geneva Conventions of 1949: Do They Protect War Victims Today?*, in London, October 1999, copy on file with the author.

Here, however, it is appropriate to reiterate the question: what is *likely* to encourage compliance? Although training may sometimes backfire, the chances are that proficient training will, in many instances, generally encourage compliance. This point had been made recently by a number of commentators, including in the Machel Report,[54] and by senior military commanders, such as Sir Peter De La Billière (British Forces Commander during the 1991 Gulf War).[55]

Other related proposals to enhance the effectiveness of the relevant law, currently being proposed by Olara Otunnu, among others, include: first, to place children's protection and welfare on the peace agenda, for example in the making of peace accords (as were recently being undertaken in Burundi, Sierra Leone, Sudan and Colombia). Second, in relation to peace operations (e.g., by UN peacekeepers), to recognise and address the needs of children in the planning stages, and to employ senior officers with the specific mandate of ensuring the welfare of children.[56] Such proposals could have a real and practical impact on the treatment of children affected by armed conflict.

Linked to the idea of training for the military and others involved in conflict situations is the concept of training, or dissemination of information on the rules of international humanitarian law to all sectors of society, children and adults. Most States in the world have signed treaties obliging them to disseminate such information (e.g., the Geneva Conventions, the Geneva Protocols, and the CRC)[57] and clearly as more people become broadly familiar with it, the more likely compliance with the law becomes. After all, children who learn the basic principles of international humanitarian law are potentially the soldiers of tomorrow. Further, in complying with their general dissemination obligations, governments may inform non-governmental forces about the rules of humanitarian law.

Another factor that may encourage compliance is the creation of a political climate, both on a national and international level, in which maltreatment of children in armed conflict becomes increasingly unacceptable. Indeed the UN seems to be gathering momentum in this direction, as evidenced by a number of recent initiatives directly or indirectly encouraging better treatment of children in armed conflict. Most relevant is the fact that the Security Council has recently passed various resolutions specifically on the protection of children in situations of armed conflict.[58] Also, the UN Secretary General has issued a bulletin stating

---

[54] Machel Report, *supra*, note 25, ¶ 110(b).
[55] From a paper delivered at the British Red Cross Conferences, *supra*, note 53, *Making the Geneva Conventions More Effective*, copy on file with the author.
[56] *See* O. Otunnu, Special Representative on Children and Armed Conflict, Statement in the Security Council on the Occasion of Open Debate on Children and Armed Conflict, Aug. 1999, New York.
[57] *See e.g.,* Geneva Convention IV (1949), Article 144, Geneva Protocol I (1977) Article 83, and CRC (1989) Article 42.
[58] *See* UN Doc. S/RES/1261 (1999). This wide-ranging resolution refers, *inter alia*, to the need for strict compliance with international law obligations regarding children in armed conflict; to the draft Optional Protocol regarding child soldiers; to the importance of protecting children in armed conflict specifically from sexual abuse, and to the work of UNICEF, Otunnu, humanitarian agencies and others working for such children.

that all UN forces should act in accordance with international humanitarian law.[59] In addition, he has recently presented a report to the Security Council on the protection of civilians in armed conflict, and the Security Council has, partly in response to that report, passed a resolution on civilian protection.[60]

In this context, the role of the Committee on the Rights of the Child should also be noted, since this Committee can exert some influence on behalf of children in armed conflict, both within the UN and more widely.[61] Thus, *inter alia*, the Committee can and does comment on State practice, including in relation to children in situations of armed conflict, when conducting its regular reviews of the country reports of States Parties to the CRC (and all countries in the world are now party to this Convention, except the US and Somalia).[62] The Committee also has other pertinent functions, such as holding days of discussion on specific topics, and, via the General Assembly, requesting the Secretary General to undertake studies on particular issues regarding the rights of children. Indeed, it was the use of these latter mechanisms that led to the Machel Report, which, in turn, resulted in the creation of the office of the UN Special Representative of the Secretary General for Children and Armed Conflict (Olara Otunnu).[63]

In addition to the mechanisms already outlined, one of Otunnu's more interesting strategies for encouraging compliance with the relevant law is to try and reinforce traditional value systems. According to him, 'Values matter, even in times of war. In most societies distinctions between acceptable and unacceptable practices were maintained, with taboos ... proscribing the targeting of civilian populations, especially women and children.'[64] He favours an 'ethical renewal', a community-based process that can be integrated with international norms. This seems a valuable approach, even if it is arguable that in some societies traditional value systems are not in accordance with principles of international humanitarian law.

INITIATIVES IMPLEMENTING THE LAW

The discussion in this chapter thus far has considered certain existing or proposed mechanisms that are likely to enhance the effectiveness of international legal principles regarding children in armed conflict. In continuing an assessment of the usefulness or otherwise of this body of law, it is now important to look to instances where the law has already been put into practice. There are many such examples,

---

[59] *See, Observance by United Nations Forces of International Humanitarian Law,* SECRETARY GENERAL'S BULLETIN UN Doc. ST/SGB/1999/13.

[60] UN Doc. S/1999/957, 8 September and UN Doc.S/RES/1265, 1999 respectively. This resolution is only one of many passed over the years by the UN relating to civilian protection in situations of armed conflict. *See e.g.,* UN GA Res. 2444(XXIII), UN GA Res. 2597(XXIV) and UN GA Res. 2675(XXV)).

[61] For more detail on the workings of this Committee in relation to children in armed conflict, see KUPER *supra*, note 2 at 130–138.

[62] UN Doc. ST/HR/4.Rev.16 (1998).

[63] *See* KUPER, *supra*, note 2 at 132–135.

[64] *See further*, Statement in the Security Council. (Aug. 1999, New York). *Supra*, note 56.

one of which is the creation of 'zones of peace'. Here, typically, combatants agree to a cease-fire during which children are immunised and supplies delivered, as has happened for example in El Salvador, the Lebanon and the Sudan.[65] In the 1991 Gulf War, too, UNICEF and the WHO managed to bring into Iraq one shipment of basic medical and health supplies.[66] Another example can be found in the results of recent visits by Olara Otunnu to various conflict areas. For instance, on a visit to Sierra Leone in August/September 1999, Otunnu negotiated an agreement with the leadership of one of the armed factions (the RUF) that they would allow a humanitarian team to visit zones under their control, as a first step to releasing children held behind their lines. He also obtained a commitment by two armed factions (the RUF and the CDF) and the Government of Sierra Leone not to recruit children under 18.[67] He has had similar discussions elsewhere, for example in Colombia.[68] It seems doutful that these agreements will be honoured in practice, but they do, at least, indicate that the issue of the treatment of children is on the agenda.

CONCLUSION

The treatment of children in situations of armed conflict remains a continuing problem, involving as it does the dilemma of trying to encourage their humane treatment in circumstances where so many of the normal rules and taboos of society are flouted, and issues of life and death are at stake. The only realistic way to ensure protection of children in conflict situations is to eliminate armed conflict itself. While the achievement of world peace would clearly be the ideal solution,[69] it seems highly improbable in the foreseeable future.[70] It is therefore necessary to confront the unpalatable task of attempting to humanise arguably the most destructive of all human activities, and of gradually raising standards so that, at least, fewer children are harmed in situations of armed conflict.

---

[65] *Supra*, note 21.
[66] *See e.g.*, UN Doc. S/22328, 4 Mar. 1991; *see also*, KUPER, *supra* note 2 at 178 and 207.
[67] Otunnu. Statement in the Security Council. *supra*, note 56; *see also* O. OTUNNU, MISSION REPORT ON VISIT TO SIERRA LEONE AND GUINEA BY THE SPECIAL REPRESENTATIVE OF THE SECRETARY GENERAL FOR CHILDREN AND ARMED CONFLICT (1999).
[68] *Special Representative of the Secretary General for Children and Armed Conflict Concludes Humanitarian Mission to Colombia*. Press Release, United Nations, New York, June 8 1999).
[69] Indeed, discussions on world peace have recently been the focus of the 1999 Hague Peace Conference. See HAGUE AGENDA FOR PEACE AND JUSTICE FOR THE 21ST CENTURY, Conference Edition (1999).
[70] One interesting possibility here, however, is that a shift towards more technologically-driven armed conflicts, or 'cyberwars', may succeed, where international law and diplomacy have failed, in drastically reducing the numbers of civilians harmed in situations of armed conflict. *See* GUARDIAN WEEKLY. Nov. 11–17 1999, at 8.

Peter Newell

8. ENDING CORPORAL PUNISHMENT
OF CHILDREN

INTRODUCTION

Corporal punishment is the issue that falls off adult agendas, even the agendas of human rights and children's rights advocates. In the past decade, however, both within States and on an international level, legal reform to give children the same protection from assault as adults is creeping onto and up political agendas. This is primarily because of the growing movement, in the context of the Convention on the Rights of the Child (CRC), to accept that children are holders of human rights.[1]

Respect for human dignity, the right to physical integrity and equal protection under the law, are three fundamental human rights principles, of supposedly universal application enshrined in the Universal Declaration of Human Rights (1948) and the two International Covenants (1966).[2]

Yet corporal punishment – smacking, slapping, beating, flogging – is a daily, sometimes hourly, occurrence in the lives of children all over the world, most often at the hands of those they should be able to trust: their parents, carers and teachers. In every case, this deliberate violence to children is a breach of their fundamental human rights. Over the centuries, adults in most countries have found it easy to overlook the reality of their treatment of children or to justify it as 'for their own good'. Corporal punishment always violates the child's physical integrity, it demonstrates disrespect for his or her human dignity and it undermines self-esteem. Furthermore, the existence of special defences for violent punishment of children – 'reasonable chastisement' or 'lawful correction' – in otherwise universally applicable laws on assault, deliberately removes the equal protection under the law which is also guaranteed by the human rights instruments. In addition, corporal punishment often reaches the level of 'cruel, inhuman or degrading' punishment, and in a significant number of cases it is the direct cause of death.

The adult invention of sordid legal concepts like 'reasonable chastisement' arises from the traditional view of children as the property of their parents. Traditional attitudes to slaves, servants and women were also reflected, only a century or two ago, in the 'rights' of their masters and husbands to beat them – and the attitudes

---

[1]   *See* United Nations Convention on the Rights of the Child UN Doc. A/44/25 (1989), reprinted in 28 I.L.M. 1457 (1989). *See generally* D. McGoldrick *The United Nations Convention on the Rights of the Child*, 5 INT'L J. L. & FAM. 132 (1992).
[2]   Universal Declaration on Human Rights, adopted December 10 1948 G.A. Res 217A (III) 3 U.N. GAOR (Resolutions, part 1) UN Doc.A/810 (1948); International Covenant on Civil and Political Rights, opened for signature December 16 1966m G.A.Res 2200 (XXI)m 21 U.N. GAOR Supp. (No. 16) UN Doc.A/6313 (1976). International Covenant on Economic, Social and Cultural Rights, 993 UNTS 3.

Deirdre Fottrell (ed.), Revisiting Children's Rights, 115–126
© 2000 *Kluwer Law International. Printed in Great Britain.*

behind these laws are still entrenched in many societies today. Challenging corporal punishment of children is the last stage in a lengthy process. Children have had to wait until last to be given equal legal protection from deliberate assaults, a protection which adults take for granted. It is surely extraordinary that children, whose developmental state and small size is acknowledged to make them particularly vulnerable to physical and psychological injury, should be the ones singled out for less protection from assaults on their fragile bodies, minds and dignity.

For women, challenging legal and social acceptance of violence, in particular the daily experience of routine violence in their homes, has been a fundamental part of the struggle for equal status. So it is with children: there is no more telling symbol of their low status as less than people than adults' continuing assumption that they have a 'right', even a duty, to hit children.

Remarkably, in the United Kingdom and other countries, corporal punishment still manages to drop off the political agenda when family violence is debated. The United Kingdom Government is happy to embrace what it sees as the consensus issue of ending violence between adult family members. Ministers launch new, well-resourced programmes and materials. 'Zero tolerance' has been adopted as a central theme. But children seem to be largely outsiders to this focus on violence in the family. Recently, there has been growing concern about the effect that witnessing violence between adults in the family has on children. But the most common form of family violence, far more common now in our society than violence between adult partners, is direct violence by adult family members to children: the slapping and smacking that starts with babies – three quarters of a large sample of English mothers in recent Government-commissioned research admitted to smacking their babies before the age of one; 97 per cent of four year olds had been hit, many of them more than once a week and a quarter of the seven year olds had been hit with an implement.[3] Thus, when corporal punishment of children is raised, policies of zero tolerance suddenly become deeply controversial.

But the visibility of family violence now, and the general acceptance of the priority of challenging it should present an opportunity to make quick progress: if everyone involved in promoting an end to family violence took a logical decision to extend the concept of zero tolerance to cover children and pursued the policy and legal implications of doing so we would quickly get the reforms which children and society so urgently need.

While it is intolerable that children should have had to wait until last for equal protection, it is understandable, because of the deeply personal nature of the issue. Most people were hit as children; most parents have hit their children. We like to think well of our parents, and of our parenting. But this can get in the way of compassionate and logical consideration of the arguments. Frankly, it is an issue which sees adults at their most hypocritical. We have invented a whole vocabulary of

---

[3] *See further* M.A. Smith, *A Community Study of Physical Violence to Children in the Home and Associated Variables*, a poster presented at International Society for the Prevention of Child Abuse and Neglect, European Conference on Child Abuse and Neglect, Oslo, May 1995, copy on file with the author.

words and phrases to make us feel more comfortable about hitting children –
smacking, spanking, tapping, a good hiding, six of the best...

Returning to the CRC, the particular purpose of the Convention is to assert that
children, too, are holders of human rights – civil, political, economic, social and
cultural. Most importantly, the CRC is the first international human rights instrument to provide explictly for the protection of children from violence in all its
forms. Article 19 requires States to take 'all appropriate legislative, administrative,
social and educational measures to protect the child from all forms of physical or
mental violence, injury or abuse, neglect or negligent treatment, maltreatment or
exploitation, including sexual abuse, while in the care of parent(s), legal guardian(s)
or any other person who has the care of the child'.[4]

Other provisions of the CRC reinforce the child's right to physical integrity and
protection of his or her human dignity. The Preamble recognises the 'inherent
dignity and ... equal and inalienable rights of all members of the human family'. It
also affirms that precisely because of their 'physical and mental immaturity',
children need 'special safeguards and care, including appropriate legal protection'.
Article 37 requires protection from 'torture or other cruel, inhuman or degrading
treatment or punishment'.

The Committee on the Rights of the Child, the body charged with supervising the
Convention, has consistently stated that legal and social acceptance of corporal
punishment of children, whether in their homes or in institutions, is not compatible
with the Convention. The Committee has recommended prohibition of all corporal
punishment, including in the family.[5] It has also suggested that governments should
support public education to ensure parents, teachers and other carers understand
the negative effects of corporal punishment and to encourage the development of
positive, non-violent child-rearing and educational practices.

In 1994, in a concluding statement to the General Discussion on Children's
Rights in the Family, organised as the Committee's contribution to the International Year of the Family, it stated

> ...As for corporal punishment, few countries have clear laws on this ques-
> tion. Certain States have tried to distinguish between the correction of
> children and excessive violence. In reality the dividing line between the two is
> artificial. It is very easy to pass from one stage to the other. It is also a
> question of principle. If it is not permissible to beat an adult, why should
> it be permissible to do so to a child? One of the contributions of the
> Convention is to call attention to the contradictions in our attitudes and cul-
> tures.[6]

---

[4] *See* United Nations Convention on the Rights of the Child, UN G.A. Res 44/25.
[5] *See* R. HODGKIN AND P. NEWELL, IMPLEMENTATION HANDBOOK FOR THE CON-
VENTION ON THE RIGHTS OF THE CHILD, 237–255 (1998).
[6] Committee on the Rights of the Child Official Reports, UN Doc.CRC/C/SR 176, October 10 1994, ¶
46; These reports are available on the Web-site of the United Nations High Commissioner for
Human Rights: < www.unhchr.ch >. On the Committee *see generally* HODGKIN & NEWELL,
supra, note 5.

The Committee has often criticised attempts to draw a line between acceptable and unacceptable forms of corporal punishment, as it did when it examined the initial report from the United Kingdom in 1995:

> ... the Committee is worried about the national legal provisions dealing with reasonable chastisement within the family. The imprecise nature of the expression of reasonable chastisement as contained in these legal provisions may pave the way for it to be interpreted in a subjective and arbitrary manner. Thus, the Committee is concerned that legislative and other measures relating to the physical integrity of children do not appear to be compatible with the provisions and principles of the Convention, including those of its Articles 3, 19 and 37. The Committee is equally concerned that privately funded and managed schools are still permitted to administer corporal punishment to children in attendance there which does not appear to be compatible with the provisions of the Convention, including those of its Article 28, paragraph 2.

The Committee went on to propose

> ... that physical punishment of children in families be prohibited in the light of the provisions set out in Articles 3 and 19 of the Convention. In connection with the child's right to physical integrity, as recognised by the Convention, namely in its Articles 19, 28, 29 and 37, and in the light of the best interests of the child, the Committee suggests that the State Party consider the possibility of undertaking additional education campaigns. Such measures would help to change societal attitudes towards the use of physical punishment in the family and foster the acceptance of the legal prohibition of the physical punishment of children.[7]

The 191 States which have ratified the CRC have to report to the Committee, first after two years and then every five years. The Committee's Guidelines for Periodic Reports, adopted in October 1996, asks

> whether legislation (criminal and/or family law) includes a prohibition of all forms of physical and mental violence, including corporal punishment, deliberate humiliation, injury, abuse, neglect or exploitation, *inter alia* within the family, in foster and other forms of care, and in public or private institutions, such as penal institutions and schools.[8]

---

[7] *See* Committee on the Rights of the Child, concluding observations on the initial report of the United Kingdom, CRC/C/15/Add. 34, February 15 1995, ¶ 16, 31. *See further*, U. Kilkelly *The UN Committee on the Rights of the Child: An Evaluation in the Light of Recent UK Experience*, 105 CH & FAM. L.Q. (1996).

[8] COMMITTEE ON THE RIGHTS OF THE CHILD, GENERAL GUIDELINES REGARDING THE FORM AND CONTENTS OF PERIODIC REPORTS TO BE SUBMITTED UNDER ARTICLE 44, PARAGRAPH 1(B) OF THE CONVENTION ON THE RIGHTS OF THE CHILD, UN Doc. CRC/C/58, October 11 1996.

Another human rights treaty body, the Committee on the Elimination of Discrimination against Women charged with the implementation of the Convention on the Elimination of All Forms of Discrimination against Women (1979)[9] has been understandably preoccupied with domestic violence to women. Similarly, the Committee on the Rights of the Child is now leading the challenge to violence to children. When representatives of these two Committees met in 1998 in Geneva to discuss action against family violence, they agreed that 'zero tolerance' is the only acceptable target. As with violence to women, the problem was recognised to be rooted in traditional attitudes and culture, sometimes underpinned by religion. But a practice which violates basic human rights cannot be said to be owned by any culture, nor dictated by any religion.

The imperative for prohibiting all corporal punishment of children is one of human rights. It has always been wrong to hit children, just as wrong as to hit adults. As the extent of legalised violence to children in their homes (and also in schools and other institutions) has become more visible, so we have begun to learn about the short- and longer-term dangers of hitting them, accumulating other compelling arguments for eliminating the practice, beyond the human rights imperative. First, there is the immediate danger of physical injury from even 'gentle' forms, because most corporal punishment is directed at very young, very small children, including babies. There is always the risk of escalation too. Then there are the longer-term effects: corporal punishment and other humiliating forms of discipline are now identified as a highly significant factor in the development of violent attitudes and actions, both in childhood and later life. Thus, ending corporal punishment must be seen as a key strategy for reducing violence to women in the family too; also for reducing school bullying and generally as a strategy for the prevention of all forms of interpersonal violence.

There are volumes of research literature on the causes of violence and on the effects of corporal punishment. Identifying cause and effect in this extremely complex area of child-rearing and family relationships is not easy. But there is no question whatsoever that – apart from the fairly obvious fact that in the very short term physical punishment may stop an undesired behaviour – the overwhelming direction of the evidence points towards bad, unwanted effects, and certainly no positive long-term effects whatsoever.[10]

In advocating for an end to any social or legal acceptance of corporal punishment, we have to be careful not to put too much emphasis on this sort of research; it can become an unproductive diversion. The fact is that even if we had excellent researchers proving that corporal punishment 'worked', it would in no way reduce the fundamental human rights case against it (can you imagine, these days, a serious research debate about the pros and cons of slapping women, or cats or dogs?).

---

[9] Convention on the Elimination of All Forms of Discrimination against Women, adopted December 18 1979, G.A. Res 34/180 (1979) 1249 UNTS 13.

[10] For a brief review of research references *see* GULBENKIAN FOUNDATION, REPORT OF THE COMMISSION ON CHILDREN AND VIOLENCE, CHILDREN AND VIOLENCE, (1995); *see also* M.A. STRAUS, BEATING THE DEVIL OUT OF THEM; CORPORAL PUNISHMENT IN AMERICAN FAMILIES, (1994).

The most useful forms of research to help speed the end of corporal punishment are studies of prevalence – detailed interview research, preferably asking children as well as their parents. And it was interesting – if obvious – to find from recent United Kingdom research that if you ask each parent in two-parent families about prevalence you get a result which roughly doubles the amount of physical punishment the child is receiving.[11]

Another unusual and valuable piece of research carried out recently in the United Kingdom interviewed 75 five-to-seven-year-old children about their perspective on smacking. These young children define smacking as hitting; most of them described a smack as a hard or very hard hit. They said 'smacking hurts ... it hurts and makes you feel sad. It hurts your feelings inside'. Children responded negatively to being smacked, that adults regret smacking and that smacking was 'wrong'. The introduction to the study states: 'For too long, one voice has been missing in the debate about children and physical punishment – the voice of children themselves, and particularly younger children'.[12]

INTERNATIONAL PROGRESS TOWARDS ENDING CORPORAL PUNISHMENT

Where corporal punishment is most visible – in penal systems and schools and so-called caring institutions – it is under serious threat now in all continents. In the home, where children are hit most often, it has only been challenged seriously in a tiny handful of countries. But the context of the CRC and the clear recommendations of the Committee on the Rights of the Child are leading to accelerating reform across the world.

Only eight countries, all in Europe, have explicitly banned all corporal punishment of children.[13] In addition, Italy's and most recently Israel's Supreme Court have outlawed it, but this is not yet reflected in statute.[14] Sweden was the first State to ban all corporal punishment, 21 years ago. When the Swedish law was coming into force in 1979, the International Year of the Child, a Ministry of Justice official explained

> By the prohibition of physical punishment, the legislator wanted to show that a child is an independent individual who can demand full respect for his or her person, and who should thus have the same protection against physical punishment or violence as we adults see as being totally natural for ourselves.[15]

---

[11] *See generally* G. Nobes and M.A. Smith, *Physical Punishment of Children in Two-Parent Families*, 2 CLINICAL CHILD PSYCHOLOGY AND PSYCHIATRY, 271–281 (1997).

[12] *See* C. WILLOW AND T. HYDER, IT HURTS YOU INSIDE – CHILDREN TALKING ABOUT SMACKING, (1998).

[13] These are: Austria, Croatia, Cyprus, Denmark, Finland, Latvia, Norway and Sweden. Germany joined them in July 2000. For an exhaustive account of moves towards prohibiting corporal punishment of children, see S.H. Bitensky, *Spare the rod, Embrace our humanity: Towards a new legal regime prohibiting corporal punishment of children*, 31 MICH. J.L. REFORM 353 (1998).

[14] Cambria, Cass., sez.v, 18 Marzo 1996 [Supreme Court of Cassation, Rome, 6th Penal Section, March 18 1996] Foro IT. II 1996, 407 (Italy); Israel Supreme Court, January 2000.

[15] For an account of the prohibition of physical punishment in Sweden, *see further* P. NEWELL, CHILDREN ARE PEOPLE TOO: THE CASE AGAINST PHYSICAL PUNISHMENT (1989).

The legal provision forms part of Sweden's family (civil) law: ... 'Children are enti-tled to care, security and a good upbringing. Children are to be treated with respect for their person and individuality and may not be subjected to corporal punishment or any other humiliating treatment.'[16] But its purpose is to emphasise beyond doubt that the criminal code on assault covers physical punishment, although trivial offences remain unpunished just as trivial assaults between adults are not prosecutable.

The purpose of criminalising all corporal punishment is not to prosecute and punish more parents.[17] Doing so satisfies human rights by giving children equal protection of their physical integrity and human dignity. It gives a clear message that hitting children is wrong – at least as wrong as hitting anyone else. Thus it provides a consistent basis for child protection and for public education promoting positive forms of discipline. As attitudes change, so the need for prosecution and for formal interventions into families to protect children will diminish.

The goals of the ban were to alter public attitudes towards corporal punishment, establish a clear framework for parent education and support, and to facilitate earlier and less intrusive intervention in child protection cases. A detailed review of research into the effects of the ban by Canadian Professor Joan Durrant shows that public support for corporal punishment has declined markedly. Whereas in 1965 a majority of Swedes were supportive of corporal punishment, the most recent survey found only six per cent of under-35-year-olds supporting the use of even the mildest forms. Practice as well as attitudes had changed; of those whose childhood occurred shortly after the ban, only three per cent report harsh slaps from their parents, and only one per cent report being hit with an implement (contrast the position in the United Kingdom and other countries where a quarter or more of young children were hit with implements). Child abuse mortality rates are extremely low in Sweden; from 1976 to 1990, no child died as a result of abuse.

As in every State, increased sensitivity to child abuse over the last three decades has led to an increase in reporting of assaults, but there has been a declining trend in prosecutions of parents, and a substantial reduction in compulsory social work interventions and in numbers of children taken into care. The proportions of young people who consume alcohol, experiment with drugs and commit suicide have also all declined. The review concludes

While drawing a direct causal link between the corporal punishment ban and any of these social trends would be overly simplistic, the evidence presented here indicates that the ban has not had negative effects. In terms of its original goals of modifying public attitudes toward corporal punishment and facilitat-ing early identification and supportive intervention, it has certainly been suc-cessful.[18]

---

[16] Swedish Children and Parents Code, Chapter 6, Section 1 (as amended in 1983).
[17] *See further* P. Newell, *Ending Corporal Punishment of Children* in THE HANDBOOK OF CHIL-DREN'S RIGHTS, 214 (B. Franklin, ed. 1995).
[18] *See* J.E. DURRANT, THE STATUS OF SWEDISH CHILDREN AND YOUTH SINCE THE PASSAGE OF THE 1979 CORPORAL PUNISHMENT BAN (1999).

In Finland, the ban on physical punishment formed part of a comprehensive reform of children's law. The Child Custody and Right of Access Act 1983 begins with a statement of positive principles of care for children, and continues

> A child shall be brought up in the spirit of understanding, security and love. He shall not be subdued, corporally punished or otherwise humiliated. His growth towards independence, responsibility and adulthood shall be encouraged, supported and assisted.[19]

Again, the purpose of this reform in family law is to put beyond doubt that the criminal law applies equally to assaults committed against children by parents and other carers. Norway and Austria implemented similar reforms in the late 1980s.[20] In 1997, the Danish Parliament approved an amendment to the Parental Custody and Care Act which reads: 'A child has the right to care and security. He or she shall be treated with respect as an individual and may not be subjected to corporal punishment or other degrading treatment'. In 1986, the Danish Parliament had amended its civil law to state that 'parental custody implies the obligation to protect the child against physical and psychological violence and against other harmful treatment'. But this was interpreted as allowing milder forms of corporal punishment, and research found that they were still prevalent; hence the need for further and more explicit reform.[21]

Cyprus, Croatia and Latvia have also passed laws that prohibit all corporal punishment, and several other European countries, including Spain and Ireland have proposals to do so under active consideration.[22] In Belgium, the recent National Commission against Sexual Exploitation of Children proposed that an article should be added to the Constitution recognising the right of every human being to physical, psychological and sexual integrity.[23] Where human rights principles are enforceable through regional or domestic courts, there has been recent progress in challenging corporal punishment, which may speed up the process of banning it in some regions and ultimately world-wide. The Supreme Court of Namibia in 1991 ruled that the constitutional guarantee of human dignity precluded the possibility of corporal punishment for both adult and juvenile offenders, as well as the use of corporal punishment in schools.[23] Namibia's initial report to the Committee on the Rights of the Child stated that the Ministry of Education

> has been advocating a new approach to discipline embodied in the concept 'Discipline from within'. In contrast to the emphasis on physical punishment in

---

[19] Child Custody and Right of Access Act, Chapter 1, Section 1, Subsection 3.
[20] Danish Act to Amend the Act on Parental Custody and Conviviality no. 387, Section 1.
[21] *Supra* note 15.
[22] In July 2000 the German Bundestag passed a law similar to Sweden's. *Supra* note 13.
[23] Ex Parte Attorney-General: In re Corporal Punishment by the Organs of the State 1991 NR 178 SC, also reported (3) SA 76 (NmS).

the schools in the colonial era, this new approach emphasises self-discipline based on the co-operative effort of students, teachers and parents.[24]

The new Constitutional Court of South Africa declared corporal punishment of juvenile offenders unconstitutional in 1995, and the Government went on to ban it and all school corporal punishment in 1996.[25] Since then, the Government has also banned corporal punishment in all other institutions and in foster care. The Supreme Court in Rome, Italy, in a landmark 1996 judgement quoted the CRC and stated

> the use of violence for educational purposes can no longer be considered lawful. There are two reasons for this: the first is the overriding importance that the legal system attributes to protecting the dignity of the individual. This includes minors, who now hold rights and are no longer simply objects to be protected by their parents, or, worse still, objects at the disposal of their parents. The second reason is that, as an educational aim, the harmonious development of a child's personality, which ensures that he/she embraces the values of peace, tolerance and co-existence, cannot be achieved by using violent means which contradict these goals.[26]

Similarly, in January 2000, Israel's Supreme Court declared all corporal punishment to be unlawful. One of the three judges declared

> If we allow 'light' violence, it might deteriorate into very serious violence. We must not endanger the physical and mental well-being of a minor with any type of corporal punishment. A truth which is worthy must be clear and unequivocal and the message is that corporal punishment is not allowed.[27]

The Director of Israel's National Council for the Child declared that the ruling established a precedent and 'finally recognised the right of children not to be exposed to violence of any kind, even when those who use violence make excuses for it, saying it is 'educational' or 'punitive'.[28] The European Court of Human Rights unanimously found in 1998 that corporal punishment of a young English boy by his stepfather constituted degrading punishment in breach of Article 3 of the European Convention on Human Rights (ECHR), and that current United Kingdom law, which allows 'reasonable chastisement', failed to provide adequate

---

[24] *See* the initial report of Namibia, UN Doc.CRC/C/3/Add.12, 1993, ¶ 79.

[25] S *v* Williams CCT/20/94; 1995 (3) SA 632 (CC). *See also S v Williams and others* 12 S.A.J. HUM. RTS. *See further* R. Kneightly *Torture and Cruel, Inhuman and Degrading Treatment or Punishment in the UN Convention Against Torture and Other Instruments of International Law: Recent Developments in South Africa,* 11 S.A.J. HUM. RTS. 379–400 (1995) ; *see also* J. Sloth Nielsen and B. van Heerden, *Proposed Amendments to the Child Care Act and Regulations in the Context of Constitutional and International Law: Developments in South Africa,* 12 S.A.J. HUM RTS. 247–263 (1996).

[26] Cambria, Supreme Court of Cassation, Rome, Italy, 6th Penal Section, 18 March 1996.

[27] *Supra* note 14.

[28] Dan Izenberg, JERUSALEM POST, Jan. 26 2000.

protection.[29] The case involved repeated caning of the boy by his stepfather between the ages of five and eight. Having found a breach of Article 3, the Court followed its usual practice of not going on to review possible breaches of other articles. Article 8 of the ECHR has been taken as guaranteeing the right to physical integrity: the punishment plainly constituted a serious invasion of the boy's physical integrity. Article 14 requires that rights in the ECHR be guaranteed to all persons without discrimination. The lack of legal protection of children from corporal punishment is discriminatory, given that such treatment of an adult is plainly unlawful. Had the Court reviewed these provisions too it seems clear that the judgement would have required action to ban all corporal punishment.

The UK Government was ordered to pay the boy £10,000 compensation and his legal costs. It accepted that the law must be changed to give children better protection and promised a consultation on how to change the law. The immediate response of one Department of Health Minister was to condemn the beating of the boy as cruel, inhuman and having no place in a civilised society, but he then distinguished between that treatment and what he called 'smacking'. He stated that 'the overwhelming majority of parents know the difference between smacking and beating. They know how to ensure good social behaviour in a loving and caring way. We respect that right...'[30]

In response to the unique opportunity to make real progress following the European Court judgment in *A v UK*, the major United Kingdom children's organisations, including the National Society for the Prevention of Cruelty to Children (NSPCC), Barnardo's and Save the Children, formed a new alliance titled 'Children are unbeatable!'. The alliance seeks a clear, Swedish-style ban in the United Kingdom, giving children the same protection as adults under the law on assault, by removing the defence of 'reasonable chastisement' altogether. By the end of 1999 the alliance included over 260 organisations and about the same number of prominent individuals – eminent professionals, celebrities and journalists.[31] The Government's consultation document was issued in January 2000 (for England – there will be separate consultations for Northern Ireland, Scotland and Wales). It includes questions only on narrow options for slightly limiting the defence of 'reasonable chastisement'. In a few years, the questions – emanating from a Department of 'Health' – will surely be viewed with some embarrassment; one asks whether punishment can ever be reasonable if it 'causes' or risks causing injury to a child's head, including brain, eyes and ears.[32]

Following the consultation, when legislation is eventually put before Parliament, it is a constitutional tradition that MPs will be allowed a conscience vote. It is to be hoped that whatever position the Government of the day takes, MPs will take note

---

[29] *See* Application No. 25599/94 A *v* UK, Eur. Ct. H.R. September 23 1998.
[30] *See* Statement by the Rt Honourable Paul Boateng, MP, Parliamentary Under-Secretary of State for Health, Department of Health Press Release (98/397) (September 23 1998).
[31] The Secretariat of the 'Children are unbeatable!' Alliance can be contacted at 77 Holloway Road, London N7 8JZ.
[32] *See* DEPARTMENT OF HEALTH, PROTECTING CHILDREN, SUPPORTING PARENTS: A CONSULTATION DOCUMENT ON THE PHYSICAL PUNISHMENT OF CHILDREN, (2000).

of fundamental human rights principles and the near professional consensus against corporal punishment of children, and will perceive that this is an issue on which they need to lead rather than follow public opinion, as they have had to on such other key social issues as ending capital punishment and homosexual law reform. In Canada, parents' and teachers' use of corporal punishment is currently being tested against all the fundamental human rights principles. A challenge under the Canadian Charter of Human Rights seeks to have section 43 of the Criminal Code, which allows the use of 'reasonable force' to correct children, declared unlawful. The Charter includes the principle of equality of protection under the law. In defending the case, the Canadian Government has to prove some demonstrable justification for breaching this and other constitutional principles. The Government has accepted that corporal punishment of children is harmful. The Ministry of Health, for example, has widely distributed material promoting positive, non-violent discipline and listing the dangers of spanking children. Nevertheless, the Government has so far mounted strong opposition to the Charter challenge, presumably because it perceives a ban on spanking to be unpopular with voters.[33] In doing so, the Canadian Government is also resisting the clear recommendation of the Committee on the Rights of the Child, which in its concluding observations on Canada's report suggested that the Government 'examine the possibility of reviewing the penal legislation allowing corporal punishment of children by parents, in schools and in institutions where children may be placed'. The Committee recommended that the physical punishment of children by parents or carers be prohibited and suggested that the Government consider the possibility of introducing new legislation and follow-up mechanisms to prevent violence within the family. These measures could be accompanied by educational campaigns aimed at 'changing attitudes in society on the use of physical punishment in the family and fostering the acceptance of its legal prohibition'.[34]

CONCLUSION

Children and their advocates need to be impatient: giving children protection of their fundamental human rights is long overdue. They also need to be aware of the threats to progress. They mostly come from what now appears to be a global network of fundamentalist Christians and extreme right-wing family campaigners who peddle absurd misconceptions about the CRC, which is in no sense whatsoever an anti-family document. In the United Kingdom, there have been recent signs that the people engaged in these campaigns have begun to retreat, seeing the inevitability of reform.

Of course law reform without public education will not achieve much, and public education will need to continue for some time after a law is passed. Sweden recently launched a new public education campaign to ensure that all sectors of the commu-

---

[33] *See* Ontario Court of Justice (General Division), Canadian Foundation for Children, Youth and the Law and the Attorney General in Right of Canada, judgment pending (February 2000).

[34] Committee on the Rights of the Child, concluding observations on the initial report of Canada, UN Doc.CRC/C/15/Add.37 (1995).

Carolyn Hamilton and Marcus Roberts

9. STATE RESPONSIBILITY AND PARENTAL RESPONSIBILITY: NEW LABOUR AND THE IMPLEMENTATION OF THE UNITED NATIONS CONVENTION ON THE RIGHTS OF THE CHILD IN THE UNITED KINGDOM

INTRODUCTION

November 1999 marked the 10th anniversary of the UN Convention on the Rights of the Child. In the same year the UK submitted its second report to the UN Committee as required under Article 44.[1] The UK ratified the CRC at the end of 1991 and the ratification came into effect in early 1992. The CRC is not incorporated into UK law, but it has, nevertheless, had considerable impact on the development of law, policy and practice, altering public and political attitudes to children in the UK. However, implementation of the Convention has been variable and the UK is not a meticulous observer of children's rights.

In the concluding observations on the initial report in 1995, the Committee on the Rights of the Child was highly critical of the UK's implementation of the Convention across a spectrum of rights.[2] In particular, the Committee expressed concern about the adequacy of measures to implement the economic, social and cultural rights of children. The principle of the best interests of the child did not, according to the Committee, appear to be reflected in legislation on health, education and social security. The Committee noted the high number of children living in poverty; the high rates of divorce, single parenthood and teenage pregnancy; and the growing number of homeless young people. In the opinion of the Committee, such phenomena raised questions about the adequacy of benefits and the availability and effectiveness of parenting education. It recommended additional efforts to combat poverty and inequality.

A further major area of concern for the Committee related to the administration of juvenile justice. The Committee found the age of criminal responsibility to be low and legislation in force in 1995 did not appear to be compatible with the provisions of the Convention which stipulate, for instance, that detention should be used as a measure of last resort and for the shortest possible time.

This chapter considers what the Government has done to address these criticisms between the reports in relation to child poverty, education and juvenile justice. It

---

[1] DEPARTMENT OF HEALTH, UNITED NATIONS CONVENTION ON THE RIGHTS OF THE CHILD: SECOND REPORT BY THE UNITED KINGDOM (1999).
[2] COMMITTEE ON THE RIGHTS OF THE CHILD, REPORT OF THE EIGHTH SESSION, UN Doc. CRC/C/38, ¶ 9–27 (1995).

Deirdre Fottrell (ed.), Revisiting Children's Rights, 127–147
© *2000 Kluwer Law International. Printed in Great Britain.*

will focus on the policies of the New Labour Government, which came to power in the UK in May 1997.[3] At a more general level, this chapter addresses an issue that remains controversial a decade on from the adoption of the CRC: the issue of responsibility. Specifically, we question how responsibility for a child's welfare and actions is divided between the child, her parents (or other carers), the community and the State.

CHILD POVERTY

Under Article 27 of the CRC the State recognises the right of every child 'to a standard of living adequate for the child's physical, mental, spiritual and moral and social development'. Article 27(2) states that 'the parent(s) or others responsible for the child have the primary responsibility to secure, within their abilities and financial capacities, the conditions of living necessary for the child's development'.[4] The State has two obligations under this article. First, under 27(4), to pursue parents who seek to evade their financial responsibilities for their children (as this and the previous Government in the UK have been doing through the Child Support Agency). Second, and more significantly, Article 27 (3) provide: 'State Parties, in accordance with national conditions and within their means, shall take appropriate measures to assist parents and others responsible for the child to implement this right and shall in case of need provide material assistance and support programmes, particularly with regard to nutrition, clothing and housing.'

Article 27 raises the questions of whether all children in the UK have a standard of living that is adequate for their development. The Institute of Fiscal Studies has recently estimated that four million children in the UK were living in poverty in 1995–96, one-third of all those under 18 and three times the numbers in poverty 20 years earlier.[5] In 1999 the British Medical Association reported that children in the poorest families in the UK are amongst the unhealthiest in the developed world and that the health gap continues to widen for children in the lowest social classes.[6] A range of other indicators, from teenage pregnancy rates to levels of homelessness amongst young people, confirm that the UK is doing very badly when it comes to

---

[3] This chapter will not attempt to refer back to the performance of the Conservative Party who were in government from 1992–97, which includes the period covered by the first report of the UK to the Committee on the Rights of the child, because in the opinion of the authors the Labour Government has taken a very different approach to the issue of children's rights.

[4] *See also*, Article 18 (1) of the CRC which makes the same point more generally:
States Parties shall use their best efforts to ensure recognition of the principle that both parents have common responsibilities for the upbringing and development of the child. Parents or, as the case may be, legal guardians, have the primary responsibility for the upbringing and development of the child. The best interests of the child will be their basic concern.

[5] *See* P. Gregg, S. Harkness, and S. Machin, *Poor Kids: Trends in Child Poverty in the Britain 1968–96* 20 FISCAL STUD. 164 (1999). Gregg et al have reported that 43 per cent of children are now living in lone parent families as compared with just 7 per cent in 1968 and that there has been a startling drop in employment in these families with only 42 per cent now in employment. However, they caution against overstating the importance of lone parenthood as an explanation for child poverty. The rise in lone parenthood per se only accounts for one-fifth of child poverty.

[6] BRITISH MEDICAL ASSOCIATION, GROWING UP IN BRITAIN: ENSURING A HEALTHY FUTURE FOR OUR CHILDREN: A STUDY OF 0–5 YEAR OLDS (1999).

the living standards of many of its children, and on many indicators, considerably worse than other European (and developed) countries.[7] But the issues of who is responsible for child poverty, and how it can best be tackled, remain complex.

ELIMINATING CHILD POVERTY IN THE UK

The New Labour Government made it clear that it considered child poverty to be unacceptable and launched an ambitious programme to tackle it. In March 1999 the Prime Minister pledged to eliminate child poverty within 20 years. He returned to the theme in his speech to the 1999 Labour Conference when he proclaimed that he would not rest so long as there remained a single poor child in Britain. This commitment points to a more general characteristic of the New Labour Government: it has been centrally concerned with issues affecting children and young people, more so than any of its predecessors, and for reasons that relate to the general shift in the philosophy of the Labour Party that has marked the transition from 'old' to 'new' Labour.[8] It is notable that the Prime Minister did not pledge himself, as previous Labour premiers have done, to eliminate poverty in general, even in the long term, but specifically and only to the abolition of *child* poverty. There are, no doubt, various reasons for this new approach, including, most obviously, that this Labour Government is more reluctant than previous Labour administrations to assume responsibility for eliminating adult poverty.[9]

This reflects a general shift in the Party's philosophy away from the redistributive approach favoured by both main political parties in the 1950s and 1960s, towards what might be described as an enabling approach. The latter approach provides that adults who are unable to work have a right to social security benefits, but that the right to benefits brings corresponding responsibilities. While the Government

---

[7] *See*, SOCIAL EXCLUSION UNIT, TEENAGE PREGNANCY, 1999, Cm 4342. *See also*, ROUGH SLEEPING, 1998, CM 4008, at 98.
[8] The Rt Hon Tony Blair MP, Beveridge Speech, Toynbee Hall (March 19 1999). The Government's pledge to eliminate child poverty is reiterated, and its strategy for doing so documented, in two recent Government publications, *see further*, HM TREASURY, THE MODERNISATION OF BRITAIN'S TAX AND BENEFIT, NUMBER FIVE: SUPPORTING CHILDREN THROUGH THE TAX AND BENEFIT SYSTEM, (1999). *See also*, OPPORTUNITY FOR ALL: TACKLING POVERTY AND SOCIAL EXCLUSION, 1999, Cm 4445. *See further*, a recent publication by the Chancellor of the Exchequer in the journal of the Child Poverty Action Group, G. Brown, *A Scar on the Nation's Soul*, 104 POVERTY, Autumn 1999, at 8–10.
[9] A recent report from the left-leaning think-tank DEMOS claims that there has been a general increase in the priority placed on services for young people by governments: 'The clearest example of this is the way in which education has become a greater priority, both for government spending and political debate. But many other policies and priorities reflect growing attention to the challenges faced by young people: employment, criminal justice, drugs, public safety, family services – the list goes on. In the UK, three out of five of Labour's early election pledges focused on children and young people' [and] 'in Australia, Canada, the US and France, major public investments are being made in measures to reduce exclusion and disadvantage among young people'. These developments are attributed to '[a] period of profound social, economic and cultural change [that] has put increasing pressure on our assumptions about the nature of youth, and on the systems and structures that support young people to become healthy, independent and self-governing adults'. *See* T. Bentley. and K. Oakley, THE REAL DEAL – WHAT YOUNG PEOPLE REALLY THINK ABOUT GOVERNMENT, POLITICS AND EXCLUSION, DEMOS, (1999).

129

continues to have a role in helping to create opportunities to work, and in legislating to guarantee that citizens are adequately remunerated for their work, it is the responsibility of individuals to take advantage of those opportunities.[10] Where adults persistently fail to take the opportunities presented to escape poverty, they themselves will be held responsible for their own situation.

Whatever one's assessment of this approach to adult poverty it clearly will not do for child poverty and for reasons that help to explain why the Prime Minister has assumed a responsibility for ending child poverty, but not for the elimination of povety in general. Children, at least up to a certain age, are economically dependent upon adults. It follows that poor children can bear no responsibility at all for their poverty: they are poor because the adults who care for them are poor. Children, it might be said, necessarily find themselves amongst the deserving poor.

ENABLING AND SANCTIONING

But there is a dilemma for the Government inherent in this approach. How is the Government to address the economic deprivation of children who are poor as a result, as the Government would see it, of the failures of adults on whom they depend? In particular, to what extent should a controversial strand of Government policy apply to parents: the sanctioning of people on benefits who fail to take advantage of opportunities to train and work?

There is little doubt that the imposition of such sanctions is a core part of the UK Government's policy, not least because of its symbolic significance: it marks an overall shift in responsibility away from Government and towards individuals. For instance, when Chancellor of the Exchequer Gordon Brown announced the most important measure to date directly addressing child poverty, the Working Families Tax Credit (WFTC),[11] he went to great pains to emphasise that the new entitlements brought new responsibilities.[12]

The purpose of the WFTC is to ensure that work pays more than benefits and thus, according to Brown, that there is no excuse for people with the opportunity to

---

[10] New Labour's insistence that rights bring responsibilities was made clear in Tony Blair's first speech as Prime Minister. He insisted that a 'one nation Britain' can only be done on the basis of a new bargain between us all as members of society. 'The basis of this modern civic society is an ethic of mutual responsibility or duty. It is something for something. You only take out if you put in. That's the bargain.' The Government would provide opportunities, but an 'inactive life on benefit' would not be an option. *See*, Rt Honorable Tony Blair, MP Address at the Aylesbury Estate, Southwark (2 June 1997).

[11] Under the Working Families Tax Credit (WFTC), a family with two children on £15,000 a year, for example, will receive £1,460 in tax credits where the mother stays at home to look after children. The Government is also introducing a children's tax credit from April 2001, which will replace the married couples tax allowance. Families will get a £416-a-year flat rate tax credit, irrespective of the number of children they have, so long as the main earner is on less than £30,000 a year. *See* HM TREASURY, THE MODERNISATION OF BRITAIN'S TAX AND BENEFIT NUMBER FIVE, *supra*, note 6.

[12] The message from the Government inherent in this policy was reflected in newspaper headlines reporting the policy. *See e.g., Go To Work Or I'll Freeze Your Giro, Warns Brown*, THE GUARDIAN, Sept. 5 1999.

work not to do so. The Chancellor made it clear that those adults who persistently refused opportunities to train or to work would risk having their benefits frozen. The WFTC, he argued, would enable responsible parents to improve the standard of living of their children, by working rather than remaining dependant on State benefits. Some months before the WFTC was announced, a similar philosophy was apparent in policies which particularly targeted lone parents. The Secretary of State for Social Security, Alistair Darling, in announcing provisions of the Welfare Reform and Pensions Act 1999, stated that lone parents would be required to attend job advice interviews or risk having their benefits frozen, a move he described as 'harsh but justifiable'.[13]

Imposing sanctions by freezing the benefits of parents who fail to attend job advice interviews, or who persistently turn down offers of work or training, will inevitably have an impact on their children. Indeed, as long as such sanctions are being imposed on adults with dependent children the Government cannot deliver on its pledge to eliminate child poverty completely. The problem for the Government is both philosophical and practical. Its policy is to shift the burden of responsibility for poverty away from the State and towards the individual: that is, to create an enabling society in which the Government fulfils its responsibilities by creating opportunities and adults fulfil their corresponding responsibilities by taking advantage of those opportunities. If adults fail to do so and are poor as a consequence, then, aside from providing minimal social security benefits (which may be frozen where adults behave irresponsibly), the State cannot be considered responsible for their predicament. However, in reality, where those people who fail to take advantage of the enabling State have dependant children, the Government abandons not just the adults but their children too. This cannot be justified by arguing that the children of 'job shy' adults are somehow responsible for the circumstances in which they find themselves.

There is another obvious sense in which the Government cannot guarantee to eliminate child poverty but only to create the conditions under which it is not responsible for any remaining child poverty. The Government could ensure that all families either receive adequate wages or adequate benefits to provide for their children. However, without drastic interventions in family life it cannot ensure that any increase in the benefits or wages received by adults with children is spent on those children (unless, perhaps, it introduced some sort of voucher scheme, which would be both difficult and controversial). While poorer parents may spend more on their children than is allowed for in their benefits (i.e., sacrifice their own interests for those of their children), the possibility also exists that money intended to relieve child poverty may not actually reach the children. Again this raises questions as to where the State's responsibility for child poverty ends and parental responsibility begins.

The Government could claim that it will have delivered on its child poverty pledge if it succeeds in creating an enabling environment in which any children who do remain poor do so as a consequence of the failures of their parents or other

---

[13] *See e.g., 'Harsh' rules to benefit poor*, THE GUARDIAN, Feb. 11 1999.

carers and not of the State. The Government's role on such a view is to create a society in which no child need remain in poverty, and any continuing poverty will remain the fault and responsibility of parents or other carers and not of Government.

FULFILLING OBLIGATIONS UNDER ARTICLE 27 OF THE CONVENTION ON THE RIGHTS OF THE CHILD

It seems that a government that enabled parents and carers to provide adequately for their children, while providing material assistance to those who could not do so, would have fulfilled its obligations under Article 27 of the Convention. The State's obligations begin only where those with 'primary responsibility' (parents or carers) are unable to provide children with an adequate standard of living. Under the Convention an enabling State which ensured that all parents could provide adequately would have no responsibility for any remaining child poverty. If the State enables parents to take their families out of poverty by providing them with training and work opportunities, then it has fulfilled its responsibilities under the CRC. If parents refuse those opportunities and the State penalises them, with the consequence that children suffer, then responsibility for those children's poverty will rest with the parents and not with the State. An enabling State, therefore, cannot properly pledge to eliminate child poverty but only to eliminate the conditions under which any child *need* be poor.

There are problems with this approach. Where children live in poverty because of the irresponsibility of their parents, it is still arguable that the CRC imposes on the Government a duty to take remedial action under Article 27. Moreover, where parents in the judgement of the State fail to act responsibly and to provide even a minimal standard of living for their children, the State may be justified in intervening to protect those children from the consequences of this form of 'parental irresponsibility'. A substantive discussion on this controversial territory is beyond the scope of this chapter. It is sufficient simply to note that this issue arises given both the Government's pledge to eliminate child poverty and its commitment to an enabling, rather than a redistributive, State.

There are other problems with the approach of the New Labour Government. For example, there is a tendency to present its enabling approach as an alternative to wealth redistribution. The Government's responsibility is to provide opportunities rather than to increase social security benefits.[14] Such a policy can be problematic, particularly in its application to lone parents.[15] This is significant given

---

[14] The New Labour Government has taken some steps to improve benefits. In particular, it raised the level of child benefit for the first child in the budgets of 1998 and 1999 by more than 35%: from £11 in April 1997 to £15.00 by April 2000. For further details see HM TREASURY, THE MODERNISATION OF BRITAIN'S TAX AND BENEFIT NUMBER FIVE, *supra*, note 6.

[15] Similar arguments would apply to a two-parent family which could only provide adequately for its children if both parents work. If lone parents should not be required to work, then presumably by extension both parents in the two-parent family should not be required to work.

that the children of lone parents are disproportionately represented amongst the disadvantaged.[16]

LONE PARENTS

The New Labour Government has introduced measures to encourage lone parents into work outside the home and to provide support systems – for example, in the form of childcare – to remove obstacles to their taking jobs.[17] This is consistent with its enabling approach. However, it has stopped short of requiring lone parents to seek employment. Lone parents may legitimately choose to remain at home to care for their children. It would appear to follow that the Government cannot fulfil its responsibilities simply by providing (lone) parents with opportunities to work, for it does not believe that they should be obliged to do so. This creates a dilemma: either the Government must review the exemption of lone parents from the responsibility to seek employment or accept that there is a significant group of poor children whose rights can be protected only by increasing benefits or through changes to the child support arrangements. It is notable that the Conservative opposition appears to be moving towards grasping the first horn of this particular dilemma. Speaking on 23 November 1999, Shadow Social Security Secretary David Willetts argued that lone parents who refused 'reasonable' job offers should lose benefit when their youngest child turned 11.[18] There are problems with this proposal that have already been noted with reference to similar sanctions introduced by New Labour. In particular, while Willetts made clear that this cut would be in the parent's personal benefit allowance, it is unclear how the Opposition propose to ensure that children do not in fact suffer as a result. The question of what constitutes a 'reasonable' job offer is also likely to be a vexed one. Leaving these problems aside, it is significant that even this 'tough' Conservative approach would not require lone parents to accept 'reasonable' job offers until their youngest child reached 11 years of age.

---

[16] *See e.g.*, P. Gregg, S. Harkness and S. Machin, *Poor Kids – child poverty in the United Kingdom*, 161 CHILDRIGHT 4 (1999). Gregg et al have reported that 43 per cent of poor children were now living in lone parent families as compared to just seven per cent in 1968. They also note that there has been a startling drop in employment in these families, with only 42% now working. However, they proceed to caution against overstating the importance of lone parenthood as an explanation of child poverty. The rise in lone parenthood per se only accounts for one-fifth of child poverty.

[17] For the most important Government initiative, *see further*, THE NEW DEAL FOR LONE PARENTS, (July 1998), the programme applied nationally from October 1998. This initiative has been accompanied by the development of a National Childcare Strategy. Voluntary organisations have been encouraged to train childcare assistants, efforts have been made to extend after-school activities, and tax changes have sought to make childcare more affordable for poorer parents. In particular, a childcare tax credit will 'put childcare within the reach of people who have never been able to afford it'. However, while the Government's focus has been on getting lone parents into work, and the Welfare Reform and Pension's Act, 1999, § 57, 58 empowers the Secretary of State to make regulations requiring lone parents to attend 'work-focused interviews' or risk a reduction in benefits, the Government has been at pains to stress that it will not require lone parents actively to seek employment. For a clear insight into the Government's approach to lone parents (and to the family), *see generally*, HOME OFFICE, SUPPORTING FAMILIES: A CONSULTATION DOCUMENT, (1998).

[18] *See e.g., Lone Parents Should Look For Work When Children Reach 11, Say Tories*, The GUARDIAN, 23 Nov. 1999.

There are ways in which the Government could improve the support available to lone parents other than by increasing benefits levels. Many poor lone parents could be helped by being permitted to keep a proportion of the child maintenance collected from non-residential parents by the Child Support Agency (CSA). Currently, any money received is deducted from income support on a pound-for-pound basis. New Labour is moving in this direction, but, its critics argue, not far enough. The long-delayed reforms to the CSA, which were introduced in the 1999–2000 parliamentary session, introduce a 'child support premium'.[19] Parents on income support will be allowed to keep the first £10 of their weekly child support maintenance payments. This will make a real difference to children in one-parent families. However, given both the Government's commitment to eliminating child poverty and its acceptance that lone parents should not be required to work, a strong case can be made for a more generous premium.[20]

It should also be remembered that some parents are also children, as defined in the CRC, and many are themselves the products of disadvantaged backgrounds. If some of these young people fail to behave 'responsibly' as parents, then, on the Government's own analysis, this will, in part at least, be because they have themselves been the victims of the very 'cycles of disadvantage' that its social exclusion programme seeks to address. It is unclear, then, if it is appropriate for the Government to sanction them for 'irresponsible' behaviour, and whether doing so will be conducive to the social inclusion of either them or their children.

Consider, for example, the Government's insistence, following a recommendation from the Social Exclusion Unit (SEU), on the need to pursue teenage fathers for child maintenance.[21] The CSA will be instructed to pursue support vigorously as soon as these young fathers leave full-time education and move into work. There is clearly a strong case for insisting that teenage fathers do have responsibilities towards their children. However, as the SEU report also found, these boys are disproportionately drawn from socially excluded groups and from the care system, and tend to be on low incomes or benefits and to have low expectations for the future. Requiring teenage fathers to make child maintenance contributions even where they are on benefits risks leaving some of them with too little money to cover even basic costs. Moreover, as the Government's CSA reforms increase the child support obligations of the poorest and youngest non-resident parents (including those on social security benefits), any other children who are living with these non-resident parents will tend to be adversely affected both socially and economically.[22]

SOCIAL EXCLUSION OR WHY 20 YEARS?

This focus on the limits of the Government's responsibilities to poor children may seem to distract from the prime consideration which is the nature and the extent of

---

[19] *See further*, the Government Green Paper, DEPARTMENT OF SOCIAL SECURITY, CHILDREN FIRST: A NEW APPROACH TO CHILD SUPPORT, (1998).

[20] *See e.g.*, S. Osborne, *Child First: The Government's Child Support Green Paper*, 150 CHILDRIGHT, Oct. 1998, at 12–13.

[21] *See further*, SOCIAL EXCLUSION UNIT, TEENAGE PREGNANCY, *supra*, note 5.

[22] *See*, Osborne, *supra*, note 20 at 12.

those responsibilities. It may be that even where Government has made genuine and concerted efforts to eliminate child poverty, some children will continue to live in poverty where parents and other carers are responsible. The real question, however, is not what is to be done about a small minority of adults who fail to properly fulfil their responsibilities and incur sanctions as a result, but how the Government can eliminate current child poverty levels in excess of three million. Thus far Government measures which directly address child poverty are aimed at working families – including the tax credits discussed above – and on improved childcare facilities to assist those parents who choose to go to work. While there are measures which will improve the position of families dependent on State benefits, children in non-working families remain well below the poverty line on the Government's own definition of poverty (i.e., where the household income is half that of an average income). This has led some organisations, which have welcomed the Government's pledge on child poverty, to ask why it needs 20 years to be fully implemented.

The New Labour Government's first annual report on poverty and exclusion is titled Opportunity For All (claimed by the Secretary of State for Social Security to 'herald the most radical and far-reaching campaign against poverty since Beveridge').[23] Setting out a 'new approach' the Government report states that past attempts to tackle poverty and exclusion have

> focused on short-term piecemeal solutions. Huge sums were spent dealing with immediate problems, very little to preventing problems occurring in the future. Our approach is radically different ... We are tackling the causes of poverty and social exclusion and not just the symptoms; creating a fairer society in which everyone has the opportunity to fulfil their full potential; and investing in individuals and communities to equip them to take control of their lives.[24]

There is repeated insistence throughout this document on the need to break the 'cycle of disadvantage' that 'has been passed from generation to generation as children inherit poverty from their parents before passing on this debilitating legacy to their own children'.[25] The Government's response to those critics who argue that it should directly attack child poverty – for example, by substantially increasing social security benefits – appears to be that this is the sort of 'short-term' approach that has spent 'huge sums dealing with immediate problems' while neglected deeper causes.[26] People are indeed poor, as the Child Poverty Action Group has put it, 'because they have not got enough money', but giving them enough money, the Government argues, is not a viable way of tackling poverty and exclusion in the long term and within the context of an enabling State. The causes of poverty need

---

[23] DEPARTMENT OF SOCIAL SECURITY, OPPORTUNITY FOR ALL: TACKLING POVERTY AND SOCIAL EXCLUSION, 1999, Cm 4445.
[24] *Ibid.*
[25] *Id.*
[26] *Id.*

to be addressed in a more robust way. Of course, low social security benefits and wages are a proximate cause, but the deeper cause, the Government insists, is the lack of opportunity that leaves families reliant on social security benefits and low wages in the first place. This helps to explain why the Prime Minister requires 20 years. It is the time required for the sort of long-term solutions, in which the Government is investing substantial resources, to achieve their ultimate aims.

A Government seeking to equip people 'to take control of their own lives' will inevitably be preoccupied with young people, most particularly with equipping them to be economically independent and to prosper, to be good parents and good citizens. Increasing benefits to poor families will not break the 'cycle of dis-advantage ... passed from generation to generation'; it may, as the Government sees it, reinforce the 'culture of dependency'. To break this cycle it is necessary, instead, to intervene to ensure that the poor children of today do not pass poverty and disadvantage on to their own children.

Much, of course, could be said about the adequacy of this approach. The Government is surely right to insist that it cannot solve the problem of child poverty simply by increasing benefit levels. It is imperative to address the 'cycles of dis-advantage' that leave too many people in the UK dependant on benefits. At the same time, the Government suggests, quite misleadingly, that the choice is between either short-term measures (such as increasing benefits) or a long-term strategy tackling the causes of social exclusion. When presented in this way it is not difficult for the Government to argue convincingly that its long-term strategy is preferable to short-term interventions such as benefit increases. However, no such choice exists: the Government could actually pursue both long- and short-term strategies. It is possible to provide adequate levels of support for those parents (and children) whom it accepts cannot or should not be required to work and insist on the responsibilities of all other parents to take 'reasonable' jobs where they have opportunities to do so.

The 'long-term' approach the Government has taken to social exclusion, in addition to explaining why it has asked for 20 years to eliminate child poverty, also explains the centrality of education to the Government's programme. It is education that is to equip young people with the qualifications and skills that they will need to arrest cycles of deprivation. New Labour has, then, placed great emphasis on the education of children as a route out of poverty. It has sought to address the numbers of children who are being excluded from schools and provide a number of funded initiatives to keep children in school. It has also sought to raise school performance targets and deal with 'failing' schools. Here again the issue of parental responsibility is central. A series of measures have been introduced which are designed to emphasise parental responsibility for children's behaviour and performance at school and for low educational attainment.

EDUCATION

The New Labour Government's strategy has been guided by the SEU report on truancy and exclusion published in May 1998. The report bluntly stated that 'parents bear the primary responsibility for ensuring that their children attend school regularly'. In reaching this conclusion the report cited research which showed that parental attitudes were a key factor in truancy; in particular when parents of persistent truants condoned unauthorised absenses – for example, for family shopping trips, or to enable their school-age children to look after younger siblings or undertake other responsibilities in the home.[27]

The New Labour Government has introduced a range of measures to address this problem and ensure that parents accept responsibility for their children's attendance at, and behaviour in, school. This idea of education as involving a 'partnership' between children, parents and schools was a central theme of the School Standards and Framework Act 1998. The Act requires maintained-schools to 'adopt a home-school agreement (HSA) for the school, together with a parental declaration to be used in connection with the agreement'.[28] The HSA sets out the school's aims, ethos and responsibilities, its expectations of pupils and significantly, 'the parental responsibilities, namely the responsibilities which the parents of such pupils are expected to discharge in connection with the education of their children while they are registered pupils at the school'.[29] While HSAs do not have the force of law, and schools are expressly prohibited from requiring parents to sign them or in any way penalising parents who refuse to do so, their introduction is a clear sign of the Government's intention to shift a greater burden of responsibility onto parents or other carers.[30]

A similar message is conveyed in the Crime and Disorder Act 1998 (CDA) which introduced a new court order: the parenting order.[31] Under this provision, the court can require a parent or guardian to comply with the terms of such an order (which may include accompanying a child to school and/or attending parenting guidance sessions) for a period not exceeding 12 months. Failure to comply with such an order can result in a fine of up to £1,000. A parenting order can be issued not only where a child is convicted of a criminal offence or is guilty of 'anti-social behaviour', but for parental failure to comply with a school attendance order and/or where parents fail to ensure regular attendance at school.[32] The Government's determination to 'get tough' on parents who fail to fulfil their responsibilities was driven home by Secretary of State for Education and Employment David Blunkett at the Labour Party's 1999 Conference when he stated that persistent failure to ensure a child's attendance at school was to be made an arrestable

---

[27] *See further*, SOCIAL EXCLUSION UNIT, TRUANCY AND SOCIAL EXCLUSION REPORT, (1998), Ch. 1, *What we know about truancy*, §. 1.8.

[28] *See* the School Standards and Framework Act 1998, §110, 111.

[29] *Id.*, § 110(2)(c).

[30] *See generally*, DEPARTMENT FOR EDUCATION AND EMPLOYMENT, HOME SCHOOL AGREEMENTS GUIDANCE – GUIDANCE FOR SCHOOLS AND HOME SCHOOL AGREEMENTS – GUIDANCE FOR PARENTS, 1998. For a summary, *see further*, 152 CHILDRIGHT, Dec. 1998, at 15–16.

[31] Crime and Disorder Act 1998, §. 8, 9 10.

[32] *See* written answer to Parliament of the Rt Honorable Charles Clarke, MP, the Minister of State at the Home Office, October 25 1999, Hansard HC Column 685, according to which 122 parenting orders had been made as of September 30 1999.

offence (with minimum and maximum fines substantially increased).[33] This change will be introduced under s. 55 of the Criminal Justice and Court Services Bill which was before parliament in the 1999–2000 session.[34]

It is reasonable to insist that parents have some responsibility for their child's attendance and behaviour, but again the question of how precisely responsibility divides between parents and Government is problematic. No doubt, parents often are failing to fulfil their obligations where their children are not attending school. However, the issue of parental responsibility only arises once children are truanting, and parental inadequacies will not usually be the cause of the disaffection and demoralisation that can lead a child to truant in the first place.

The SEU report on truancy and exclusion insists that parents have primary responsibility for ensuring attendance at school and provides evidence that some parents do not take those responsibilities sufficiently seriously. However, the report also acknowledges that the causes of truanting are many, and include anxiety about bullying, coursework deadlines and dissatisfaction with particular lessons, teachers or the national curriculum (which some young people see as lacking relevance to their lives). In addition, it reports, that in some schools poor attendance is centred on children who are poor readers. None of these failings can be blamed on parents, although some parents undoubtedly do less than they should to address these causes or the resulting truancy.

In addition, there is a group of children whose disproportionate representation amongst truants and the excluded is clearly not the responsibility of parents: looked-after children. The figures in the SEU report make startling reading: the permanent exclusion rate amongst children in care was 10 times higher than average at this time 'with perhaps as many as 30 per cent of children in care ... out of mainstream education, either excluded or truanting'.[35] New Labour has introduced a range of initiatives which have improved the care system.[36] Worthy as the Government's objectives are, however, its ambitions are depressingly low. In its response to the Utting Report it set the following targets for educational attainment amongst children in care: by 2001 50 per cent of children leaving care should possess at least one GCSE or GNVQ qualification rising to 75 per cent by 2003.[37]

---

[33] *See e.g., Truants' parents under threat of arrest and fines*, THE TIMES, 30 Sept. 1999. The Government estimates that at present around 9,000 parents a year are prosecuted for this: few turn up for court hearings, and many end up paying only the minimum fine of £20. Under the Government's proposals, persistent failure to ensure a child's attendance will become an arrestable offence so that parents are compelled to appear in court. The maximum fine will also be increased from £1,000 to £2,500 per parent and the minimum from £20 to £200.

[34] The Education Act 1996 § 444, provides that if a registered child of compulsory school age fails to attend school regularly, his parent is guilty of an offence. Currently a parent convicted under this section is liable to level 3 on the standard scale – a fine of up to £1,000. The Criminal Justice and Court Services Bill §55 increases the maximum fine to level 4 – a fine of up to £2,500 – and introduces the possibility of a custodial sentence. The use of a custodial sentence is at the discretion of magistrates and is intended to ensure parents attend court.

[35] *Supra*, note 27, ¶ 2.19.

[36] DEPARTMENT FOR EDUCATION AND EMPLOYMENT, THE EDUCATION OF CHILDREN BEING LOOKED AFTER BY LOCAL AUTHORITIES, 1999. Its commitment to addressing the educational problems of looked-after children was most recently evidenced by the publication of draft guidance on education for looked-after children.

Perhaps to aim so low is justifiable given the difficulties that remain within the care system and the time it will take for the Government to resolve them adequately. Nevertheless, the targets show that there is some way to go before the equality of expectation and opportunity at the core of the New Labour social justice vision is reached.

THE RESPONSIBILITIES OF GOVERNMENT

The responsibilities of Government with respect to education include the content of the national curriculum and the framework of legislation and regulation within which the Local Education Authorities (LEAs) and the schools operate. Article 28(b) of the CRC requires States to make 'secondary education available to every child' and Article 28(e) 'to take measures to encourage regular attendance at school'. The New Labour Government has taken measures to encourage regular attendance but, disturbingly, some groups of children, in particular those with special educational needs (SEN), those in care and those from certain minority ethnic communities, are seriously over-represented among children who are permanently excluded from school. An emphasis on parental responsibility for truancy, exclusion and poor educational performance is difficult to reconcile with some of the statistical evidence, much of which implies that aspects of the education system itself are the source of pupil disaffection and of resulting behavioural and educational problems. For example, it is hard to reconcile the fact that SEN children were seven times more likely to be permanently excluded from school in 1997–98, with a policy which hinges on parental responsibility for behavioural problems, other than on the assumption that the parents of SEN children are much more likely to have inadequate parenting skills.

Further, LEAs and, ultimately, Government itself might be responsible for bad behaviour and truancy amongst such children. In the case of SEN children, it may be that the education system is failing the children; that the provisions made for them are too often inappropriate or inadequate. They are therefore prone to disaffection and, consequently, to the sort of behaviour that can lead to permanent exclusion. Similarly, it may be that the disproportionate representation of black children among the permanently excluded is, in some part, the result of a national curriculum that fails adequately to engage them, as well as of experiences of racism (including racist bullying) at school. The Government is ultimately responsible for the curriculum, the SEN system, for setting out the obligations of LEAs and schools to tackle racism, etc.

It is reasonable then to conclude that where these children are excluded from school, the Government bears some responsibility for that misbehaviour and for

---

[37] *See further,* DEPARTMENT FOR EDUCATION AND EMPLOYMENT, THE GOVERNMENT'S RESPONSE TO THE CHILDREN'S SAFEGUARD REVIEW, 1998. *See also* W. UTTING, PEOPLE LIKE US, REPORT OF THE REVIEW OF THE SAFEGUARDS FOR CHILDREN LIVING AWAY FROM HOME, July 30 1997. *See further* J. Templeton, *Listening to looked-after children: The Government's response to the Utting Report,* 153 CHILDRIGHT, Dec. 1998, at 10–11.

failing to address its underlying causes. In addition, of course, the Government has a responsibility to ensure that children are not disadvantaged in other ways that may affect their performance at school, such as poor health and inadequate nutrition.[38]

The New Labour Government, it should be said, has made much of the duties of schools and LEAs to tackle truancy and exclusion. In July 1998, the Government set ambitious targets for reductions in exclusion and truancy: learning time lost through truancy and exclusion to be cut by one-third by 2002 with new LEA targets to reduce exclusion. Three months later, in October 1998, the Secretary of State for Education announced a Pupil Support Grant of nearly £500 million to cut truancy, bad behaviour and exclusions. More significantly, the Home Secretary Jack Straw recently announced that 100 schools would share £12 million in funds from the Government's Crime Reduction Programme.

The Government has also introduced a series of circulars to improve arrangements for children with SEN and other pupils at particular risk of being in trouble at school. In November 1999 it announced the introduction of a SEN Bill. This built on *A Programme for Action – Meeting Special Educational Needs*, published in November 1998, which set out a programme to improve provision for SEN children (and to ensure closer co-operation between parents, schools and LEAs). Particularly significant are two recent circulars that address the issue of pupil support and provide guidance for schools and LEAs.[39] These circulars recognise that the failures of schools and LEAs contribute to pupil disaffection and bad behaviour. For example, *Social Inclusion: Pupil Support* insists on the importance of the early identification of SEN so that action can be taken to address educational needs before disaffection sets in. Recognising the high rates of exclusion amongst pupils from certain minority ethnic communities, it also exhorts schools to address the problem of racism and to cultivate non-racist environments. In addition, the School Standards and Framework Act 1998 places a duty on head teachers to 'determine measures to be taken with a view to ... preventing all forms of bullying among pupils'.[40] That headteachers now have a

---

[38] That children can be disadvantaged before they even start school as a result of inadequate nutrition and health care (as well as lack of parenting skills) is acknowledged by the Government's Sure Start Scheme (in which it has invested £540 million), which is targeted at children from 0–3 and, significantly, led by the Department for Education and Employment, despite the fact that the children it targets are not yet of school age. The reasons for this were explained by the Secretary of State for Education and Employment, as follows: 'Sure Start will bring together early education, health services, family support and advice on nurturing for families when they need it most. It will enhance the life chances of children by ensuring that they are ready to learn and to thrive when they start school.' Speech by the Rt Honourable Alastair Darling, Gingerbread Conference (Jan. 19 January 1999). *See further, DfEE Press Release 23/99, 19/01/99*). For a Government so concerned about equality of opportunity it is salutory to recognise that *inequality* of opportunity can be evident so early in a child's life. For an up-to-date introduction and guide to the Sure Start Programme, *see further*, DEPARTMENT FOR EDUCATION AND EMPLOYMENT, SURE START: A GUIDE FOR SECOND WAVE PROGRAMMES, 1999.

[39] *See generally*, DEPARTMENT FOR EDUCATION AND EMPLOYMENT, SOCIAL INCLUSION: PUPIL SUPPORT, Oct. 1999. *See also*, SOCIAL INCLUSION: THE LEA ROLE IN PUPIL SUPPORT, Nov. 1999.

[40] School Standards and Framework Act 1998, § 61(4)(b).

legal duty to tackle bullying is of significance here given that bullying often causes its victims to truant and leads to the exclusion of its perpetrators.

Perhaps the clearest acknowledgement by the Government that the failures and mismanagement of schools and LEAs may be implicated in the bad behaviour and truancy of pupils is in the provisions of the School Standards and Framework Act which empower the Secretary of State for Education to intervene and close down schools which are 'failing' their pupils'.[41] Predictably, the schools giving cause for concern tend to be found in the most economically deprived areas of the country. Where truancy and exclusion rates are high, and educational performance is poor, the New Labour Government has, then, introduced measures both to reinforce the duties of parents and to hold schools and LEAs to account. However, the debate about respective responsibilities and roles remains a heated one. Schools complain about uncooperative parents and unruly pupils. Parents criticise teaching standards and discipline regimes in schools. Schools argue that the Government is insufficiently sensitive to the problems of providing education to children in areas of the country suffering from poor housing, high crime rates, widespread unemployment and all the multiple elements of social exclusion. Educationalists debate whether branding certain schools as failing and publishing school league tables contributes to the solution of these problems or further entrenches them by further demoralising children, parents and teachers.

These issues of responsibility are of considerable practical importance given a social exclusion agenda which aims to extend opportunity to all and recognises that a universally high standard of education is of fundamental importance if this is to be achieved. If the 'cycles of disadvantage' are to be broken and the obligation under Article 28 to provide secondary education for every child implemented, it is important that the Government does not abandon children excluded from school or children in conflict with the law. Adequate provision must be made to ensure that these children are not deprived of education, which would, in all likelihood, condemn them to social exclusion in adulthood, with the consequence that the 'cycle of disadvantage' passes to their own children. A recent example illustrated both the difficulties which schools in deprived areas face in tacking the problems of particularly difficult children and the unacceptable though often understandable reaction which sometimes results in a school abandoning entirely its efforts to educate the child. Firfield School in Newcastle found itself at the centre of a political storm when it cut its truancy figures dramatically to meet Government targets, but did so, in part, by encouraging the parents of persistent truants to sign their children off the school role on the pretext that they would be educating them at home.[42]

---

[41] *Ibid.*, § 8,19

[42] The revelations about Firfield School appeared on Channel 4 News on December 10 1999 and were reported in many national newspapers on December 11 1999. *See e.g.*, *Teachers 'fiddled school role'*, THE GUARDIAN, Dec. 11 1999. The headteacher, Carole McAlpine told Channel 4 News that 'five' or 'six' serial truants were removed from the school role after parents had signed forms, at the invitation of the school, agreeing to educate their children at home. The General Secretary of the National Association of Schoolmasters, Union of Women Teachers, Nigel deGruchy, responded that these revelations 'show how targets [i.e. for reducing truancy and exclusion] corrupt'.

Education is at the very core of the Government's social exclusion agenda. Its policies, and the debates surrounding them, have once again highlighted the issue of responsibility and in particular the division of responsibility between parents and other carers, public institutions and the State. The Government is confronting the problems in this area, and has introduced a legislative and policy framework which extends and reinforces the responsibilities of parents, schools and LEAs. There is much to be said in favour of the approach it has taken, and yet there is also room for some sympathy with parents, schools and LEAs who complain that the Government has been insufficiently sensitive to their problems and has passed down edicts to them rather than engaging in dialogue.

The SEU report, for example, highlighted the 'considerable disadvantage excluded pupils generally experience with evidence of high levels of stress including unemployment, low income and family disruption'. Schools working in such environments face formidable challenges, as the revelations about Firfield School make clear. The Government's quite reasonable insistence on the responsibilities of parents and schools for truancy and exclusion could, perhaps, be tempered by a greater sensitivity to the problems such schools face and the wider context, for which the Government has responsibility. There may be something of a 'chicken-and-egg' dilemma in the Government's approach to education: it is difficult to extend educational opportunity to all so long as social exclusion persists and yet at the same time extending such opportunity is the principal means by which the Government aims to reduce social exclusion.

CRIME AND DISORDER

Thus far we have been concerned with the respective responsibilities of parents, public authorities and governments to and for children, with little reference to the responsibilities of children. This is in keeping with the tone and content of the wider public debate on both child poverty and education in the UK. Obviously children are not responsible for being poor. More significantly, in the area of education, the focus has been on the responsibilities of parents, schools and LEAs for the misbehaviour of truanting and excluded pupils, and their role in ensuring that such children are not condemned to social exclusion. The pronouncements and policies of the Department for Education and Employment rarely, if ever, include any direct condemnation of children who misbehave at school. They are viewed as failed children rather than bad children and as children to whom the community and the State has responsibilities to address their problems and provide them with opportunities. But the approach, policy and practice of New Labour changes dramatically when one moves from the departments of Health, Social Security and Education to the Home Office, for here condemnation of children for their crimes and misdemeanours is routine.

This is evidenced in New Labour's conspicuous failure to address the criticisms of the UK's youth justice system made in the UN Committee's response to the UK's First Report. While the Government can justly claim that the Second Report shows it to be making significant progress to address most of the other problems highlighted by the Committee, it has not only failed to move towards addressing the low age of criminal responsibility in the UK (10 in England, 8 in Scotland) and the incarceration of young offenders, but appears to be heading in precisely the opposite direction.[43] It is, in particular, arguable that New Labour has lowered the age of criminal responsibility, de facto if not de jure, through the removal of *doli incapax* from UK law.

The punitive elements in New Labour's youth justice policy are difficult to square with the approach to social exclusion and education. As discussed above, New Labour recognises the link between social exclusion and truancy and bad behaviour at school and it emphasises the responsibilities of parents, schools and LEAs to those children most at risk. But in many cases it is precisely these children who are most likely to find themselves in conflict with the law. For example, the Audit Commission's report *Misspent Youth* (1996) found that 42 per cent of school age offenders have been excluded from school and a Home Office report of 1995 found that 98 per cent of boys and 61 per cent of girls permanently excluded from school admitted to offending.[44]

While the Government's crime and disorder policy has been concerned with the rehabilitation of young offenders the emphasis has been much more on the responsibility of children and young people (at least, those above the age of criminal responsibility) for their own actions. The Government's position was clearly set out in November 1997 in a White Paper, significantly entitled *No More Excuses*, which set out the framework for youth justice, subsequently introduced in the CDA 1998.[45] The Government, in an accompanying summary, emphasised that 'allowing young people to drift into a life of crime undermines their welfare and denies them the opportunity to develop into fully contributing members of society'.[46] The purpose of the youth justice system, therefore, was not primarily a punitive one but

---

[43] *See generally*, HOWARD LEAGUE FOR PENAL REFORM, PROTECTING THE RIGHTS OF CHILDREN, SUBMISSION TO THE UN COMMITTEE ON THE RIGHTS OF THE CHILD, 1999, where this case is set out with great clarity and force. For a critical assessment of the approach of the New Labour Government to juvenile crime, *see further*, YOUTH JUSTICE: CONTEMPORARY POLICY AND PRACTICE (B. Goldson, ed. 1999); *see also* S. CURTIS, CHILDREN WHO BREAK THE LAW OR EVERYBODY DOES IT, (1999).
The retention of such a low age of criminal responsibility is difficult to reconcile with other age-based legislation affecting children and young people in the UK. A 10-year-old child is not considered sufficiently mature to consent to medical treatment (unless, as is unlikely, judged to be Gillick competent), vote, enter into sexual relationships, marry, manage his or her financial affairs and so on. However, a child of this age is, under UK law, regarded as having the cognitive and other capacities to be held fully responsible for his or her actions in the criminal courts. It is difficult to see how a child who is considered in need of protection from the consequences of bad choices and decisions when it comes, for example, to health care and sexual relationships, can be held fully responsible in criminal law for bad choices and decisions that produce offending behaviour. There is surely a fundamental inconsistency in Government thinking and legal practice here.

[44] Figures cited in D. Gilbertson, *Exclusion and Crime*, in SECOND CHANCES – EXCLUSION FROM SCHOOL AND EQUALITY OF OPPORTUNITY, 24 (N. Donovan, ed. 1998).

[45] *See generally*, HOME OFFICE, NO MORE EXCUSES – A NEW APPROACH TO TACKLING YOUTH CRIME IN ENGLAND AND WALES, 1997, CM 3809.

[46] *See also*, HOME OFFICE, NO MORE EXCUSES – A NEW APPROACH TO TACKLING YOUTH CRIME IN ENGLAND AND WALES, Summary, 1997.

to 'prevent offending by the young people with which it deals'.[47] It also emphasised that 'parents have a crucial role in preventing their children committing criminal and antisocial acts', and the parenting order (discussed above) was included in the CDA.[48] This approach is in keeping with the Government's approach to social exclusion and education.

However, *No More Excuses* proceeded to state that 'to prevent offending and re-offending by young people, we must stop making excuses for youth crime [that is, for children]. Children above the age of criminal responsibility are generally mature enough to be accountable for their actions and the law should recognise this.'[49] Children of 10 and above were therefore to be held responsible for their antisocial and criminal actions. In particular, the CDA abolished the assumption of *doli incapax* for children aged 10 to 14.[50] The prosecution no longer has to establish that these children understood that their offence was seriously wrong and not just naughty or mischevious: children of 10 are now treated as having the same criminal intent and maturity as adult offenders.

This is all somewhat curious in the light of the Government's sensitivity to the vulnerability of certain groups of children, evident in its approach to the care system, social exclusion and education. Its sympathy appears to expire as soon as a child commits a criminal offence. Not infrequently, the children who end up in the youth courts will have been failed by parents or the care system, condemned to grow up in socially and economically deprived areas, and truanting or excluded from the very schools that the Department for Education and Employment deems as failing. Up to this point, the Government's approach is that such children have been let down by parents, the care system, schools and, ultimately, previous governments. As a consequence, these children are both the victims of, and at risk of perpetuating, those 'cycles of disadvantage' that it is determined to arrest. Once they commit an offence, however, they fall under the 'no more excuses' approach.[51]

Delinquency and the consequences of delinquency will tend to further deepen social exclusion. Children who break the law, and particularly those who spend time in prison, will have particular trouble in keeping up with their education and finding their way into work. It might be concluded that New Labour would be at particular pains to ensure that its policies to tackle social exclusion reach them. One element of such an approach would be to minimise, at least, the numbers of children detained in penal institutions. In fact there has been a further extension of the use of custodial sentences for children since the initial UK report to the

---

[47] *Ibid.*
[48] *Id.*
[49] *Id.*
[50] The Crime and Disorder Act 1998, § 34.
[51] As noted above, the Government has also insisted on the responsibilities of parents. However, this raises an obvious question: if children are to be held fully responsible for their actions in the criminal courts at the age of 10, then how can their parents *also* be held responsible. After all, parental responsibility is not an issue that is ever considered when it comes to adult offenders. Its importance for the Government's youth justice strategy suggests that here, at least, it does see some difference between child and adult offenders when it comes to respective responsibility for offending behaviour, but, with the abolition of *doli incapax,* this difference in no longer recognised in law.

Committee.[52] In particular, the New Labour Government has pressed ahead with the establishment of Secure Training Centres (STCs) for the detention of 12–14 year olds who commit non-grave offences. This has occurred despite the provisions of Article 37 of the CRC which advocates non-custodial sentences where appropriate and the concluding comments of the Committee to the initial UK report which suggest that such units run counter to the spirit and the letter of the CRC.[53]

Under the CDA young offenders can be incarcerated in STC's if they are subject to a Detention and Training Order (DTO) (which replaced the Secure Training Orders introduced under the Criminal Justice and Public Order Act 1994).[54] The DTOs are not intended simply to be punitive: with detention comes training, including continued study of the national curriculum. Children at STCs are, therefore, known as 'trainees', rather then inmates or prisoners. However, on the evidence of a report on the first STC at the Medway Centre, the reality falls far short of the ideal. The report noted routine use of physical restraint by often untrained staff, unsatisfactory educational provision, failure to address offending behaviour, a culture of bullying, intimidation and self-harm, frequent disturbances and occasional riots. The obvious conclusion is that the rehabilitation and reintegration of young offenders is not well served by detaining them, together with other young offenders, in custodial institutions.

It should be said that many of the Government's youth justice policies do address the multiple problems of children in conflict with the law. For example, under s. 39 of the CDA, local authorities are placed under a duty to establish one or more youth offending teams in their area. The team has responsibility for the co-ordination of youth justice services and carries out any additional functions assigned to them by the youth justice plan, which is formulated by the local authority. Teams are composed of a social worker and a person nominated by both the health authority and the chief education officer, along with police and probation officers. This demonstrates clear recognition by the Government that youth offending is a social exclusion issue. It is, therefore, the responsibility of social services, health authorities and LEAs. This kind of 'joined up' approach to offending is also intended to inform and shape the development of Youth Justice Plans, under s. 40 of the Act, and the work of the Youth Justice Board, set up under s. 41. Similar recognition that young offenders may face a wide range of problems, and that in addressing their offending behaviour it is necessary to address its causes, is also evident in the composition and role of youth offender panels as set up under the Youth Justice and Criminal Evidence Act 1999.[55] These developments have been welcomed by organisations such as the Howard League on Penal Reform, which have

---

[52] Since 1995 the number of children serving custodial sentences has increased by 17 per cent. The number of girls given custodial sentences increased by 45 per cent between 1995 and 1997. *See also* F. Russell *Juvenile Crime and Youth Justice*, 155 CHILDRIGHT 7–8 (1999) *see further*, Howard League, *supra*, note 43.

[53] The first STC at Medway was the subject of a very critical report by the Social Services Inspectorate, *see further*, DEPARTMENT OF HEALTH, INSPECTION OF MEDWAY SECURE TRAINING CENTRE, SEPTEMBER–OCTOBER 1998, 1999.

[54] The Crime and Disorder Act 1998, § 73.

[55] *See* the Youth Justice and Criminal Evidence Act 1999, Part I Referrals To Youth Offender Panels.

in the past been highly critical of other aspects of the Government's crime and disorder policy.[56] The difficulty is that, as the experience of Medway shows, the punitive elements of the Government's youth justice policy may actively impede its rehabilitative intentions and it may prove impossible to combine incarceration with both reintegration and the national curriculum.

All this is not to say that the Government ought to concentrate exclusively on improving the care system, parenting education, tackling exclusion and similar issues, rather than on directly addressing offending behaviour with young offenders. For example, increasing emphasis on restorative justice means that more young offenders are required to face the consequences of their offences for victims and to make reparation either to individuals or communities.[57] There is a great deal to be said in favour of such an approach. However, it is important to note that the philosophy underpinning it is not narrowly punitive but is also educative. Being forced to confront the impact of offending is intended as much as a contribution to the 'moral education' of young offenders as it is a punishment and accordingly serves a rehabilitative purpose.

Finally, it should be added that while the age of criminal responsibility is too low in the UK and the high rates of incarceration are contrary to Article 37 of the CRC, it is not easy for those committed to the principles of the CRC to advocate a system where no child should be held responsible for criminal or antisocial actions, if the child is defined in accordance with Article 1 as a person under 18 years. Such a position is not only implausible in itself, but also difficult to reconcile with a commitment to Article 12. It is hard to argue, at one and the same time, under Article 12 that 'States Parties shall assure to the child who is capable of forming his or her own views the right to express those views freely in all matters affecting the child, the views of the child being given due weight in accordance with the age and maturity of the child', with a policy which is based on the presumption that children have no responsibility for their actions. For the same capacities in virtue of which a child's views should be given weight, such as the ability to make decisions and think independently, also imply some responsibility for action. While an age of criminal responsibility of 10 is hardly in 'accordance with the age and maturity of the child'; determining precisely what would be is an altogether more difficult matter.

It is very difficult to reconcile the progressive intent of New Labour policy on poverty and exclusion with its tough stand on juvenile crime and delinquency, other than by taking account of the wider political environment within the UK. It is evident that the New Labour Party regards a tough stand on crime (and, indeed, on immigration and asylum) as electorally expedient given the public mood on these issues in the UK. This is not the only explanation for New Labour's failure to respond positively to the CRC Committee's criticisms of the youth justice system in response to the UK's initial report, but it is undoubtedly a reason. There is an important lesson here for advocates of children's rights who are seeking to influence Government policy. It is not enough simply to address arguments to the Govern-

---

[56] Howard League, *supra*, note 43.
[57] The Crime and Disorder Act 1998, §§ 67, 68.

ment; it is important also to influence public opinion so that the policies which are progressive from a children's rights perspective have the sort of public support that will convince the Government that they do not involve high political risks. This said, it is in the nature of international human rights obligations that they should be upheld by States regardless of popular clamour and public opinion.

CONCLUSION

Hopefully, this survey of New Labour policy in the UK has brought out some general points about the implementation of the CRC, with a wider significance for individuals and organisations committed to promoting the rights of the child. The CRC raises questions that do not arise with other human rights instruments for the obvious reason that its subject is the child. In particular, there are a whole range of unresolved issues regarding the division of responsibilities for the welfare and actions of children between young people themselves, parents and other carers, local government and the State. These issues have been of particular significance in the UK recently given New Labour's determination to shift more of the responsibility for children's welfare and actions onto parents and other carers (as well as its commitment to retaining a very low level of criminal responsibility despite the concerns of the UN Committee). They remain as fraught as they are important. One reason why it is necessary to address these issues is that the signatories of the CRC are States and it is, therefore, crucial to clarify where the State's responsibility for children begins and ends. The points developed in this chapter with specific reference to New Labour's approach in the UK should convey some idea of what is at stake in such questions and why they remain so controversial.

Patricia Tuitt

10. THE STATE, THE FAMILY AND THE CHILD REFUGEE

INTRODUCTION

In an essay entitled *States and Refugees: A Normative Analysis*, Joseph Carens sought to advance reasons for the continued support by States of the institution of asylum.[1] Arguing that the existence of refugees challenged the rational basis of the State system, Caren's employed the familiar analogy of the State and the family. In the final analysis both State and family must justify their primacy as a means of access to civil and political society of individuals as citizens and as family members. Such justification would be found where those denied State or family protection (refugees and orphans) were embraced by substitute States through the institution of asylum or substitute families through the process of adoption or fostering.

Speaking principally of refugees defined within international legal instruments and specifically those refugees falling within the definition of Article 1.A(2) of the Geneva Convention Relating to the Status of Refugees,[2] Carens's family model served as little more than a vehicle within which to present a set of normative propositions concerning the responsibilities of States in the provision of asylum. However, the rapidly increasing presence of displaced children in world refugee statistics illustrates just how apt this model was.[3] Children represent some 65 per cent of refugees of concern to the United Nations High Commissioner for Refugees and while, in general, the fundamental human rights of adults are secured through membership of the political community known as the State, the child's civil, political and welfare rights depend ultimately upon membership within a family. This is

---

[1] *See* J. Carens, *States and Refugees: A Normative Analysis* in REFUGEE POLICY: CANADA AND THE UNITED STATES, 18–29 (H. Adelman, ed. 1991).
[2] Geneva Convention Relating to the Status of Refugees, 28 July 1951, 189 UNTS 150.
[3] Under the United Nations Convention on the Rights of the Child, UN Doc. A/44 (1989) 28 ILM 1456, children are defined as individuals below the age of 18 under Article 1. Aproximately 45 per cent of the world's refugees and displaced persons are children within the meaning of the Convention. The vast majority are from countries in the developing world, although an increasing number are emerging from the war-torn countries in Eastern Europe. Displacement among children occurs for reasons common among forced population movements in general: as a result of breaches of human rights amounting to persecution on grounds specified within the Geneva Convention, Article 1.A(2) or as a result of famine or other natural disaster or generalised violence within the terms of Article 1(2) of the Organisation of African Unity Convention Governing the Specific Aspects of Refugee Problems in Africa, 1 UNTS 4691 (1969). Children, however, are displaced for reasons specific to their status as children: forced abduction in times of unrest, forced military recruitment, sexual abuse and forced labour are examples of forms of refugee-producing phenomena which are either peculiarly meted out to children or which take on a dimension that can only be experienced by child refugees. *See further* UNHCR, GLOBAL REPORT 390 (1999).

Deirdre Fottrell (ed.), Revisiting Children's Rights, 149–155

because of an ideology of children's rights which attributes to adult family members, usually parents or legal guardians, the responsibility of exercising 'rights' on behalf of the child.[4] As recent large-scale refugee crises have shown, the various phenomena that lead to the production of refugees undoubtedly trouble the State system and pose a threat to the existence of individual States; however, they threaten to the very core the institution of the family. Individual family units are routinely and permanently destroyed or fragmented in refugee crises.

Focussing upon child refugees, this chapter attempts to highlight some of the problems inherent in the conventional tie-in of fundamental human rights: civil, political, social, economic and cultural rights, with, at least in the refugee context, two failing institutions. I argue (somewhat tentatively) that dominant solutions to the problem of child refugees – tracing and reunion, inter-country or third country adoption and fostering – mirror almost exactly the old, anti-holistic approach to broader population displacements. In other words they represent a rather desperate attempt at suturing the institution (in our example the family) through a process of substitution. Whilst the substitution process, as exemplified in the right of asylum, is effective for some refugees seeking a new State, where the substituted entity is the family, arguably a less durable entity than the State, the substitution process is likely to break down, leaving the child's 'civil rights in suspense'.[5] In an exploratory vein, this paper seeks ways in which the refugee child's protection needs can be met in a way that acknowledges the important role of the family unit, but does not see the child refugee's protection needs and rights as being reducible to family membership. The argument that the child refugee's needs are too closely tied to one of the most vulnerable institutions in time of civil disturbance – the family unit – depends on two related claims: first that the status of child refugees within legal discourse is largely inseparable from their status as family members, in other words that the child's rights in this context are derivative; and second that the child's derivative status has adversely affected the nature and scope of protection afforded to them. The chapter will focus on a discussion of these two arguments.

The Status of the Child Refugee Within Legal Discourse

While the Geneva Convention Relating to the Status of Refugees sets out many obligations binding on States, these do not specifically extend to child refugees, nor is there any specific mention of children within the Article 1.A(2) definition of refugee. Displaced children form one of several groups of refugees, of increasing concern among the international community, who have been omitted or marginalised from the dominant terms of refugee law and the broader human rights discourse. These groups include women, the elderly and refugees displaced on account

---

[4] *See e.g.*, M. de Langen, *The Meaning of Human Rights for Children* in THE IDEOLOGIES OF CHILDREN'S RIGHTS 255–264 (M.D.A. Freeman & P. Veerman, eds. 1992).

[5] *See* G. Goodwin-Gill, *Protecting the Human Rights of Refugee Children: Some Legal and Institutional Possibilities* in CHILDREN ON THE MOVE: HOW TO IMPLEMENT THEIR RIGHT TO FAMILY LIFE 105 (J. Doek, H. Van Loon & P. Vlaardingerbroek, eds. 1997).

of their sexual orientation – refugees with 'special needs'.[6] These needs are 'special' insofar as these groups call into review the entire concept of the protective regime available to refugees: its exilic bias, its complex and highly individualised forensic process and its narrow conception of the form of tortious wrongs upon which protection depends.

These 'special' refugees form an open category for above all they challenge the view that the causes and consequences of refugeehood can be reduced to a set of fixed definitions. They demand new regimes and newly articulated rights against which both conventional and 'special' needs of refugees can be measured and addressed. What in particular distinguishes these groups is the fact that they have traditionally fallen to the margins of refugee discourse, not as a result of a deliberate policy of exclusion but rather because of the instrumental application of the terms of the discourse that has served to privilege rights discourse in favour of male, adult, heterosexual and able-bodied asylum-seekers. In other words, these refugees have 'special needs' within the institution of asylum and the broader protective regime, because such institutions and regimes operate within a broader legal culture within which their status is at best uncertain.

Returning to the particular example of the child refugee, legal culture perceives the child as being principally defined through the social entity known as the family. The philosophy that children's rights belong to parents is endemic within rights discourse.[7] It is hardly surprising, therefore, that the philosophy permeates the rights regime established under the 1951 Geneva Convention. It is most strongly in evidence in the Convention's silence over child refugees. This silence does not attest to ignorance on the part of the drafters of the Convention of the fact that children are displaced alongside adult family members in times of political, economic and social crises. Rather, it asserts that the Convention's extension of protection to adult refugees of a certain class was a necessary and sufficient basis of protection to child refugees also. The practice of States is to automatically confer refugee status on dependants where the 'head of the family' is recognised as a Convention Refugee. The immediate authority behind this practice is Recommendation B of the Final Act of the Convention. Concerning Family Unity, Governments are encouraged to take necessary and appropriate measures to protect 'refugees who are minors, in particular unaccompanied children and girls, with special reference to guardianship and adoption'.

Expressed within the principle of family unity is both the derivative status of the child and the policy of preserving the integrity of the family unit through the process of substitution. Importantly, the family is to be preserved not merely because of its obvious social value, but as the conduit to the civil, political and welfare rights of the displaced child.

---

[6] *Ibid.*, at 97.
[7] *Supra*, note 4.

THE APPLICATION OF THE BEST INTEREST PRINCIPLE IN TIMES OF REFUGEE
CRISES

The principle of family unity can be traced beyond Recommendation B of the Final
Act of the Geneva Convention to the often cited, overarching principle that in all
matters concerning the child, the child's best interest is the paramount consideration. The 'best interests' or 'welfare' principle is expressed in numerous international treaties and in States' domestic legislation and was incorporated in the
Convention on the Rights of the Child (CRC) in Article 3. Whilst the principle
expresses a largely undisputed standard of protection, it must also be said that concepts such as 'best interests' or 'welfare' are somewhat indeterminate. The best
interest of the child could arguably be achieved if her rights to self-determination
were paramount in rights discourse. This, according to Michael Freeman, is
emphatically not the case, with the discourse of rights firmly favouring a child's
welfare rights over her rights to self-determination. The distinction is important for
welfare rights – the right to care, education and general well-being – are distinguished by the fact that they are amenable to protection through an agency other
than the child – most often a family member. Since the child's interests are defined
as interests predominantly in 'welfare', the content of the best interest principle –
that indeterminate category – is presented conversely as 'determinate' and moreover
absolutely dependent upon the promotion of the family unit.

The principle of family unity directly embraces and applies to the refugee
context a firmly entrenched ideology concerning the nature of harms to which
children are exposed. It is assumed that these are mainly composed of threats to
their welfare. The principle also assumes that the best way to protect the child
from such harms or threats to their security is to vest rights in the head of the
family unit, exercisable for both her benefit and for the benefit of dependants. It is
beyond the scope of this essay to call into question the philosophy of children's
rights as it is generally applied; however, it does fall to be determined whether
securing a child's right to welfare was ever a sufficient basis of refugee protection
where displaced children were concerned. This in turn is dependent on the nature
of the harms thought to befall the majority of children in situations of conflict or
hardship.

In general it appears to be argued that the welfare philosophy is appropriate at
least in relation to accompanied refugee children. Often in these situations, the persecution or other form of harm afflicting the child is derivative and therefore it is
appropriate that a child's rights should also be derivative. In many given cases children become targets because of the religious or political associations or social
group membership of adult family members. In wars, armed conflicts and situations
of general unrest, children are still largely associated with the civilian population
harmed by the 'indiscriminate methods and means of warfare'.[8] There is in fact a
sense, amounting almost to a presumption, that in all civil wars children were non-

---

[8] *See further* F. Krill *The Protection of Children in Armed Conflicts* in THE IDEOLOGIES OF
CHILDREN'S RIGHTS, *supra* note 4 at 347–356.

combatants,[9] a presumption that only begun to be challenged during the later half of the 1970s.[10]

In essence children are ascribed an essentially 'passive' role in refugee-like situations – a role which significantly posits the view that something or someone other than the child was the real focus of harm. In such circumstances the welfare notion dispels the need to confer refugee status on children. Rather, should they be fortunate enough to escape their situation, rights are granted indirectly to them through the entity – the family – most concerned with their welfare.

Unfortunately, what may appear to be a quite logical and rational explanation for the nature of protection traditionally extended to refugee children is compromised by two factors. The first is that under the law as it developed, the question as to whether the child is declared a refugee according to the Convention or through the principle of family unity is not determined after a close scrutiny of the nature of the harm to which they would be exposed upon return to the state of origin, but according to whether they are accompanied or not.[11] Thus, for accompanied children the presumption of their innocence in field combat and other refugee-producing situations remains firm – a factor which is crucial in explaining their still rather nebulous status under international refugee law.

The second factor that tends to undermine the supposed rational basis of the protection afforded to child refugees, the argument that children took a 'passive' role in conflict situations, whether one refers to historical or contemporary conflicts, is seriously disputed, particularly as a result of the growing recognition of the phenomenon of the child soldier. The involvement of children in wars not only provides states or agents of the State with a clear motive to target children as individuals, on the basis of a political opinion expressed by or attributed to the child; it also attributes to children a level of consciousness and autonomy which belies the passive role traditionally ascribed them. For example, in exploring the reasons why children take up arms, Ilene Cohn and Guy Goodwin-Gill identify factors that would supposedly be common to adults (males) whose status under refugee law is not uncertain or disputed. Reasons cited include 'the militarization of daily life and questions of loyalty to religious, nationalistic or political ideology'.[12] Whilst they rightly state that these motives cannot be used to argue 'voluntary participation' (because of the clear presence of 'youth indoctrination'), the existence of child soldiers and less formal involvement of children in armed conflicts seriously undermines the notion of their innocence because that innocence in this context denotes that the child remains a passive and untargeted casualty in refugee crises.

SUTURING THE FAMILY: THE CHILD REFUGEE SOLUTION

The paramount welfare principle, with its reliance upon the family entity in securing children's rights, has been severely tested in recent times of civil unrest resulting

[9] *See* F.A. Mann, < > 58.
[10] *Supra* note 8 at 348.
[11] *See* G. GOODWIN-GILL, THE REFUGEE IN INTERNATIONAL LAW 357 (1996).
[12] *See* I. COHN & G. GOODWIN-GILL, CHILD SOLDIERS (1994).

Patricia Tuitt

in the separation and fragmentation of the family unit. In positive terms it has resulted in the greater visibility of children within the refugee determination process, much to the enrichment of refugee discourse, which now embraces dimensions brought about through the acknowledgment of the particular suffering of refugee children. It is undoubtedly the case that child refugees only acquired real visibility within the legal regime once they had become separated not only from their State of origin but from their families too. Thus, although child refugeehood as a sociological phenomenon was known to the world, the child refugee as denoting an identifiable legal category owes its presence within contemporary legal discourse to the existence of the unaccompanied refugee child.

Much less positively, the refugee child phenomenon has tested the institution of the family in ways that the largely abstract entity of the State could not be tested. The large number of displaced children encouraged international organisations to place child refugees high on the list of priorities. The urgency of the child refugee phenomenon, together with the philosophy that makes the family paramount in a solution to the problem of refugee children, means that the most desired solution is the return of the child to the unit that would best secure her civil, political and welfare rights. As Goodwin-Gill recently observed this has meant that 'all too frequently in the past ... the rush to find solutions for refugee children deprived of their family has led to premature insistence on resettlement, adoption or foster placement'. This is done, he argues, without sufficient attention to 'standards and procedures'.[13]

Tracing families and subsequent family reunification is clearly the preferred objective, with inter-country or third country adoption and fostering being desirable alternatives. These solutions clearly have a sound juridical basis. Article 22(3) of the CRC (1989) emphasises the need to trace the child's family with a view to eventual family reunification. Unfortunately, there are difficulties in the way of each solution caused, I would argue, by a rights regime that privileges adult asylum-seekers. Tracing and reunification has proved difficult not merely because of the obvious problems inherent in trying to trace family members left behind in an increasingly disordered society, but also because many States, including the United Kingdom, have made reservations to the principle of family unit on immigration grounds. For example, the United Kingdom is reluctant both to extend rights of residence to asylum-seekers and to permit family reunification in circumstances where the person exercising the right has less than full refugee status. This is without sufficient regard to the effects of such reservations on child refugees who require the family unit to enforce their legal and other rights.

Alternative solutions, such as adoption, are also problematic, particularly where third country adoption is sought. The 1980 Hague Convention on Inter-country adoption[14] appears to set out the principles upon which States are guided. The Convention grants power to the government of the State to arrange adoptions of persons habitually resident within the State. Again, as few refugees are immediately

---

[13] See Goodwin-Gill, *supra* note 5 at 100.
[14] See The Hague Convention on Protection of Children and Co-operation in Respect of Intercountry Adoption, concluded May 29 1993, 1134, I.L.M. (1993).

determined 'habitual residents' of a State, the government of the State may prove unwilling to take responsibility for arranging adoption.

CONCLUSION

What the foregoing illustrates is that increasingly children are finding that there are no natural or substitute families to go to. This absence suspends not only their welfare rights; their civil and political rights are temporarily suspended within a legal culture that has failed to find a way of creating a discourse of rights within which the child is both visible and central. In the refugee context this should mean at the very least that formal refugee status and therefore permanent residence is vested in the child displaced as a result of refugee-producing phenomena that leave them without a family. Thus, absence of family brought about by individually targeted threats to the civil and political status of the child or family member, or general violence affecting a child or family member, should become an independent ground of refugee status. This would not displace the family's symbolic or institutional importance; however, it would ensure that child refugees are not forced to float in a 'legal limbo' until the process of substitution is complete.

Maggie Black

11. CHILD DOMESTIC WORKERS: SLAVES, FOSTER CHILDREN OR UNDER-AGE EMPLOYEES?

The use of children to skivvy and 'help about the house' has a very long history, as folk literature from all over the world attests. The story of 'Cinderella' – an archetypal child domestic worker – is one of the best known and best loved in the pantheon and has its counterparts in many non-European languages.[1] Today there are maybe as many as 100 million real life Cinderellas in countries all over the world who do not get to marry Prince Charming or live happily ever after. Their story is more often the classic one of benign (or less benign) neglect, casual exploitation, and the subjugation of their childhood into the rendering of service to others more privileged than themselves.

As a start then, we should deconstruct the eighteenth century version of Cinderella's servant girl process from rags to riches (eighteenth century because it is usually visualised on the stage or screen in high baroque). Cinders is the daughter of Baron Hardup, her mother died when she was very young, and her father has since married a spiteful woman who is mean in the matter of hiring servants. The Stepmother has two ugly and unpleasant (note the equivalence) daughters and they depose the existing daughter, Cinderella, who becomes their drudge. The father is the eighteenth-century equivalent of 'absent', making no effort to care for or champion the rights of his own child (he is sympathetically depicted as harried by women). Cinders lives in the kitchen with the mice, she has no room or bed of her own, she works round the clock and has barely a decent set of rags to wear. She is lonely and isolated, she has no friends and never gets to play.[2]

How does Cinderella manage? She has her dreams and aspirations, which can be a potent force in keeping unhappy children going. Today's children in 'especially difficult circumstances' – street children, children in institutions, children who have been orphaned or abandoned – often survive on their dreams. Children in Manila who work on the city's notorious Smokey Mountain rubbish dump talk of others who have found gold bars in the trash, or brown paper bags full of dollar bills, believing that a lucky find will bring them miraculous delivery from their lot.[3] Children who work as maids in Sri Lanka's coastal resorts have heard of the

---

[1] The Cinderella story turns up in many guises, for example, in pantomime (Buttons), in film (The Rose and The Slipper) and in opera (Rossini's La Cerentola); similar stories exist in Russian and Chinese folk literature.

[2] In the Cinderella story school is not mentioned as schooling for girls was not heavily rated in the eighteenth century. If a tutor comes to the house to instruct the stepsisters Cinderella is an onlooker at best.

[3] *See* M. BLACK, CHILDREN OF THE RUNAWAY CITIES (1991). *ICDC UNICEF Florence.*

Deirdre Fottrell (ed.), Revisiting Children's Rights, 157–168
© 2000 *Kluwer Law International. Printed in Great Britain.*

serving girl who married a rich and handsome client and was carried away to become a bejewelled wife in a land of plenty.[4] The pages of today's glossy magazines yield similar tales of humble teenaged waitresses swept off Parisian sidewalks and away to Hollywood by passing celebrities. In the Cinderella story her dream comes true. That is part of the point of the story: to give other Cinderellas hope. The other part is to keep them good, submissive and perfectly behaved while they wait for their day of transformation to come.

We know what happens to Cinderella: the fairy godmother, the transformation, the dance with the Prince who falls instantly in love and her ultimate triumph over the ugly sisters. Thus, it all ends with the lovely Cinderella's wedding to a gloriously good-looking and delightful prince.

Apart from the ending, the situation of many of today's Cinderellas is remarkably similar to that of their forbear. Children in domestic work in the twenty-first century typically work around the clock, eat scraps and leftovers, sleep in the kitchen, are isolated and spoken to roughly by their 'betters', and criticised for the slightest thing.[5] These young domestic workers, whether they are in Bangladesh, the Philippines, Kenya, India, Togo, Haiti, or Peru, typically receive very little or nothing in the way of remuneration and are exploited as if this were their natural lot in life. There is an important difference between these children and Cinderella. She has been artificially relegated to a servant status. She is, in fact, a daughter of the household. Undoubtedly, there are girls today in a similar situation, whose parent or step-parent is the source of abuse or exploitation. However, Cinderella's advantage is that when her great break comes, she can look and act the part. That is much less likely to be the case with today's servant girls (probably also in the eighteenth century), who usually come from a socially and/or ethnically deeply 'inferior' world. In fact, it is systems of social hierarchy and entrenched attitudes about social inferiority which keep this practice going, and make it so oppressive.

My own first conscious exposure to the use of children as domestic workers was in Bangladesh. Like other societies in the Indian sub-continent, Bangladesh is deeply and profoundly hierarchical. It is not a caste society like India, but its poorest people are almost as 'untouchable', belonging to a totally different world from the rich and well appointed who live in garden suburbs and drink lime sodas at the Sheraton Hotel.

I went to Bangladesh in 1993 on behalf of Anti-Slavery International. My initial brief was to examine the predicament of Bangladeshi children in bonded labour. However, there are no market dynamics to support bonded labour in Bangladesh. Classic forms of slavery in which labour is 'owned' or bound to the employer as a purchasable commodity only tend to occur in environments where labour is scarce: hence the need to create unbreakable bonds between the employee and the employer. In Bangladesh, labour is so abundant that there will always be a replace-

---

[4]   *See* N. TATNAPALA, CHILD LABOUR IN THE HOTEL, CATERING AND TOURISM SECTOR: A SRI LANKAN CASE STUDY, (unpublished paper 1993), quoted in M. BLACK, IN THE TWILIGHT ZONE (1995).
[5]   *See further* UNICEF/INNOCENTI, *Child Domestic Work*, INNOCENTI DIGEST (1999).

ment, quite possibly a cheaper replacement, for any labour lost. So on this visit, I soon decided to look at other contemporary forms of child slavery or servitude, using as my starting point the 1956 UN Supplementary Convention on Slavery.[6] Article 1(d) specifically prohibits

> any institution or practice whereby a child or young person under the age of 18 is delivered by either or both of his natural parents or by his guardian to another person, where for reward or not, with a view to the exploitation of the child or young person or of his labour.

My visit to Bangladesh was facilitated by the Oxfam Field Director (Anti-Slavery International was not well liked in Bangladesh at that time, due to work on another human rights issue which had upset the Government.) Oxfam booked me into a local guesthouse – let us call it the Acacia – and I set off around Dhaka asking researchers and non-governmental organisations (NGOs) all about child labour. In Bangladesh this is a vast field as there is no occupation – from manufacturing to transport, farming, trading, prostitution, begging and crime – in which children are not employed.

The Acacia was a family-run guesthouse whose owner was extremely helpful. Every morning, I was greeted by a five-year-old whooping around the master's car and throwing soapy water on the bonnet. Whenever I pressed the bell outside my room, an older boy brought tea, or ironed my trousers, or went to fetch a rickshaw. This was all very hospitable and normal in Bangladesh, and I switched easily into a *memsahib* persona – the smiling and authoritative lady patron.

Before long I had settled on the key lines of my inquiry. I was horrified by an incident reported in the newspaper. An employer had attacked her girl domestic with a red hot iron and nearly blinded her. Such news items were not uncommon, I was told. The usual motive was sexual jealousy. A wife might attack the maid because the husband was molesting her. Or it might be 'maid rage' against a clumsy child who broke things. Sexual abuse and personal violence against child domestics marked out this occupation as highly vulnerable. Sex was just one form of exploitation. Many domestics – some as young as six or seven years – were on duty around the clock, without holidays or rest breaks, they never left the house and only saw their parents back in the village maybe once a year for the *Eidd* festival.[7] This was not just 'child labour'. This was clearly servitude – even slavery according to the definition in the Supplementary Convention.

One day there was an episode at the Acacia. I had given my trousers to be ironed without removing my money from the pocket. It disappeared. I spoke to the manager. Only when he instituted a search of the boys' sleeping quarters did it dawn on me that I was staying in an establishment almost entirely staffed by child

---

[6]   The UN Supplementary Convention on the Abolition of Slavery, the Slave Trade, and Institutions and Practices Similar to Slavery (UN, 1956).

[7]   *See futher* H. RAHMAN, CHILD DOMESTIC WORKERS: IS SERVITUDE THE ONLY OPTION? (1995).

domestic labour. The search was productive. He found a blue plastic wallet just like mine among a boy's possessions. But the money in it was in a thick bundle in tiny denominations; this was not the few, pristine, large-denomination notes I had been given by the bank. Clearly the boy had collected his tips and this was his savings. So here was a new revelation. A child domestic worker at the Acacia could save the equivalent of $50. So was this servitude too?

Of my reactions to this episode, the one which remained with me most power-fully was the degree to which I had been able to discuss, research, and contemplate a particular phenomenon, and not notice it around me. The boys at the Acacia had been an important part of my support system – as no doubt for all other NGO visi-tors staying there. What on earth had I thought? That they were the manager's sons? Naturally, *his* children were in school. Actually, I had not thought. I had not been looking at the trees, only at the wood. And I was far from being the only one. You can discuss child servitude with the most sincere Bangladeshi child rights acti-vist, while your tea is served by a teenage maid. It would be far more unusual if your hostess served the tea herself – in Bangladesh that would be very uncommon.

This episode at the Acacia – at $50 the lesson was cheap at the price – was my introduction to what I have since described as the 'attitudinal invisibility' surround-ing children in domestic employment. If someone belonging to a society where live-in domestic servants are almost unknown, an anachronism, could slip into a persona where she took for granted the use of 12-year-olds to cater to her domestic needs even while closely examining issues of child servitude, then how totally normal such a thing must seem to those brought up with such a custom. This is the case in most third world countries. Not just in the Indian sub-continent, but in Africa, the Middle East, other parts of Asia, Latin America, and most of the Car-ibbean, domestic management still depends not on the labour-saving device but the employment of 'helpers' or whatever word they are known by. There are differences of age, and of sex: in East Africa, domestic work is often undertaken by men. Most servants are adult, or at least not as young as is common in Bangladesh; although I have to confess that I employed a 15-year-old secondary schoolboy in Nairobi in the late 1970s as my servant. His father had run off and left him unsupported in the servants' quarters attached to the house I was renting, and this was the only way – as far as I could see – of giving him a place to live and helping him complete school. It never occurred to me that he was enduring 'child servitude', and it still seems somewhat laughable to describe it that way now.

Invisibility, however, is an important aspect of this whole practice. At the time of my visit to Bangladesh, child domestic work was invisible from every point of view. Very few NGOs or researchers anywhere had addressed the issue, either as a sub-set of child labour or from a human rights perspective. There was a complete dearth of information. At that time the only available international research data was a report from Haiti about *restavek* children[8] – children given by poor families to richer ones to work in their households – and a couple of other studies from Kenya

---

[8] Minnesota Lawyers International Human Rights Committee, 'RESTAVEK: Child Labour in Haiti', case report, Minneapolis, 1990.

and Sri Lanka. That has since changed radically. There are now many studies from many different countries, admittedly many small scale and several unpublished; but still a much fuller picture is emerging.[9] In September 1999, Save the Children UK hosted a regional workshop in Lima on the subject of 'children working in other people's households' all over South America – a great advance in terms of challenging the invisibility of the practice in that part of the world.[10] Similar meetings have been held by the African Network for the Prevention and Protection against Child Abuse and Neglect (ANPPCAN) in East Africa, in West Africa by UNICEF, and internationally by ILO/IPEC (the ILO International Programme for the Elimination of Child Labour). The subject of child domestic workers is therefore now 'in'. Indeed, no discussion of child labour today seems complete without references to the 'invisible millions' of child domestic workers. The numbers of these 'millions' are still only guesses and may remain that way. But it can be stated with confidence that domestic work is the largest employer of girls under 16 around the world (ILO's assessment).[11] There is, too, much more qualitative information available about the practice than there used to be. This is owing, in considerable part, to the work of Anti-Slavery International and IPEC, and their joint efforts to encourage local NGOs to undertake action-research studies.[12]

Gathering information on the issue is difficult because of the nature of the employment which is another aspect of its invisibility. Almost all child domestics are employed in separate households, so there is no group setting, such as the factory, the plantation or the shopping mall, in which to count them. Child domestics are behind closed doors in private homes and consequently very difficult to reach. And if researchers conduct door-to-door household surveys and interview the children in their workplace (where else can they be interviewed if they never leave it?) they say very little. They have almost no capacity for self-expression. They fear being punished or losing their job. Certainly, they will not describe episodes of violence or sexual abuse to strangers.[13] It takes a great deal of time and confidence-building, usually in a setting such as a drop-in centre, before they can do any such thing. So information about them often remains hidden or is anecdotal.

The jobs are invisible too. Domestic work is unregistered and not part of employment statistics. And the arrangements for hiring a child domestic, even where 'recruiters' are involved, are very informal. A go-between, often a woman from the girl's village, makes a deal with the employer on behalf of the child's parents; who knows what these deals consist of? Many placements are not perceived as 'jobs' at all. A typical reaction in an employer household may be: 'We aren't employing her, no. She is a poor girl from our village who my wife has kindly taken in. Naturally she helps about the house.' Is this a child domestic servant or a foster child?

---

[9] *Supra* note 5.
[10] REUNION TECNICA INTERNACIONAL: NIÑEZ TRABAJADORA EN EL HOGAR DE TERCEROS, LIMA, PERÚ; SCF (1999).
[11] See note 5.
[12] *See further* M. BLACK, CHILD DOMESTIC WORKERS: A HANDBOOK FOR RESEARCH AND ACTION (1997).
[13] M. BLACK, RESEARCH METHODS RELATING TO CHILD DOMESTIC WORKERS, REPORT OF AN ASI SEMINAR, ASI (1996).

Thus the situation of child domestic workers is very ambiguous. As the story of Cinderella illustrates, the deployment of young girls to skivvy in the household is a practice with a long tradition. In fact, it can be seen as an even older occupation than sexual services, with which it sometimes interacts. The death of one or both parents was until very recently the commonest of family tragedies and often when a child was orphaned and where parents were extremely poor and over-burdened, it was common in every society and in some is still common today, to send a child to live in another household – usually, but not necessarily related. This circumstance is now again becoming increasingly common in eastern and southern Africa in the wake of orphanhood due to parental AIDS. The child performs tasks 'in the house of others' in return for shelter, care, nurture and education or useful instruction. And what could be more useful for girls in many societies than preparation for a life of marriage, procreation, child-raising, and proficient domestic management? Such ideas were common in our own society as recently as the nineteenth century as Jane Eyre and Bleak House both bear out.

In some settings, child domestics are seen as additional family members as if they were 'adopted'. Legal forms of adoption or guardianship may also be used for the purposes of exploiting such children's labour – there are cases where people in the US today 'adopt' children from Eastern Europe for motives which are suspiciously close to the intention to add a live-in maid to the household.[14] Thus the difference between adoption and employment can be difficult to pin down. Certainly, in Latin America and elsewhere, many employers perceive themselves as being totally beneficent towards a young girl domestic under their protective and nurturing wing. And they may genuinely have set her off on a good path in life, given her an education and even found her a Prince Charming. Cecilia Endara, the Director of the Fundación María Guare in Ecuador, described to a recent meeting in Lima the case of her own girl domestic, who started work in her household at the age of 13, has been a close family friend ever since, and is today married to a very successful architect.[15] Endara's organization is, among other things, a progressive employment agency for such girls, helping them to defend their rights and to use this occupation as a path for self-advancement. Thus there is evidence for employer empowerment of such girls, as well as for employer exploitation. Generalisations about the practice between households, let alone between countries, are dangerous.

Still the fact is that for many such children their working situation is indistinguishable from slavery. The worst general case is that of Haiti. Here, a society which is still effectively feudal accepts as normal that a child may be given away by a poor mother to a better-off family for good. These children are known as *restavek* – meaning 'staying with' from the French '*reste avec*' – and are treated as the living equivalent of a broom or a dishwasher. They receive no pay, can be as young as five, frequently lose all contact with their families, and are profoundly discriminated against in the household.[16] At least 300,000 children are thought to be working as

---

[14] Personal communication between the author and a journalist on the New York Times.
[15] *See* note 10.
[16] *See further* IPSOFA/UNICEF, RESTAVEK: LA DOMESTICITÉ JUVENILE EN HAÏTI (1998).

restavek domestics but a definitive count is almost impossible. A recent study conducted for UNICEF by the Institut Psycho-Social de la Famille in Port-au-Prince paints a truly shocking picture of maltreatment. Of 850 children surveyed, 77 per cent reached 17 years of age without ever going to school. Their '*patronnes*' did not regard them as entitled to play or make friends. Few received any word of encouragement (8.5 per cent) and only one-fifth were ever given money for their families; 60 per cent had never received anything at all. The same proportion were frequently physically punished by the master or mistress of the house and sometimes by their children, a situation which they found particularly humiliating. The most frequent form of punishment was to be whipped (44 per cent), and there were many instances of torture.[17]

By any definition, *restavek* children are in slavery. The practice is, in fact, illegal in Haiti, but as in so many cases of child employment or labour or adoption around the world, the law is regularly flouted and ignored; it is both unenforced and unforceable. However, it would be completely wrong to characterise all situations of child domestic work in this way – perhaps even in Haiti. It is often said that child domestics may be the most numerous, most exploited, and most vulnerable child workers in the world. But my experience at the Acacia Guesthouse, where at least one boy had managed to save the equivalent of $50 from his tips, indicates that it would be utterly misleading to suggest that servitude and gross abuse are the inevitable pattern. That gross abuse and exploitation exists is indisputable: that was the case for the girl branded with a hot iron by her mistress, whose case had reached the newspaper. But I had had no sense of a connection between the boys at the Acacia and the girl with a permanently scarred face, in excruciating pain at the hospital as a result of her *memsahib's* behaviour. Nor would most people in Bangladesh, who would be equally appalled by such cruelty.

Wherever it occurs in the world, the practice of employing children as domestic workers, or sending them to 'live' in other people's households, has to be viewed in the context of life-styles, belief systems and employment patterns. If it is to be brought out of the shadows and made visible, this needs to happen without introducing distortions. Analysis should be grounded in the socio-cultural and economic setting.

If there is a general contemporary trend in the developing world, it is that 'work as upbringing' in the child's own home or that of a relative is giving way to a commercialised and therefore more potentially exploitative arrangement. Long hours, low rewards, lack of childhood development opportunities, lack of affection and other forms of deprivation therefore ensue. Increasingly, the sending out or the taking in of a child is not primarily designed to serve the child's interests, but is the outcome of a transaction in which the traded commodity is the child's labour. In a rapidly urbanising and industrialising world, the demand for cheap household labour – for girls that 'do what they're told and don't answer back' – is growing.[18] At least one commentator on the situation in the Americas regards 'feminists' as

---

[17] *Ibid.*
[18] *See note 5.*

partly to blame, because they need to employ household help so that they can go out to work.[19] In many countries their supply is also becoming more organised and the involvement of recruiters and agents more common. In West Africa and parts of Asia, this can mean the involvement of traffickers, bringing boys and girls in from neighbouring countries.[20] More children and young people today are working in households of people who are in no way related to them, often at a considerable distance from home. They are under the control of adults who, whatever their intention, have as their first concern not the child's well-being but that of their own household. Where a recruiter has acted as an intermediary and brought children from far away including across borders, the sense of distance is enhanced; and where the child is barely literate, the possibility of writing home or maintaining any contact with his or her family during the employment period is non-existent.

Given this trend, the possibility of abusive or discriminatory behaviour towards children who cannot retaliate or defend their rights increases dramatically. The perception of their employment by the children concerned is very different from that of many of their employers. Those who are not regarded as 'employed' suffer an even greater degree of subjugation than those who have an employee status. In West Africa especially, where upbringing in the houses of others has a long traditional history, many such children are regarded simply as living in surrogate parental households where their role is to cook, clean, and fulfill other domestic obligations as a preparation for adulthood.[21] Children in such situations are clearly vulnerable to overwork, exploitation and neglect. Yet many 'employers' or 'carers' think that the situation is advantageous to the child. They point to the fact that their child domestics eat better, live in nicer – usually urbanised – surroundings, and are better looked after than they would be in a village or distinctly poorer home, or in street-based occupations, factories or workshops where they would be exposed to other dangers. But almost all children in domestic work who have been asked what they feel, tend to view their situation negatively.[22] When invited to list their preferred type of working occupation, child workers, whatever job they are currently in, rate domestic work very low in the choice list. They would prefer to work on the street, or do almost anything other than occupy a position of servility and subjugation to others.

The impacts of their working situation on domestic child workers cannot be viewed in a simple framework of physical survival and health on the one hand, and vulnerability to violence, cruelty and neglect on the other, the somewhat crude frameworks which are too often used to assess children's well-being. An important

---

[19] *See* E.M. Chaney, of the University of Iowa and Confederation of Latin American and Caribbean Household Workers, paper presented at SCF REUNION TECNICA INTERNACIONAL NIÑEZ TRABJADORA EN EL HOGAR DE TERCEROS, Lima, Peru, September 1999. Copy on file with the author.

[20] LAETITIA VEIL, THE ISSUE OF CHILD DOMESTIC LABOUR AND TRAFFICKING IN WEST AND CENTRAL AFRICA, (1988).

[21] *Ibid.*

[22] *See* MARTIN WOODHEAD, CHILDREN'S PERCEPTIONS OF THEIR WORKING LIVES (1998).

reference is the 1989 Convention on the Rights of the Child (CRC).[23] Although the CRC does not contain any article that specifically proscribes employment of a child as a live-in domestic as definitively as the 1956 Supplementary Convention on Slavery, a number of rights articulated in the CRC are actuallly or potentially relevant, especially if the child is under the age of 14 – the legal minimum age of employment according to the relevant ILO Convention (No. 138).[24] (The more recent ILO Convention on the Worst Forms of Child Labour No. 182, does not specify domestic work as a 'worst form', but it does include 'practices similar to slavery' and repeat the validity of the 1956 Slavery Convention.) The application of the CRC is more complex: the rights it expresses provide a model of childhood and are best used as a checklist or benchmark.

There are certain general rights in the CRC that may be breached by the use of a child for domestic work: the right to development (Article 6), to non-discrimination (Article 2) and respect for the child's best interests (Article 3). Among the specific rights that a child domestic worker does not, or may not, enjoy are the following: rights of independent identity, selfhood, physical integrity and freedom (Articles 8, 13, 15 and 37); parental nurture and guidance (Articles 7, 8 and 9); physical and psychological well-being (Articles 19, 27); educational development (Articles 28, 32); psycho-social, emotional and spiritual development (Articles 31, 32); and protection from exploitation, including sexual exploitation, sale and trafficking (Articles 32, 34 and 35). In all these contexts, the nature of the work or the terms governing both work and living conditions, may – or may not – lead to serious deprivation. Everything, in the end, is at the whim of the employer. This is the feature of the situation of child domestics most frequently emphasised in the relevant studies as potentially damaging.

For the child workers themselves, the worst aspects of their situation are usually the isolation, the loneliness, the discrimination, the lack of love, the loss of a sense of self, the imprisonment in a servant *persona*. Projects specifically aimed at helping child domestics often focus on providing them with an alternative social setting for days off, one with friends and peer companions. And, of course, with catch-up classes. There are also a growing number of crisis intervention programmes, which can consist of emergency medical and legal and psychological counseling services, often within a drop-in centre. Such centres, of which the Casa Panchita in Lima, Peru, is a typical example, provide a place where young maids can find the substitute parent figures and the socially equal peers which provide a real surrogate family. Here they can relax, enjoy themselves, make close affective relationships, take up their own interests, and learn how to be someone in their own right instead of a permanently fixed social inferior to others whose fundamental attitude is that of patron and supreme boss.[25]

---

[23] *See* the United Nations Convention on the Rights of the Child, UN Doc.A/44/25 (1994), reprinted in 28 I.L.M. 1457 (1989).

[24] ILO Convention Concerning Minimum Age for Admission to Employment (1973), No 138, ILO, Geneva.

[25] PANCHITA, published by LA CASA DE LA PANCHITA DE LA ASOCIACIÓN GRUPO DE TRABAJO REDES; see also note 10.

What – other than service interventions – can be done to help repair all the many kinds of invisibility and deprivation child domestic workers suffer? Advocacy certainly has a role but this must be sensitively handled. 'Shock, horror' tactics and international outrage against the practice is, in the main, inappropriate. In societies where the hiring of young maids or the taking-in of children from other families is regarded as normal, outrage may come across as simplistic and neo-colonial condemnation of the entire society. Certainly, some child domestics are subjected to violence and sexual abuse: there is indisputable, if sketchy, evidence that this is the case. But neither is integral to child domestic employment, any more than to being a stepchild, though there, too, evidence shows that the correlation is more likely than in the case of a conventional family upbringing. In order to address the practice, it is necessary to enlist, not alienate, the employers of child domestics. Where social values condone the use of child domestic labour, this is not a reprobate minority group of clearly identifiable child abusers – such as pimps or traffickers – but ordinary respectable members of society – including child rights activists themselves. If advocacy is handled sensitively, minds can and do change, sometimes quite quickly. This has already begun to happen in Bangladesh in the years since my first visit to examine the issue in 1993.

The way to start is by tackling 'attitudinal invisibility' within the society. Awareness-raising needs to be led by local people and local organisations, and based on local research and proper data, not scare-mongering and synthetic generalisations. This research, well publicised, may be able to persuade people with entrenched ideas of social patronage and hierarchy to become more self-aware. If they are to acknowledge the dignity and self-worth of the maids that they hire, the example has to come from within their own ranks. At present, in Bangladesh and in some other parts of the Indian sub-continent, the English language newspaper columns and magazines, and other contexts in which society women express themselves, tend to lament the bad behaviour and attitudes of the maids, not of their employers. The idea that 'a poor child from the village who I have kindly taken in' is a child with as many needs and rights as their own children is truly extraordinary and basically unacceptable to people whose sense of their own standing is relatively elevated. But it does not need to stay that way.

At the SCF meeting on 'children working in the houses of others' in Lima in September 1999 it was sometimes unavoidable to feel a whiff of hypocrisy. In the meeting room were several representatives of local domestic workers' associations. It was an achievement that they were present. But their own personal experiences and insights which would have been so valuable, given that many began work at a very young age, were drawn upon inadequately. It was as if they had been invited to listen to 'the experts'. One speaker, an 'expert', arguing the case for attitudinal change, said courageously: what about *'nosotros tambien'* – us too?[26] Too many people at the meeting, many of them men in suits with fancy Power-Point presentations about child labour, wanted to believe that a major study could be launched and a law passed and somehow this problem of domestic child worker exploitation would go

---

[26] *See* note 10.

away. After the meeting, representatives from Casa Panchita (*casa Panchita* means a 'house' or room where young *Panchitas* or maids could come for classes, counselling or recreation) invited me to visit their project. Casa Panchita, which was taking employers to court and doing all sorts of pioneering things, was run entirely by volunteers on a shoe-string. Few men in smart suits had ever visited it or tried to help find it support. Probably many people at the Lima meeting had maids at home who might well be below the age of school completion or the minimum age of employment, if they had ever thought about it. '*Nosotros tambien*' is important indeed, and applies as much to those of us who have lived in, or spend time in, countries where domestic service is the norm, as my own experience bears out.

It is also important to realise that the use of the law is not going to be much help. In most countries where the practice is widespread, laws, even if they exist, and most countries have plenty of laws against abusive child work and exploitation, are quite unable to be implemented in the child domestics context. Most domestic work around the world, including in a highly lawyered society such as Britain, is unregulated. Labour inspectorates, the standard child labour preventive, can be sent into factories and mines to remove children from the workplace. But what happens in private households between a woman and a child worker or a surrogate foster child, is beyond the reach of law enforcement agents. Certainly, in cases of gross abuse where they are revealed, for example, when a child is admitted to hospital with burns, it is important to see that the employers be taken to court and successfully prosecuted. This has been done effectively in Sri Lanka, which set up a 'helpline' for children to telephone the social services confidentially about abuse. But outside this context there is not much of a role for laws or law enforcement. The use of international instruments such as the CRC is mainly confined to awareness-raising, or to guide the development of interventions. In this context, the views of lawyers on how to develop voluntary codes of practice for the employment of young and older domestics is also valuable; these codes of practice can be propagated as part of advocacy directed at employers. But again, this activity is essentially about changing attitudes rather than about applying law.

Whatever action is undertaken, the principle should still be observed that at the international level, such action promotes and takes its cue from local action. It is there, in Dhaka, in Haiti, in Lima, in Kenya and elsewhere that the attitudinal change will come which will release these girls from servitude and give them back their childhoods.

So to return at last to Cinderella. It is not possible to save all the Cinderellas of the twenty-first century world from their fate, and no-one would support a strategy of mass marriage to multiple Prince Charmings. However, I do not believe that the mean-minded stepmother is totally beyond redemption, nor the poor ugly sisters (with whom I have always had a sneaking sympathy). Baron Hardup could usefully be given some lessons in parenting or a visit from the Child Support Agency to make him shape up. The idea should be put across that employment is employment under all circumstances, even when the employee is very young. The household employer should fulfill all suitable employment rights and obligations, especially to allow time off for education, social life and recreation. It should also be put across

Judith Ennew

12. WHY THE CONVENTION IS NOT ABOUT STREET CHILDREN

INTRODUCTION

Although most international agencies working with children now refer to their work as 'rights-based', the majority of policies continue to focus on adult definitions of children's needs and problems and adult-designed services and solutions. Indeed there is no general consensus about what 'rights-based' programming may or may not be, and many child rights workers are woefully ignorant of the wider human rights agenda. One obstacle to the development of a genuine child rights approach to programming has been a tendency on the part of planners to think of child rights as belonging in the sphere of protection from abuse and exploitation, while continuing to use conventional welfare and service provision approaches in areas such as health and education. Moreover, civil and political rights tend to be sidelined, with the exception of a romantic approach to 'participation', which is little more than a rights gloss on pragmatic project decisions that encourage 'beneficiaries' to become 'participants' in the interests of sustainability.[1]

As a result of this confusion between protection and child rights, policymakers have tended to focus on children who epitomise childhood vulnerability because they are outside adult control.[2] The groups of children who have come to be called 'street children', who excite both pity and fear because they live without families on streets and other public urban spaces, attract a disproportionate amount of so-called 'rights-based' programming. As a target group for policymakers, street children have hijacked the urban agenda, together with associated planning budgets, to the detriment of other groups of disadvantaged urban children.[3] Similarly, the topic of street children has, to a large extent, hijacked the child rights agenda and attached it to welfare philosophy, obscuring the actual rights issues that apply to these children as well as to all children everywhere.

WHAT AND WHO ARE 'STREET CHILDREN'?

'Street children' of one kind or another have existed as long as there have been urban streets but have become a particular topic of fascination since attention was

---

[1] J. Ennew, *How Can We Define Citizenship In Childhood?* in THE POLITICAL PARTICIPATION OF CHILDREN (R. Rajani, & A. Ledward, eds.), 2000.
[2] J. Ennew, *Outside Childhood: Street Children's Rights,* in Franklin B., (ed.) CHILDREN'S RIGHTS: A HANDBOOK OF COMPARATIVE POLITICS AND PRACTICE (B. Franklin, ed. 1994) at 201.
[3] *See further* Rakesh. Rajani, 1997, Presentation to the 'Children out of Place' Symposium, Urban Childhood Conference, Norwegian Centre for Child Research, University of Trondheim (June 9–12, 1997).

Deirdre Fottrell (ed.), Revisiting Children's Rights, 169–182
© 2000 *Kluwer Law International. Printed in Great Britain.*

drawn to them by a number of non-governmental organisations (NGOs) in 1979, the UN International Year of the Child. In the decade that followed, the exposition of child rights in the drafting process for the UN Convention on the Rights of the Child (CRC), the current idea of 'street children' and the development of a particular model of child-related NGO shared a simultaneous historical appearance.[4] In this discourse, street children are always new, always (re-)discovered and always increasing in number (although, because the arithmetic is as symbolic as the children involved, the numbers quoted have remained the same for nearly two decades). Almost every article on the topic begins with a definition of children 'on' or 'of' the street, based on some early Latin American descriptions, even though this division does not work well even in Latin America.[5]

In all parts of the world, 'street children' became a major target of welfare concern in the 1980s. Thanks to media-driven donor interest and the rapid development of an NGO sector devoted to their welfare, programme models from Latin America were exported to other regions. Whether or not the numbers had actually increased (and there is no reliable statistical evidence to prove or disprove this) the social visibility of this particular group of 'problem children' did increase. Although Latin American models have been employed as a recipe for success, there are in fact no criteria for what counts as success, which means there can be no systematic evaluation, little control (other than financial reporting to donors) and no generally agreed qualifications for, or supervision of, the worker-heroes who have become known as 'street educators'.

Within the world of national and international NGOs, street children have become, both mythically and actually, big business. This has been well documented in Brazil, where some newspapers claim that there are three NGOs on the street for every 'street child'.[6] This amounts at its worst to a 'child industry' in which the continuation of misery is a guarantee for the continuation of the pseudo-philanthropic activities of certain NGOs.[7] By now this has become a global phenomenon. For example, the literature on street children in Tanzania mimics the fables of Brazil. Conventional wisdom has produced a myth of origin in a particular seminar held in Dar es Salaam in 1989.[8] This raised the social visibility of children who had previously been a taken-for-granted feature of urban life, and created both a social problem for policymakers and the rationale for establishing NGOs to solve the

---

[4] *See further*, J. Ennew, Address for the Seminaire de Sociologie, Universite de Fribourg, Switzerland (May 1999).

[5] *See* B. Glauser, *Street Children: Deconstructing A Construct*, in CONSTRUCTING AND RECONSTRUCTURING CHILDHOOD (A. James, & A. Prout, eds. 1999).

[6] *See* F. Impelizieri, *Street children and NGOs* in RIOA/CRIAN çAS DO RUA E EONGS NO RIO, (Amais/IUPERJ, 1995); *see also* T. HECHT, Introduction, AT HOME IN THE STREET (1997) for a similar point about children in Recife.

[7] *See* F. Rosemberg & L. Feitosa Andrade, *Ruthless rhetoric: child and youth prostitution in Brazil*, 6 CHILDHOOD, Feb. 1999, at 113–32.

[8] *See e.g.*, Seminar on Street Children in Tanzania, Dar es Salaam, March, 7–8 1989; for comment *see further* SOCIAL WELFARE DEPARTMENT, A REPORT ON RESEARCH ON STREET CHILDREN, Feb. 1991; *see also* Mwakyanjala, T.E., Problems and Dilemmas of Street Children in Tanzania: A case study of Dar es Salaam Region, MA dissertation (1993), University of Dar es Salaam, Institute of Development Studies (on file in the University library).

problem. According to Tanzanian mythology, there were no street children in the country until the 1980s, nor were there any street children organisations. In contrast, by 1994, 35 organisations devoted totally or in part to work with street children attended a conference.[9] The activities and structures of the NGOs themselves have been said to be weak[10] and an academic thesis refers to the 'selfish motives of the would-be philanthropists' and 'mushrooming of NGOs' that had 'one and the same purpose' of accumulating wealth.[11] Children in Dar es Salaam also know how to manipulate these mythologies through what Tanzanian programme workers call 'shopping around' for the best project options. This seems to be a general tendency. In several Latin American countries, long-term research has shown street children altering their life histories and self-presentation according to the agency or domain in which they are operating, and even referring to NGOs as their 'clients'.[12]

STREET CHILDREN IN STATES PARTY REPORTS

In 1992, the first examples of an entirely new genre of text were produced – States Party reports to the Committee on the Rights of the Child. Inevitably these are country reports, which have more to say about States than about the children whose rights are supposedly the *raison d'être* of the texts. The writing subject is the State and the main narrative is the constitutional context of childhood, which is paradoxical given that children are by definition disenfranchised citizens. States Party reports epitomise the triangular relationship between State, child and family, or in other words the relative strengths of States and civil society and the power this gives to penetrate into the private sphere, using children as hostages.[13] Even the word 'child' may appear for the first time a considerable way in to the text. Among the first twenty reports to be received for example, Mexico was unusual in mentioning children in the first sentence and Costa Rica was the only report that used the actual words of a child.

The way the impossibly constructed category of street children occupies disproportionate space and pops up in odd places in country reports is symptomatic of a number of issues in international work with children. The fact that these children are generally conceptualised outside childhood entails that they have no particular place within country reports. They appear variously under the headings of separa-

---

9   The Conference was organised by the Association of American Allumni of Tanzania (AAAT, 1994). *See further Final Report of the conference on the plight of street children in Tanzania*, 15 September 1994, Pearl Club Conference Hall, Dar es Salaam; Dar es Salaam, American Alumni Association of Tanzania.

10   *See* T. Mulders, *Children en route: A situation analysis of street children and street children's projects in Dar es Salaam*, unpublished manuscript in UNICEF Dar es Salaam library.

11   *See* Mwakyanjala *supra* note 9. at 106.

12   B.E. Turnbull Plaza, *Street Children and their Helpers: A Social Interface Analysis*, PhD Thesis (1998) University of Sussex (on file in the University library); *see further* R. Lucchini, *Theory, method and triangulation in the study of street children* 3 CHILDHOOD, May (1996) at 167–70; *see also* by the same author in the same publication *The street and its image*, at 235–46. *See further*, T. Hecht, *supra* note 6.

13   *See* P. MEYER, THE CHILD AND THE STATE (1983).

tion from parents, juvenile justice, economic exploitation, but more frequently under the catch-all division of 'other types of exploitation' provided by Article 36 of the Convention. The assumption therefore is that, whatever they may be and wherever they may be found, street children are being exploited one way or another, even if the form of exploitation or violation cannot be precisely defined. It just has to be happening.

There are other paradoxes in the treatment given to street children in States Party reports. For example, these children were given large amounts of space in the texts of preliminary reports of certain countries where it is clear to any urban observer that very few children live or even work on the streets. Yet they are not mentioned at all in the preliminary report of the Government of Colombia, despite that country's world-wide identification with the construction of the street child category.

Regardless of the welfare philosophy espoused by a State, all country reports seem to assume that homes are the location of play, culture and family life. Yet this is more typical of a Northern experience of family life in private (and relatively spacious) dwellings, where the front door is shut against an apparently hostile world. For the majority of families in Southern countries, life in slums and shantytowns does not display this privacy; overcrowding forces play, culture and family life out on to the streets. Indeed, for most of human history, socialisation and family relationships have taken place to a very large extent outside houses and, in urban areas, this meant in the streets. This is still the case for most deprived communities. But children playing on the streets within their own communities are not 'street children' even though they are disadvantaged and may be particularly vulnerable to violation of their rights. A street child is not just a child on any street but a child *out of place*, on thoroughfares that are intended for circulation of pedestrians and traffic. No one calls a child working or playing on the streets of a slum or shanty town a 'street child' yet many of these children are likely to have the same, or even worse, problems than visible children out of place. This emphasises the symbolic nature of the street child category.[14]

The ubiquity of the category 'street children' in discourses of child rights and welfare draws attention to the influence of what might be called international civil society (international NGOs) and indirect government from outside (intergovernmental organisations – IGOs) in many aid-dependent countries. The Namibian preliminary report to the Committee on the Rights of the Child explicitly mentions and praises this intervention.[15] Costa Rica and Sudan, on the other hand, complain, the first about the lack of co-ordination among external organisations, particularly IGOs, the second about the cultural aggression of NGOs.[16]

---

[14] *See Children out of Place*, special issue, 3 CHILDHOOD (M. Connolly & J. Ennew, eds. 1996).

[15] *See* PRELIMINARY REPORT OF THE GOVERNMENT OF NAMIBIA, UN DOC CRC/C 3/ Add.12 (1993) at 70.

[16] *See* PRELIMINARY REPORT OF THE GOVERNMENT OF SUDAN, UN DOC CRC/C/3 Add.20 (1992) at 10–11.

STREET CHILDREN AND HUMAN RIGHTS

The curious position of 'street children'in States Party reports leads to questions about their location within human rights discourses and instruments. Just as children who live and work on the street have been with us for centuries, so they were the targets of human rights concern before the CRC was adopted by the United Nations General Assembly in 1989. A report on 'Street Children' made in 1982 by Anti-Slavery International (ASI)[17] to the UN Working Group on Slavery[18] referred to 'millions' around the world being 'denied the barest elements of social justice', constituting 'a disenfranchised group' and 'totally vulnerable to many forms of exploitation'.[19] At that time, the Working Group on Slavery was one of the few international fora to which concerns about working children could be brought. This Report was the first time ASI brought street children to the notice of the Working Group on Slavery and the text (which I drafted) contains many of the preconceptions and misinformation that characterised (and still characterise some) attempts to deal in legal terms with the 'problem'. This report flounders around with ideas of 'social justice' because it cannot conceptualise rights violated in such general terms. Later in the 1980s, but before the adoption of the CRC, a well-publicised and widely distributed book on street children was sponsored by the Independent Commission for International Humanitarian Issues. The author stated that the violation of street children's rights should be understood in terms of omission as much as commission so that 'street existence without a family to protect intrinsic rights must be considered the sum of all individual violations even though one cannot single out its perpetrators'.[20] Like the ASI submission, this approach reveals much the same imprecision as one notes in the insistence on using Article 36 of the CRC for inserting street children into the texts of States Party reports to the Committee on the Rights of the Child. What was described as the sum of all individual violations in the 1980s became the sum of all possible exploitations in the 1990s.

In a sense, this problem with the sum of violations or exploitations is also symptomatic of the changing mood of human rights law, which has been moving since the 1970s from concern with violation of civil and political rights to non-achievement of economic, social and cultural rights, after the International Covenant on Economic, Social and Cultural Rights entered into force in 1976. The UN Commission on Human Rights had first begun to take economic, social and cultural rights seriously in the 1970s when the right to development was being considered. By the 1980s it had become necessary to define exactly what was entailed in statements about the right to work, housing, education, health care and food.[21] Meanwhile, the UN General Assembly, like the international community as a

---

[17] Anti-Slavery International was then known as the Anti-Slavery Society.

[18] Since 1990 this has been known as the Standing Committee on Modern Forms of Slavery.

[19] ANTI-SLAVERY SOCIETY, (1982) STREET CHILDREN, SUBMISSION TO THE UN WORKING GROUP ON SLAVERY, Geneva, July 1982.

[20] *See* S. AGNELLI STREET CHILDREN: A GROWING URBAN TRAGEDY (1986) at 108–109.

[21] *See* P. ALSTON, THE BEST INTERESTS OF THE CHILD: RECONCILING CULTURE AND HUMAN RIGHTS (1994).

whole, entered a long and continuing debate about the relative importance of civil and political rights on the one hand, and economic, social and cultural rights on the other. The idea of street children, whose civil and political rights to identity and equal treatment under the law are violated, while their rights to family, schooling, food security, health and shelter are not met, becomes thus coterminous with the sum of all violations and non-achievements. In this sense, therefore, the CRC is precisely about street children. But this runs the risk of reducing children's rights to a set of deficiencies experienced by a particular group of children. And this is particularly unsatisfactory if one considers that even many of those who work with street children claim that the category cannot be defined.

STREET CHILDREN IN THE CONVENTION

Thus street children seem not only to have hijacked the urban agenda, but also to have hijacked child rights. No other category of children is so repeatedly discussed in States Party reports, not even child workers, who far outnumber them. Yet, street children are not mentioned in the text of the Convention. Perhaps the closest reference is in the phrase 'children in especially difficult circumstances', which appears in the Preamble. In reports to the Committee and many other arenas within international discourses on children, street children have become virtually synonymous with 'Children in Especially Difficult Circumstances'. Commonly referred to the world over as 'CEDC', this term was originally coined by UNICEF in the mid-1980s to describe a mixed category of vulnerable children that included working and street children, unaccompanied children in disaster or conflict situations, refugee children, children affected by war and children with disabilities.[22] Over the years other groups of children were informally included as CEDC. Sometimes the inclusion was almost universal. For example, throughout the 1990s 'the girl child' has been frequently included, particularly in Asian countries.[23] But categories may also be locally defined. In line with the concerns of the regional OAU instrument, the African Charter on the Rights and Welfare of the Child, many African countries include a category of children involved in early marriages and pregnancies, which is not included in Latin American countries. Other categories may refer to particular local terms. The *talibe*, or disciples in Qranic schools who are sent to beg on the streets are included in Senegal for example. Thus the list of CEDC categories included in any national context in UNICEF Situation Analyses, country reports to the Committee on the Rights of the Child and studies carried out by local researchers is specific to that country.

Meanwhile, the conceptualisation of vulnerable children used by UNICEF world-wide has been revised. Ten years after the Executive Board had established an organisational policy for CEDC, world-wide awareness of child exploitation and

---

[22] *See further* UNICEF, CHILDREN IN ESPECIALLY DIFFICULT CIRCUMSTANCES, Executive Board Report (1986).

[23] *See* J. Ennew, *Defining the Girl Child: Sexuality, Control and Development*, in VENA, 1994, *Special Edition on The Girl Child*, edited by Henk van Beers.

abuse had grown, and the problems involved also appeared to have multiplied. A policy review in 1996, which had the aim of moving beyond the idea of children in especially difficult circumstances' provided a new perspective based on the concept of 'special protection measures', which had been 'formulated by the Committee on the Rights of the Child, to describe the actions required to redress special vulnerabilities of children so as to enable them to enjoy all of their rights'.[24] Typically, UNICEF also reveals an internal contradiction in that many national and regional offices have ignored this dictat from the New York Headquarters and blithely continue to use CEDC as key term in their programming. Moreover, CEDC is also included as a category in the instructions for writing UNICEF Situation Analyses, published two years after the Executive Board revision of terminology. The section of a programme manual devoted to situation analyses states that 'The Convention specifies these circumstances in Articles 9–11, 19–23, 25, 27, 32–4 to which it is necessary to add street children and adolescents at risk of premature pregnancy'.[25] Nevertheless, there is nothing in this manual to explain why 'it is necessary'.

Whether with respect to CEDC or the new UNICEF acronym for Children in Need of Special Protection (CNSP) and whatever the context of the category, street children appear to obscure all other groups of vulnerable children, in reports and discussions as well as in the priority and budgetary provision accorded. By the early 1990s, 'street children' had relegated other CEDC categories to relative obscurity.[26] Whatever the actual group of children that is the focus of local and international debates and policymaking forums that I attend, the discussion quickly slips to an elision with 'street children' – even though (or perhaps because) most of those who have been working in the street children field for the past two decades agree that this is a category that defies definition.[27] Thus it is assumed that 'orphans' will become (or are) street children, while 'all' street children are orphans; 'AIDS orphans' will become street children; child domestic workers have no alternative but to become street sex workers; street children have no choice but to become child sex workers, and all child sex workers (despite evidence to the contrary) are street children. According to these tenets, child soldiers, if not rescued, will become street children when the conflict ends – and so on. In Vietnam, I have encountered government researchers who even searched for street children in rural villages with no recognisable streets, so convinced they were that they had to report to the Committee on the Rights of the Child on this category.

WHICH RIGHTS?

The writer of an UNICEF report claims that 'no less than seven' Articles of the CRC cover children outside adult love and care in difficult circumstances.[28] Yet, I

---

24 *See* ECOSOC, REVIEW OF UNICEF POLITICS AND STRATEGIES IN CHILD PROTECTION, E/ICEF/1996/14, April 1996.
25 UNICEF 1996, Book D Programme Preparation, Chapter 3, Section 3 'Situation analysis' para 2 presumably based on the UNICEF 1996 Mission statement.
26 *See* M. Connolly & J. Ennew, *supra* note 14.
27 *Ibid.*
28 *See* BLACK, M., STREET AND WORKING CHILDREN, Innocenti Global Seminar, Summary Report, Florence (1993).

would suggest that some 32 Articles have direct relevance to these children most days of their lives, whether by violation or non-achievement. This results not only from taking the view that the rights of street children can only be encompassed in the sum of omissions, violations and exploitations. It is also the result of the all-encompassing (and therefore not very useful) definitions used for 'street children'. More importantly, it is the outcome of the realisation that 'street children', however they are defined, are first and foremost children, which means that, like all other children, human rights and children's rights apply to them at all times.

Although the rights in the Convention can be categorised under the headings of protection, provision and participation, the emphasis for all children tends to be on the first two; the last is offered to them by adults reluctantly, if at all. Street children, however, are seldom protected; they often have to provide for themselves, and have grasped participatory rights by accident, because they must. In brief, the Articles of greatest relevance to children who live and work in the streets encompass at least the following:[29]

- The Articles that have come to be known as 'general principles' (Articles 2, 3, 6 & 12): Protection against discrimination is denied to street children, who are stigmatised by the street children image, which causes the public and State agents such as the police to view them as asocial and amoral (Article 2). With very few exceptions, State provision for street children is taken less in their best interests and more in the interest of cleansing the streets of their presence (Article 3). The 'inherent right to life' and to 'survival and development' is denied to those street children who are gunned down in Brazil, Colombia, Guatemala and South Africa (Article 6). The right to have their opinion taken into account in all decisions taken in their interest is denied to street children by many caring agencies as much as by the State authorities that clean them off the streets into orphanages and prisons (Article 12).
- Civil and political rights: The rights to name, nationality and identity are denied to many street children, who usually not only have no birth certificates or registration documents, but also have no means of obtaining any (Articles 7 and 8). All too often street children are deprived of their liberty. In many cases, after summary justice, they are confined in adult prisons, where they suffer ill treatment at the hands of both staff and other prisoners (Articles 37 and 40). The Articles that provide for children's participation in society are of particular importance to street and working children (Articles, 12, 13 and 15). For a good part of their daily lives they operate outside the adult surveillance system that constructs and controls childhood. They participate in society not just as children but also as providers, carers and decision-makers in families and in child-centred groups. They are also workers, income generators and, often, sexual actors. These roles are ideologically repressed, in the sense that they are usually unrecognised or even denigrated by society.

---

[29] See J. Ennew, *supra* note 2. *See also* I. BYRNE, THE HUMAN RIGHTS OF STREET AND WORKING CHILDREN: A PRACTICAL MANUAL FOR ADVOCATES (1998).

- Rights to provision of services and support: The CRC assumes that families will be the main providers of rights to children, and that the obligation of States is to support this function. All the provisions of Articles dealing with the support of family life, as well as with separation from parents, family reunification and adoption, apply with particular force to street children (Articles 9, 10, 18, 20, 21 and 27). The facts that children have to seek an income on the streets and that their families are unable to provide sufficient overall support to keep them from living on the streets are extreme symptoms of this widespread social neglect of the most vulnerable social groups (Articles 26 and 27). Children outside childhood are already marginalised by society and not in receipt of any welfare provision, either from families or from the State (Article 4). Specific service provision for children who live and work on the street is usually left to NGOs. Although rehabilitative care is provided for some street children, mostly by NGOs, the coverage is patchy and there is little agreement on objectives, methods or evaluation, and the same applies to non-formal education schemes, which tend not to prepare children for return to State education systems but rather to provide very basic vocational training (Articles 28, 29 and 39). Curative health care is often denied to these children and preventative health care almost entirely absent even though life on the streets can be particularly unhealthy and unhygienic (Article 24). Some children find themselves on the streets because they have a disability. In other cases children become disabled as a result of life on the streets (Article 23).
- Protection rights: As all street children work for survival it is axiomatic that they are not protected from economic exploitation (Article 32). Sensational accounts of street children often state or imply that they are all involved in prostitution because there is no other way in which they can earn money, and that they are exploited and trafficked by wealthy international criminal gangs. The truth is less exciting and more sordid. Many children, both male and female, sell sex at some time or other and in some form or other during their lives on the streets. However, they are not all prostitutes, many who are would rather not be and sell sex only as a last resort. Many others do not sell sex at all (Articles 34 and 35). The reasons why children appear on the street may be an expression of the violation of their rights to protection. They may have been abused by their parents or guardians (Article 20), affected by armed conflict (Article 38), be refugees (Article 22), or addicted to drugs (Article 33).

IMPLICIT RIGHTS?

As this brief review of the relevant provisions of the CRC reveals, street children do not enjoy their rights to protection and provision. Indeed, this very non-enjoyment makes them appear to be unnatural children. In order to combat this marginalisation within the scope of the CRC, I would suggest that children in exceptionally difficult conditions, such as street children, might need special rights, or special consideration within the rights as written. In other words the interpretation of the rights in the CRC may not have the same texture for street children as it does for children safely nurtured within family homes.

For example, the stigmatising category 'street child' leads to unfair and sometimes abusive discrimination, from which it follows that children on the street have a right to expect correct information to be collected from and disseminated about them. Because research has so often been based on misconceptions, carried out badly or not carried out at all, many service provision projects for street children are inappropriate. For example, it is often assumed that children who are taken off the street for rehabilitation have been rescued from sexual activity until they become adults. They may be taught that their sexual experiences were bad and should be forgotten and rejected. But their sexual experiences were real and are a part of their developing identity. The close relationship with another street child may have been meaningful and powerful, more important than any other relationship thus far. They have a right to expect that this will be addressed with respect by adults. In addition, emphasis on the importance of families in the CRC is based on the modern conception of families as private arenas for the correct performance of childhood. There is no provision for respect and support to be paid to children's own friendships and support networks. Moreover, until such time as welfare provision reaches a level at which children do not have to work to provide for themselves and their families, working children should be protected from hazardous conditions, as well as given security of employment and equal wages when they perform the same or similar tasks to those carried out by adults.

INEXCUSABLE HARM

As a result of these considerations, I would argue that the Articles of greatest importance for street children (and to all children who, temporarily or permanently lack the supportive care of families), are not those referring to their need for families, schools or health care, but rather those regulating the behaviour of agencies from whom they do receive attention. Unfortunately, street children not only suffer from inadequate provision from society, but also from inappropriate provision from well-meaning intervention projects. In addition, they are frequently subjected to physical, sexual and emotional abuse within projects by those whom society empowers to care for them. This is inexcusable harm.

The rights to be protected from these violations are implicit in the CRC. The fight against inexcusable harm has three components, which depend on interpretation of Articles 12, 13 and 36 of the CRC, as well as on the somewhat neglected aspect of Article 3 dealing with professional standards of provision, that is overshadowed by 'best interests' discussions. These components are research, publicity and intervention.

RESEARCH

The CRC has opened new possibilities in child research by creating a demand for better information on children and childhood. Yet there is no unified discourse on 'street children'. Research tends to be characterised by lack of conceptual clarity and poor methodology as well as inadequate methods and poor analysis. It is rarely possible to compare results between one study and another, even within the same town. Methods are usually limited to questionnaire surveys and so called 'case studies', neither of which are good approaches to use alone in social science, much less in research with children.[30]

Although the CRC does not mention research as such, it does provide the framework for a more satisfactory approach to research with all children, according to both scientific and ethical criteria. In the first place, according to the provisions of Articles 12 and 13, it is obligatory for researchers to seek children's own views about their lives, and not just those of adults, and to find ways in which children can express themselves in 'any media of their choice'. It also follows that children must be able to give their informed consent (or dissent) to research objectives, processes and publications. With respect to street children in particular, researchers must comply with Article 2 by ensuring that the research objectives, assumptions and publications do not have any stigmatising effects.

1. Publicity

Research about street children is generally of poor quality and media outputs, which are after all market products and are often misinformed, vary from glamorising to victimising. Yet the outputs of both research and media are used to raise money for programmes and individuals as well as for so-called advocacy on behalf of street children. Media, human rights activists, and fundraising departments of development NGOs are all guilty of exploiting the histories of children, in stories that emphasise their vulnerability, exaggerate their weaknesses and turn them into victims.

Images of 'street children'are so compelling that it is inevitable that media investigations should take place on a regular basis, providing information in a steady stream of articles, photo reports, documentary videos and films, some of which are sponsored and/or used in advocacy campaigns by IGOs, NGOs and INGOs. The information presented and the language used tend to be repetitive. There is a tendency for those who publicise children's difficulties to deal in huge numbers, in hundreds of millions, which are pure guesswork. Unfortunately these are seldom questioned and often enter the official record, where they become 'fact'. It may suit the newspapers to be able to deal in shocking figures of hundreds of millions, but this exploits children rather than helping them. With respect to the 'ruthless rhetoric' employed, two Brazilian authors comment that

> efforts to sensitise public opinion regarding the violence to which children and adolescents are exposed, mainly in underdeveloped countries, have generated a specific language, now making the rounds world-wide, that in its attempts to convince frequently incorporates catastrophic and unreliable diagnoses, distant from reality and inadequate as benchmarks for action and which tend to stig-

---

[30] *See* J. BOYDEN & J. ENNEW, CHILDREN IN FOCUS: A MANUAL FOR PARTICIPATORY RESEARCH WITH CHILDREN (1997); *see also* M. Connolly & J. Ennew (1997), *supra* note 14.

matise poor families, children and adolescents ... [W]e encounter the same sources as benchmarks for the data, the same laxity in the calculations, the adoption of the same theory 'that to combat [its] misery the poor family will do anything, including selling its children.[31]

As these two researchers argue, 'street children', especially if they are female, are frequently assumed to be involved inevitably in sex work. The result of this linguistic contrivance, as the co-founder of a Tanzanian 'street children' project would agree, is a 'waste of ... international and foreign resources' on high-profile curative projects, when funds might be better invested in preventative schemes with the far larger groups of deprived children living in urban slums and squatter settlements. In addition, and ironically, concentration on these small groups of children tends to stigmatise all urban children living in poverty.[32]

Street children are not just outlaws or waifs appearing in photographs as part of the urban scenery. They are human beings, each with their own history, problems, necessities and hopes. Popular images of 'street children' are one extra problem that they simply don't need. Some object to being called 'street children' because of the negative connotations, others act up to the image, especially for tourists, photographers and NGO workers, from whom they can obtain benefits. They are not objects of concern but individual children who are subjects of human rights. In this respect they should be protected by the provisions against secondary exploitation that are implicit in the general terms of Article 36. All those who engage in publicity about street children, in the media, in fundraising and in advocacy, have an obligation continuously to review their activities in the light of this Article.

2. Intervention

Perhaps because of the extensive publicity about them, work with 'street children' forms one of the most powerful images of charity. Interventions tend to be made on the basis of arbitrary information, by well-intentioned people, without taking children's views into account.[33] This violates Article 12, but more importantly raises the question of maintaining and supervising appropriate standards of professional care provided for children, which are the concerns of Articles 3(3) and 25. Largely because the provision for street children tends to fall within the sphere of non-governmental action, there are no internationally accepted criteria for the qualifications and supervision of street children projects and few cases in which national standards are applied, supervised or subjected to routine inspection. The result is that most children in street children projects are not protected against neglect, abuse and exploitation at the hands of those licensed by society to care for them. Article 3(3) in this case is a general principle underlying health care, educa-

---

[31] *See further* Rosemberg & Andrade, *supra* note 7.
[32] *Ibid; see also* Rajani, *supra* note 3.
[33] *See* B. Glauser, *supra* note 5.

tion, discipline, substitute family care, rehabilitation and all forms of protection (affecting at the very least Articles 9, 16, 19 24, 28, 29, 34, 37 and 39).

Even if no direct abuse takes place in a street children project, the standard of care may not be adequate and this amounts to a form of societal neglect. A novel aspect of street children literature in Tanzania is the extent to which it focuses on the institutions established to provide for their needs. A survey of 10 of the projects in Dar es Salaam carried out in 1992 covered six run by separate NGOs, five by churches and one established by the Government. The author noted that 'In general the target group mentioned by the project is a very general one.'[34] Through interviewing staff of these projects, as well as 253 children, she identified certain common problems that are frequently associated with street children projects, which tend to be very small, often started by individuals of good will but little experience. This brings with it certain consequences:

- These NGOs are vulnerable and tend to lack sustainability;
- Administration especially of finance is very time consuming;
- Long term strategies are absent; and
- There is little or no sharing of experiences, or institutional learning. Indeed the field tends to be characterised by extremes of competition.

The result, in Tanzania as elsewhere, has already been noted. Children find that they can benefit little from the activities established for their benefit and make this clear by 'shopping' between projects in search of the best services or the services they want at a particular moment in time.

At the other end of the scale one can point to certain international dimensions of inexcusable harm in the sexual exploitation of children by paedophiles employed by non-governmental organisations. A case in Ethiopia that came to light in 1999 can be cited as an example of a far too frequent occurrence.[35] The children concerned were defined as orphans, but many would in fact have been displaced children found on urban streets. The case concerned two expatriate staff members, one British and the other Canadian, both of whom had dubious employment records in previous work with children in developing countries, one of whom was under investigation for abusing Ethiopian children in his care in Australia. The international NGO that employed them eventually found both these men to be guilty of sexual abuse of boys in the project. They were dismissed, but the Ethiopian authorities were not informed of the offence.

Attention to the provisions of Articles 3(3) and 25 should raise questions about the way projects are managed and supervised and the responsibility for checking references and qualifications as well as for providing expatriates with visas and work permits. Yet cases such as this also raise issues about international obligations to report and share convictions and ongoing prosecutions for paedophilia as well as

---

[34] *See* Mulders, *supra* note 10 at 36.
[35] *See e.g.*, A. Gillan, *Charity's haven for Famine Children Destroyed by Paedophile*, THE GUARDIAN, Thur. July 22 1999.

of exploring the use of extra-territorial legislation for this exploitation through development aid as well as for the more highly publicised 'sex tourism'.[36]

CONCLUSION: WHY THE CONVENTION IS NOT ABOUT STREET CHILDREN

The first and most important conclusion is obvious – the Convention is not specifically about street children, or indeed about any children in need of special protection, because it is about all human beings under the age of 18 years. The text does not mention street children and, in so far as particular provisions might be said to refer to street children, it is difficult not to come to the conclusion that just about every article does. This illustrates the facts not only that children cannot be lumped together, in groups or categories, but also that the category of 'street child' is indefinable, mythological even to those who work with them.

Having said that, one has to admit that the *idea* of street children exists and has some important effects in human rights terms. In the first place, the notion that urban streets are increasingly invaded by street children obscures the fact that most urban children do not live in the streets, and that in developing countries most urban and rural children live in conditions of considerable deprivation. It might therefore be argued that the financial and political attention paid to the small, indefinable group of street children operates to violate the rights of their contemporaries living in slums and shantytowns.

The second general conclusion is that, in so far as some children do live and work on urban streets their rights are being violated, less in the ways publicised by those who are likely to profit from being their researchers, publicists, advocates and service providers, but rather from the lack of control exercised by responsible authorities over these people, be they well-meaning, cynical or downright exploitative.

---

[36] *See e.g.*, INTERNATIONAL BUREAU FOR CHILDREN'S RIGHTS, THE INTERNATIONAL DIMENSIONS OF CHILD SEXUAL EXPLOITATION: GLOBAL REPORT (1999).

CONTRIBUTORS

Maggie Black is a journalist and author who has written extensively on children's rights issues. She has acted as a consultant to numerous international organisations and non-governmental groups including UNICEF, Save the Children and Oxfam. Recent publications include *Children First, The Story of UNICEF*, Oxford University Press (1997).

Judith Ennew is a Senior Fellow of the Centre for Family Research at the Cambridge University and a Visiting Research Fellow at the Anthropology Department, Goldsmith College. She has written widely on the topic of children's rights and has acted as a consultant to international organisations and non-govermental organisations. Her recent publications include *Monitoring Children's Rights* (1999).

Deirdre Fottrell is a lecturer in international human rights in the law department at the University of Essex. From 1997–2000 she was the Director of the human rights programme at the Institute of Commonwealth Studies, University of London. Her recent publications include *Minority and Group Rights in the New Millennium*, (edited with Bill Bowring), Kluwer Law International (1999).

Michael Freeman is a Barrister and Professor of English Law at University College London. He is the editor of the *International Journal of Children's Rights* and has published widely on the rights of children. His recent publications include *The Moral Status of Children*, Kluwer (1997).

Carolyn Hamilton is the Director of the Children's Legal Centre, an independent charity based at the University of Essex dedicated to the promotion of children's rights. She is also a Reader in the Law Department at the University and a practising Barrister. She is author of *Family, Law and Religion* (1999) and edits Child-RIGHT, the monthly journal of the Children's Legal Centre.

Ursula Kilkelly is a lecturer in the law faculty at Univeresity College Cork. She was previously on the faculty at the University of Wales, Swansea. She is a graduate of the University of Limerick and Queen's University Belfast, where she completed her doctorate in 1997. Her recent publications include *The Child and the European Convention on Human Rights* (Ashgate, 1999).

Jenny Kuper is a visiting research associate at the London School of Economics based in the Law Department and the Development Studies Institute. She is a graduate of UCLA and King's College London and she worked as a solicitor in the

Children's Legal Centre. She has written on all aspects of children's rights; her publications include *International Law Concerning Child Civilians in Armed Conflict* (Oxford University Press, 1997).

Hilary Lim is a principal lecturer in the law department at the University of East London. She has written extensively on land law, children's rights, gender and postcolonialism. Her recent publications include *Cesarians and Cyborgs* 7 Feminist Legal Studies, 1999.

Peter Newell is Co-ordinator of EPOCH – End Physical Punishment of Children, and of the international network of organisations campaigning to end all physical punishment of children, EPOCH-WORLDWIDE. In the UK he chairs the Council of the Children's Rights Alliance for England. He is the author of various books and articles on children's rights and together with Rachel Hodgkin prepared UNICEF's *Implementation Handbook for the Convention on the Rights of the Child*, UNICEF, 1998.

Katherine O'Donovan is Professor of Law at Queen Mary and Westfield College, University of London. She has previously taught at Queen's University Belfast, University of Addis Ababa, University of Hong Kong and the University of Kent. She has published widely in the fields of family law, law and medical ethics and feminist jurisprudence. Her recent publications include *Who is the Father? Access to Genetic Information*, in *Children's Rights and Traditional Values* (G. Douglas and L. Sebba eds.) (Ashgate 1998) and *Family Law* (Pluto 1995).

Jeremy Roche is a senior lecturer in the School of Social Welfare at the Open University. He has published extensively on children's rights. Recent articles include, FEMINISM AND CHILDREN'S RIGHTS in FEMINIST PERSPECTIVES ON CHILD LAW (with Hilary Lim) (J Bridgeman & D. Monk, eds., 2000).

Marcus Roberts works at the Children's Legal Centre at the University of Essex. He has written widely on issues relating to children's rights in the UK in both the academic and popular press.

Siraj Sait is a senior lecturer in the law department, University of East London. He is a graduate of the Universities of Madras, Harvard and the Institute of Commonwealth Studies, University of London. He practiced as a barrister in India for ten years and has also worked as a Commissioner on Bonded Labour to the Supreme Court, and has been an associate in the office of the Solicitor-General. His publications include *Reorienting Federalism; Process and Substance in Indian Constitutionalism*, in *Federalism and Decentralisation* (G.W. Kueck, S.C. Mathus and K. Schindker eds.) (Mudrit 1998).

Index